Systems of Innovation

Systems of Innovation

Selected Essays in Evolutionary Economics

Christopher Freeman

Emeritus Professor, SPRU, University of Sussex, UK

Edward Elgar
Cheltenham, UK • Northampton, MA, USA

Published by
Edward Elgar Publishing Limited
Glensanda House
Montpellier Parade
Cheltenham
Glos GL50 1UA
UK

Edward Elgar Publishing, Inc.
William Pratt House
9 Dewey Court
Northampton
Massachusetts 01060
USA

A catalogue record for this book
is available from the British Library

Library of Congress Control Number: 2008924167

ISBN 978 1 84720 385 4

Printed and bound in Great Britain by MPG Books Ltd, Bodmin, Cornwall

Contents

Acknowledgements

The author and publishers wish to thank the following who have kindly given permission for use of the following copyright material:

The OECD for C. Freeman, 'Technological Infrastructure and International Competitiveness', Draft paper submitted to the OECD ad hoc group on science, technology and competitiveness, August 1982, © OECD and Oxford University Press for 'Technological Infrastructure and International Competitiveness' 2004, Introduction by B-Å. Lundvall, *Industrial and Corporate Change*, **13** (3), 541–69.

Continuum International Publishing Group for 'Structural Crises of Adjustment, Business Cycles and Investment Behaviour' (with Carlota Perez), in G. Dosi, C. Freeman, R.R. Nelson, G. Silverberg and L.L.G. Soete (eds), *Technical Change and Economic Theory*, London and New York: Pinter Publishers, 1988, pp. 38–66.

Liverpool University Press for 'Family Allowances, Technical Change, Inequality and Social Policy', *The Eleanor Rathbone Memorial Lecture*, Liverpool: Liverpool University Press, 1997, 23pp.

Elsevier for 'Continental, National and Sub-national Innovation Systems – Complementarity and Economic Growth', 2002, *Research Policy*, **31**, 191–211 and 'A Hard Landing for the "New Economy": Information Technology and the United States National System of Innovation', 2001, *Structural Change and Economic Dynamics*, **12**, 115–39.

The Journal of Economics and Business Administration for 'Rise of East Asian Economies and the Computerisation of the World Economy', 1994, *Journal of Economics and Business Administration*, (Kobe University), Special Issue in honour of Professor Masaaki Hirooka, **170** (6), November, 21pp.

Palgrave Macmillan for ' "Catching Up" and Innovation Systems: Implications for Eastern Europe', in K. Piech and S. Radosevic (eds), *The*

Knowledge-based Economy in Central and Eastern Europe, New York: Palgrave-Macmillan, 2006, pp. 13–32.

Oxford University Press for 'The ICT Paradigm', in R.E. Mansell, C. Avgerou, D. Quah and R. Silverstone (eds), *The Oxford Handbook of Information and Communication Technologies*, Oxford: Oxford University Press, 2007, pp. 34–54, and 'Conclusions: A "Theory of Reasoned History"', based on a section of *As Time goes By* (with Francisco Louçã), Oxford: Oxford University Press, 2001, 124–34.

Every effort has been made to trace all copyright holders but if any have been inadvertently overlooked the publishers will be pleased to make the necessary arrangements at the first opportunity.

Chapter 4 first appeared as Chapter 7 in M. Dodgson and R. Rothwell (eds) (1994), *Handbook of Industrial Innovation*, Aldershot, UK and Brookfield, USA: Edward Elgar, pp. 78–93.

Chapter 11 first appeared as Chapter 8 in H. Hanusch and A. Pyka (eds) (2007), *Elgar Companion to Neo-Schumpeterian Economics*, Cheltenham, UK and Northampton, MA, USA: Edward Elgar, pp. 130–41.

Foreword

Giovanni Dosi*

Being asked to write a foreword to Chris Freeman's *Selected Essays* has been for me an honour and a privilege. Chris has been for almost thirty years a loved friend, an influential mentor and an extremely insightful collaborator. However, he does not need any introduction. As one of the most prominent founding fathers of the economics of innovation as a distinct sub-discipline of social science and as influential *maître-à-penser* within and outside evolutionary economics and economic history, he has deserved for quite a while the most prestigious recognition in economics, together with social scientists like Myrdal, Arrow, Simon, North, and a few other seminal contributors to the contemporary 'political economy'. A preface praising the intellectual achievements of Chris Freeman would inevitably be both partial and redundant. Rather, it might be more useful, especially for the younger readers, to briefly flag some of the themes discussed in the essays which follow and highlight the ways they relate to the ongoing evolutionary research programme in economics as well as other streams of socio-economic analysis.

Chris Freeman (together with a small number of scholars on the other side of the Atlantic – prominently Richard Nelson and Nathan Rosenberg) has established the very foundations of the economic analysis of scientific and technological research and of the ways technological knowledge becomes incorporated into new products and processes and ultimately turns out as a fundamental engine of economic growth. Freeman has indeed been one of the pioneers investigating difficult but fundamental questions such as the inter-relation between scientific and technological advances, the characteristics of innovating firms, the nature of institutions supporting technological innovation: the reader is still going to find fresh insight in the old Freeman (1962) and (2004), Freeman et al. (1963) and (1965), while of course the classic Freeman (1982) and (1994) are a must in the field of economics of innovation.[1]

The foregoing analyses are also at root of the essays which follow. However the emphasis of most of them (and also of Freeman (1987)) is on the institutions grounding 'capitalism as an engine of progress' as Nelson (1990) put it.

A major theme which offers a unifying thread across the essays, and also provides the title of the collection, concerns the nature of systems of innovation and in particular *National Systems of Innovation and of Production* (hereafter NSIP). In fact, a careful reading of the following essays and more emphatically the conclusions reveal that NSIP are for Freeman a privileged level of analysis of the interactions and co-evolutionary dynamics among five sub-domains, and related institutions, governing

1. the generation of scientific knowledge;
2. the development, improvement, adoption of new artefacts and new techniques of production (that is, the domain of technology);
3. the 'economic machine' which organizes the production and distribution of goods, services and incomes;
4. the political and legal structure; and finally,
5. the cultural domain-shaping values, norms and customs.[2]

It is indeed a formidably challenging research programme, posing basic interpretative questions, at the same level of generality – even if different in their ingredients – as the 'theories of history' addressed by Adam Smith, Marx, Weber, Keynes and Schumpeter, among a few distinguished others. One could call it the 'grand political economy', trying to answer some of the questions which, frankly, I consider to be among the ultimately interesting ones: what has triggered and what keeps the momentum to self-sustained exponential growth in developed economies since the Industrial Revolution? How do we explain the patterns of catching-up, falling-behind and forging-ahead historically observed among different countries? What are the factors underlying the long-term fluctuations in the time profile of economic aggregates such as GDP, productivity, employment, and so on at both 'world' and national levels? What is the relative importance, in the answer to the foregoing questions, of technological versus organizational versus institutional factors?

Chris Freeman's conjectures together with his enormously insightful exercises of 'appreciative theorizing' – as Nelson and Winter (1982) call the *genre* of bottom-up history-based interpretations – are nearly opposite to any quest for the 'magic bullet' enterprise. Hence, as Chris remarks in the conclusions, the 'ultimate driver' of socio-economic history is unlikely to be an invariant Marxian tension between 'forces of production', 'relations of production' and 'political/ideological superstructures'. By the same token, one is equally unlikely to find any ultimate 'Schumpeterian driver' of long-term growth just based on technological innovation – as important as it is – always holding irrespective of the (institutional and cultural) context conditions. And, needless to say, any account of the magic bullet in terms of 'just get the incentives right and you will be OK' is so far away from Chris's views that he does not even mention it (I happen to fully agree with him, but I shall briefly get back to the issue below since it features such a big part in the contemporary 'spirit of the times' in social sciences).

Freeman's first fundamental conjectures entail that each of the foregoing domains of analysis maintains a good degree of 'evolutionary autonomy': to give a few examples, science to a significant extent (even if not fully) evolves according to its own selection criteria; so do political institutions and cultural traits; collectively shared norms might well self-reinforce even when driving to technological downgrading and income deterioration; and the list is much longer.

The second interpretative conjecture, further developed also in his joint works with Carlota Perez and Francisco Louçã (see among others Freeman and Perez (1988) and Freeman and Louçã (2001)) is that the observed dynamic properties of the various (national) economies and their relative performances as well as the dynamics of international economy as a whole, ought to be interpreted in terms of *congruence* (or, alternatively, varying degrees of *mismatching*) among the foregoing sub-domains. Ambitious as it is, I find the elements of a 'theory of contemporary history' sketched out in Freeman and Perez (1988), Perez (2002), Freeman (2002), and Freeman and Louçã (2001) both highly suggestive and quite convincing. In such an interpretation the national specificities in the coupled dynamics among the above five domains account for, for example, the English emergence to leadership in the first Industrial Revolution, the subsequent catching-up and forging-ahead of the USA and Germany, all the way to the contemporary success of far-eastern economies like Korea. It is an interpretation which bears major overlappings with the – to a good extent French – 'regulation school' (see Boyer (1988a) and (1988b), and, among the non-French contributors, Dosi and Orsenigo (1988), and also Coriat and Dosi (1998), for discussions of the links between such a breed of institutionalism and evolutionary theories in economics). If anything, there is relatively more emphasis upon science and technology in Freeman and colleagues and more emphasis on politics, conflict and governance institutions in Aglietta, Boyer, Coriat, and other 'regulation' colleagues. However, this should be a second-order issue, in principle to be clarified on the grounds of finer comparative historical evidence.

Some basic 'congruence' or 'combinatorics' story is also at the core of the *variety of capitalism* approach to the comparative assessment of the political economies and revealed performances of for example 'laissez-faire' Anglo-Saxon capitalism versus 'corporatist', German or Japanese, breeds of capitalist socio-economic organization (see Hall and Soskice (2001), and also Cimoli et al. (2006) on development patterns). And, finally, Freeman's history-based generalizations are well in tune with more formal explorations of the *consistency properties* (or lack of them) among forms of governance of information, incentives, financial flows and product markets (see the seminal work of Aoki (2001); for some links with evolutionary theories of technological change see also Aoki and Dosi (1992)).

A major methodological element shared by Freeman and colleagues with these other streams of analysis is the explicit focus upon *comparisons among discrete institutional forms*[3], which distinctly combines mechanisms of knowledge generation and of governance of economic coordination. So for example, in Aoki, the archetypal 'Japanese firm' differs from the archetypal 'American firm' in terms of distinct organizational attributes determining among other features the way information flows across the hierarchical layers of the firm, the relationships between internal promotion mechanisms and modes of access to the labour market, and the links between the firm itself and finance (Aoki, 2001).

The emphasis of Aoki, as well as 'variety-of-capitalism' streams of analysis, is largely, although not exclusively, *cross-sectional*, addressing the structural differences between, say, the USA, Japan, Germany and Sweden over the last fifty years or so. The recurrent question is whether such differences, even if they existed in the past, will continue to exist in the 'globalization era'. Chris Freeman convincingly argues that they will. I fully agree with him and shall add some brief comments below. Come as it may, Freeman puts an even greater emphasis on the *historical* evolution of distinct political-economy regimes associated with distinct techno-economic paradigms shaping the overall organization of knowledge accumulation and production under for example an electricity/internal-combustion/mass production mode versus an ICT-driven one (see Freeman and Perez (1988), and Freeman and Louçã (2001) among others).

I cannot enter here into the details of the overlaps and differences between different analyses however grounded into some institutional combinatorics concerning the performance comparisons between different 'institutional types' and the assessment of their genesis, mechanisms of self-maintenance and evolution. The common bottom line is the focus upon the identification of the combinations which make, say, the 'research university' mode of generating scientific knowledge congruent with the modes of its industrial exploitation which in turn might or might not be congruent with the ways labour and financial markets work, and so on. From a modelling point of view one is still at the beginning, but the already mentioned works by Aoki offer suggestive hints (see also Marengo (1992) for a largely unexploited style of micro institutional comparisons). In any case, note that in such a style of analysis, complementarities – or lack of them – and congruence – or mismatching – are the name of the game.

Hence, to illustrate, in such a perspective it might not come as a surprise, say that 'Confucianism' under some institutional set-ups might appear as a hindrance to industrial development while in others might be a source of 'progressive' social norms; that 'labour market rigidities' in some contexts are just 'rigidities' while in others are powerful drivers to within-firm knowledge accumulation and cooperative behaviours.

To repeat, let me emphasize the still preliminary stage of such types of formal analysis – as distinct from a long and noble pedigree of 'qualitative' historical analyses, ranging from Adam Smith to Cipolla, from Marx to Landes, from Weber to Dore, indeed to Chris Freeman. As an almost symmetric opposite term of comparison, many of the younger readers are certainly familiar with the 'political economy' with solid formal neoclassical roots (for a thorough statement see Persson and Tabellini (2000)). Call it the 'Neo Political Economy' (NPE). In the NPE world, one studies the equilibrium effects of different policies and political set-ups grounded in rational responses of invariantly maximizing agents. Philosophically germane to that stream of analysis is the search for some sort of invariant 'meta-production function' that is supposed to parsimoniously describe the transformation of whatever 'inputs' which might range from physical capital investment all the way to the protestant ethic, the propensity to reproduce, the resistance to malaria, the degrees of education, the distance from the equator, and so on, into some socio-economic performance 'output'. (A concise example of the *genre* is Sachs and Warner (1997); elements of caution on the outcomes of the whole exercise are in Easterly (2001).) The device is simple and deceivingly innocent: in fact, on a couple of occasions even Chris Freeman in the essays which follow makes a heuristic use of production functions of the kind! Personally, I am all in favour of the search for statistical regularities possibly characterizing the development process and its underlying political economy. However, as I voiced earlier my scepticism regarding the quest for the 'magic bullet' explanations, I am equally sceptical about the enterprise of estimating some kind of 'meta-recipe' able to sort out the relative contributions of for example democracy, degrees of distributional inequality, knowledge, the rule-of-law, and so on within some invariant 'meta-cuisine' (as extreme in that vein, I once heard a very famous economist presenting his own 'theory of history' grounded into a production function which was supposed to be invariant in its functional form from the Stone Age to the present!). In fact, in a world ridden with complementarities the search for the 'meta-recipe' loses much of its interpretative power.[4]

What does one do then? Well, first, we should all continue and refine upon the exercises of 'reasoned history' of which Chris Freeman has offered convincing templates. Second, we certainly should refine our knowledge of the stylized facts of development, trying to identify the invariances and the discontinuities both in time series and cross-sectionally across different groups of countries (building upon some of the early classic contributions of Burns, Mitchell, Kuznets and Kaldor, and adding novel micro economic knowledge; on this point see also Dosi et al. (1994)). A third, complementary, line of investigation, involves in my view the construction of models – 'as simple as possible, but not simpler', as Einstein once put it! – able to generate (and thus, in some sense explain) the foregoing 'stylized facts'. Not surprisingly my preference goes for models of an evolutionary kind but I wholeheartedly welcome a healthy competition between evolutionary and more mainstream models aimed at interpreting a commonly recognized set of phenomena, ranging from the long-term properties of the time series of economic aggregates such as GDP, productivity, employment, and so on all the way to micro phenomena such as those concerning the patterns of innovation, corporate performance, and the dynamics of industrial structures.

The subtitle of Chris Freeman's selection of writings is 'Essays in Evolutionary Economics'. They are in fact genuinely 'evolutionary' at least in the sense of the evolutionary research programme whose building blocks one tries to spell out in different ways in Nelson and Winter (1982), Dosi and Nelson (1994) and Dosi and Winter (2002). At a first look, the spirit of Freeman's essays significantly differs from a good deal of contemporary evolutionary contributions, which mostly address micro and industry-level aspects of technological and organizational change (although not exclusively: for recent assessments also covering progress in the – formal and 'qualitative' – understanding of growth as an evolutionary process, see Nelson and Winter (2002) and Verspagen (2005)). In my view, there is indeed a fundamental complementarity between micro investigations and the more macro perspective running through Chris's essays. In fact, the latter are remarkable examples whereby thoroughly evolutionary micro stories are the underlying thread of the much broader, macro co-evolutionary histories. In Freeman's world this running back and forth between the micro, the macro and the range of complementary institutions is natural, as it should be. So the reader will appreciate in the essays that follow insightful pieces of analysis of the painstaking emergence of the ICT-centred techno-economic paradigm and of the national specificities influencing the modes and rates of its diffusion. In all that, as already mentioned, Chris Freeman's thesis is that also in the 'globalization era' nations (and 'quasi nations', such as the European Union) will continue to play a fundamental role as entities driving policy-making and institution-building. As so will the 'visible hand' of large enterprises play such a role, even if their organizational structure and their sectors of principal activity are changing as compared to the earlier 'Fordist' electro-mechanical paradigm.

I was mentioning the fact that Chris Freeman's works – those reproduced in this book and his whole production – are a template of an analytical style continuously relating micro events (say, specific innovations), 'meso' dynamics (for example the competitiveness and the patterns of evolution of particular industries) and macro patterns concerning income growth, employment, relative success/decline of particular countries. Such a style of analysis is indeed too rare a virtue, also in the evolutionary camp. As a correlate, even in the latter there is far too little reflection on the broad collective implications of the dynamics of innovation, 'creative disruption' and industrial evolution. Putting it telegraphically, in the large fuzzy 'evolutionary community' – in my view – there is a bit too much Schumpeter and far too little Keynes. And the imbalance is so high that sometimes one suspects that some evolutionary scholars are not too uncomfortable to see all their micro foundations summarized by, say, some neat equilibrium trajectory at a macro level. And some might not even shiver at the *mother of all evolutionary mistakes*, that is Milton Friedman's 'hand waving theorem' restating Mr Pangloss's proposition that 'everything we observe must be optimal, otherwise any superior competitor would have wiped it out . . .'. At this point in time, one ought to leave one of the numerous falsifications of the statement to graduate students: however, for those just educated in Chicago and intellectual surroundings, early criticisms are in Winter (1964) and (1975).

Chris Freeman on the contrary belongs to that group of evolutionary scholars who believes in the widespread possibility of multiple evolutionary paths (incidentally note that such multiplicity erodes any interpretative value to the proposition that evolution is a sort of decentralized optimization device: more on it in Castaldi and Dosi (2006)). Chris, if I understand him well, is quite comfortable with varying degrees of path-dependence in technological and institutional dynamics. In fact I trust he is quite comfortable with Paul David's proposition that 'institutions are carriers of history' (David, 1994) with all the inertia that they entail. Granted that, the whole – personal and intellectual – history of Chris Freeman has been marked by the passionate search for the degrees of freedom for purposeful human action apt to steer the evolution of socio-economic institutions toward progressive social objectives – including the international diffusion of new technologies and industrial development, equitable patterns of income distribution, employment and democratic rights, the reduction of environmental rape. I am sure to interpret also Chris's thoughts in stating that in fact these objectives have been what motivated him and quite a few of us to understand in detail how the socio-economic machine works precisely in order to identify the levers and the 'windows of opportunity' in order to change it. Chris has done a lot in this respect, trying also to spell out normative proposals at an institutional and policy level (see Freeman (1992), Freeman and Soete (1993) and also the essays in this volume).

Few others, in the past and in the near present have voiced overlapping objectives (see among others, Nelson (1977), Hirschman (1973 and 1995), Dore (2004), Stiglitz (2006)). However it is only fair to admit the minority role that all these voices, (indeed, our voices) have played especially over the last quarter of a century as compared to a 'spirit of the time' roughly grounded into some version of the neoclassical orthodoxy, but – even more importantly – into some unquestioned faith in the 'magic of the market', 'put incentives right and everything will turn out in place', and other dangerous acts of faith of this sort. Chris Freeman has been one of the few who basically did not care about this tide. At last, the world is (reluctantly) sobering up from a sinister illusion whereby 'globalization', 'the new Economy', 'more market, less policies', and so on should have been the universal panaceas. That might indeed correspond also to a 'window of opportunity' at the policy level. But one will not be able to seize it if the 'projects for better worlds' are not accompanied by a careful, dispassionate, rigorous analysis of the anatomy and evolution of the contemporary socio-economic fabric. This is one of the precious lessons that my friend Chris continues to give us.

NOTES

* Scuola Superiore Sant'Anna, Pisa, and Visiting Professor, University of Manchester. Thanks to Giulio Bottazzi, Luigi Marengo and Angelo Secchi for their comments on an earlier draft.
1. For a reconstruction of some elements of the history of the 'economics of science', see Nelson (2006).
2. In fact, as Chris Freeman implicitly suggests – and I happen to agree – it is at a national level where the interaction among these five domains appears more clearly. See also Nelson (1993) and Lundvall (1992). This does not mean to say that a germane notion of systems of innovation cannot be fruitfully applied at a sectoral level: on the latter, see Malerba (2004).
3. The merits of such methodology, on more micro economic grounds, are stressed also by Williamson (1999).
4. And of course, the fact that one is able to estimate interaction terms is a far cry from the 'combinatorics' property that, say, A when together with B and C might have a beneficial effect on growth while it may have a negative one when it comes just together with C and in the presence of D. For a similar argument concerning the simpler domain of production theory, see Dosi and Grazzi (2006).

BIBLIOGRAPHY

Aoki, M. (1990), 'Toward an Economic Model of the Japanese Firm', *Journal of Economic Literature*, **28**(1), 1–27.

Aoki, M. (2001), *Toward a Comparative Institutional Analysis*, Cambridge, MA: MIT Press.

Aoki, M. and G. Dosi (1992), 'Corporate Organization, Finance and Innovation', in V. Zamagni (ed.), *Finance and the Enterprise. Facts and Theories*, New York: Academic Press, republished in Dosi (2000).

Boyer, R. (1988a), 'Technical Change and the Theory of "Regulation"', in Dosi et al. (1988).

Boyer, R. (1988b), 'Formalising Growth Regimes', in Dosi et al. (1988).

Castaldi, C. and G. Dosi (2006), 'The Grip of History and the Scope for Novelty: Some Results and Open Questions on Path Dependence in Economic Processes', in A. Wimmer and R. Kössler (eds), *Understanding Change. Models, Methodologies, and Metaphors*, London: Palgrave Macmillan.

Cimoli, M., G. Dosi, R.R. Nelson and J. Stiglitz (2006), *Institutions and Policies Shaping Industrial Development: An Introductory Note*, Pisa, Scuola Superiore Sant'Anna, LEM Working Paper 2006/02, forthcoming in M. Cimoli, G. Dosi and J. Stiglitz (eds), *Industrial Policies and Development*, Oxford and New York: Oxford University Press.

Coriat, B. and G. Dosi (1998), 'The Institutional Embeddedness of Economic Change: An Appraisal of the "Evolutionary" and "Regulationist" Research Programmes', in K. Nileson and B. Johnson (eds), *Institutions and Economic Change: New Perspectives on Markets, Firms and Technology*, Cheltenham, UK and Lyme, USA: Edward Elgar, republished in Dosi (2000).

David, P.A. (1994), 'Why are Institutions the "Carriers of History"?: Path Dependence and the Evolution of Conventions, Organizations and Institutions', *Structural Change and Economic Dynamics*, **5**(2), 205–20.

Dore, R. (2004), *New Forms and Meanings of Work in an Increasingly Globalized World*, Geneva: International Labour Office.

Dosi, G. (2000), *Innovation, Organization and Economic Dynamics. Selected Essays*, Cheltenham, UK and Northampton, MA, USA: Edward Elgar.

Dosi, G. and M. Grazzi (2006), 'Technologies as Problem-solving Procedures and Technologies as Input-output Relations: Some Perspectives on the Theory of Production', *Industrial and Corporate Change*, **15**(1), 173–202.

Dosi, G. and R. Nelson (1994), 'An Introduction to Evolutionary Theories in Economics', *Journal of Evolutionary Economics*, **4**(3), 153–72, republished in Dosi (2000).

Dosi, G. and L. Orsenigo (1988), 'Coordination and Transformation: An Overview of Structures, Behaviours and Change in Evolutionary Environments', in Dosi et al. (1988).

Dosi, G. and S.G. Winter (2002), 'Interpreting Economic Change: Evolution, Structures and Games', in M. Augier and J. March (eds), *The Economics of Choice, Change and Organizations: Essays in Memory of Richard M. Cyert*, Cheltenham, UK and Northampton, MA, USA: Edward Elgar, (an earlier version is in Dosi, 2000).

Dosi, G., C. Freeman and S. Fabiani (1994), 'The Process of Economic Development. Introducing some stylized Facts and Theories on Technologies, Firms and Institutions', *Industrial and Corporate Change*, 3(1), 1–45.

Dosi, G., C. Freeman, R.R. Nelson, G. Silverberg and L. Soete (eds) (1988), *Technical Change and Economic Theory*, London: Pinter and New York: Columbia University Press.

Easterly, W. (2001), *The Elusive Quest for Growth*, Cambridge, MA: MIT Press

Fagerberg, J., D. Mowery and R. Nelson (eds) (2005), *The Oxford Handbook of Innovation*, Oxford and New York: Oxford University Press.

Foray, D. and C. Freeman (eds) (1993), *Technology and the Wealth of Nations*, London: Pinter.

Freeman, C. (1962), 'Research and Development: a Comparison between British and American Industry', *National Institute Economic Review*, 20, 21–39.

Freeman, C. (1982), *The Economics of Industrial Innovation*, London: Frances Pinter, 2nd edition; 3rd edition (1997) with L. Soete, MIT Press.

Freeman, C. (1987), *Technology Policy and Economic Performance: Lessons from Japan*, London and New York: Pinter.

Freeman, C. (1992), *The Economics of Hope: Essays on Technical Change, Economic Growth and the Environment*, London and New York: Pinter.

Freeman, C. (1994), 'The Economics of Technical Change', *Cambridge Journal of Economics*, 18, 463–514.

Freeman, C. (2002), 'Continental, National and Sub-national Innovation Systems – Complementarity and Economic Growth', *Research Policy*, 31, 191–211, republished in this volume, Chapter 6.

Freeman, C. (2004), 'Technical Infrastructure and International Competitiveness', *International and Corporate Change*, 13(3), 541–69.

Freeman, C. and C. Perez (1988), 'Structural Crises of Adjustment: Business Cycles and Investment Behaviour', in Dosi et al. (1988).

Freeman, C. and L. Soete (1993), *Information Technology and Employment*, Report prepared for IBM Europe, Datawyse, Maastricht.

Freeman, C. and F. Louçã (2001), *As Time Goes By: From the Industrial Revolutions to the Information Revolution*, Oxford: Oxford University Press.

Freeman, C., J.K. Fuller and A.J. Young (1963), 'The Plastics Industry: a Comparative Study of Research and Innovation', *National Institute Economic Review*, **26**, 22–62.

Freeman, C., C.J.E. Harlow and J.K. Fuller (1965), 'Research and Development in Electronic Capital Goods', *National Institute Economic Review*, **34**, 40–97.

Hall, P.A. and D. Soskice (eds) (2001), *Varieties of Capitalism. The Institutional Foundations of Comparative Advantage*, Oxford: Oxford University Press.

Hirschman, A.O. (1973), *The Strategy for Economic Development*, New Haven, CT: Yale University Press.

Hirschman, A.O. (1995), *A Bias for Hope: Essays on Development and Latin America*, Westview, CO: Encore Edition.

Lundvall, B.-Å. (1992), *National Systems of Innovation: Towards a Theory of Innovation and Interactive Learning*, London: Pinter Publishers.

Malerba, F. (ed.) (2004), *Sectoral Systems of Innovation: Concepts, Issues and Analyses of Six Major Sectors in Europe*, Cambridge: Cambridge University Press.

Marengo, L. (1992), 'Coordination and Organizational Learning in the Firm', *Journal of Evolutionary Economics*, **2**, 313–26.

Nelson, R. (1977), *The Moon and the Ghetto*, New York: Norton.

Nelson, R. (1990), 'Capitalism as an Engine of Progress', *Research Policy*, **19**, 61–87.

Nelson, R. (ed.) (1993), *National Innovation Systems*, New York: Oxford University Press.

Nelson, R. (2006), 'Reflections on "The Simple Economics of Basic Scientific Research": Looking Back and Looking Forward', *Industrial and Corporate Change*, **15**, 903–17.

Nelson, R. and S. Winter (1982), *An Evolutionary Theory of Economic Growth*, Cambridge, MA: The Belknap Press of Harvard University.

Nelson, R. and S. Winter (2002), 'Evolutionary Theorizing in Economics', *The Journal of Economic Perspectives*, **16**(2), 23–46.

Perez, C. (2002), *Technological Revolutions and Financial Capital: The Dynamics of Bubbles and Golden Ages*, Cheltenham, UK and Northampton, MA, USA: Edward Elgar.

Persson, T. and G. Tabellini (2000), *Political Economics: Explaining Economic Policy*, Cambridge, MA: MIT Press.

Rothwell, R., C. Freeman, A. Horsley, V.T.P. Jervis, A.B. Robertson and J. Townsend (1974), 'SAPPHO Updated – Project SAPPHO Phase II', *Research Policy*, **3**(3), 258–91.

Sachs, J.D. and A.M. Warner (1997), 'Fundamental Sources of Long-Run Growth', *American Economic Review*, Papers and Proceedings, **87**, 184–8.

Stiglitz, J.E. (2006), *Making Globalization Work*, New York: Norton.

Verspagen, B. (2005), 'Innovation and Economic Growth', in Fagerberg et al. (2005).

Williamson, O. (1999), 'Strategy Research: Governance and Competence Perspectives', *Strategic Management Journal*, **20**, 1087–108, reprinted in Nicolai Foss and Volker Mahnke (eds) (2000), *Competence, Governance, and Entrepreneurship*, New York: Oxford University Press, pp. 21–54.

Winter, S. (1964), 'Economic "Natural Selection" and the Theory of the Firm', *Yale Economic Essays*, **4**, 225–72.

Winter, S. (1975), 'Optimization and Evolution in the Theory of the Firm', in R.H. Day and T. Groves (eds), *Adaptive Economic Models*, New York: Academic Press, pp. 73–118.

1.   Introduction

I hesitated before deciding to go ahead with the publication of this set of chapters because they were written for a variety of different purposes and at rather different times. Therefore, they lacked the coherence of a book written at one time and for a specific goal. Moreover, the rapid advances of information technology meant that students and other scholars could usually obtain copies of the essays even though they were originally published in a variety of journals and countries, and sometimes as chapters in other books.

However, I was ultimately persuaded to embark on publication by several counter-arguments. First of all, a book is still a simple, convenient and comfortable way to impart, store and present a variety of accumulated ideas and information. The publishers, Edward Elgar, were extremely helpful in handling all the preliminary formal arrangements necessary for the publication of such a diverse set of papers. I am very grateful for their help throughout. Second, as on many previous occasions, I was greatly helped in the final processing of the papers by Susan Lees and I am indebted, as always, to her too. Finally, although of course there are inconsistencies and gaps in the story, there is actually a thread connecting most of the papers – the development of the concept of 'national systems of innovation' (NSI). There is something to be said for presenting the evolution of these ideas 'as they happened'.

Consequently, after this brief introduction (Chapter 1), Chapter 2 goes back to my first use of this expression in 1982. Fittingly, this old paper was resurrected by my friend and colleague, Bengt-Åke Lundvall. To the best of my knowledge, he was the first person to use the expression NSI informally and in seminars and I picked it up from him during a visit to Aalborg. I used it in this paper written for the OECD and Lundvall came across it when he himself was working at the OECD in Paris some 20 years later.

During the 1980s, the idea passed into general currency among people interested in the social studies of science and technology, so that when Giovanni Dosi and others hit upon the idea of a textbook on *Technical Change and Economic Theory* (Dosi et al., 1988), in a chapter on business cycles and structural crises of adjustment which I contributed together with my colleague, Carlota Perez, we used the technology systems concept as part of a general taxonomy of innovations and technical change (Freeman and Perez, 1988). This chapter introduced a discussion on the relationship between technological revolutions, economic fluctuations and changes of techno-economic paradigms which became a feature of the prolonged debate on 'Kondratiev waves' which Schumpeter had already unleashed in the 1930s. Carlota Perez went on to pursue her research on finance and technical change in a book on *Technological Revolutions and Financial Capital: The Dynamics of Bubbles and Golden Ages* (Perez, 2002). In this, as in her earlier work, she insisted on the importance of institutional changes in the diffusion of innovations. This meant that in her work as well as in my own and that of others using the NSI concept, such as Lundvall (1992) and Nelson (1993), social change was always accepted as an interdependent process, together with technical change.

Sociologists, as well as historians and economists, developed the concept of NSI. In his *A Contemporary Critique of Historical Materialism*, one of the leading sociologists of the late-twentieth century, Anthony Giddens (1981, 1995) defined a 'social system' as a society embodying an intermingling of four criteria:

1. Association with a 'social space' or 'territory of occupation';
2. A 'legitimated series of prerogatives over occupied social space', especially 'over the material environment to provide food, water and shelter';
3. 'An institutional clustering of practices among the participants in the social system', not necessarily implying total consensus or lack of dissent;
4. An overall awareness of 'belonging to an inclusive community', but again not necessarily implying consensus about values or policies (Giddens, 1995: 45–6).

Although Giddens did not use the expression 'national systems of innovation', or refer to the concept, there is some similarity between his earlier 'social systems' concept and the NSI concept as it was developing in the 1980s. However, they also differ in some important respects. While both refer to 'subsystems' of society, the NSI of course place emphasis on 'science' and 'technology', whereas these do not figure at all as subsystems in the work of Giddens. The concluding chapter (Chapter 12) of this book returns again to the theme of subsystems and possible conflicts between them in the process of economic growth (Freeman and Louçã, 2001). The idea of contradictions between the 'productive forces', the 'relations of production' and the 'superstructure' was the central feature of Marx's materialist conception of history. But the approach here again differs from this. The chapters which deal with economic growth in different parts of the world and different types of society again concentrate mainly on the science and technology subsystems (Chapters 6–9).

This does not mean that they abandoned the idea of a continuous interaction between technical change and social change, nor yet that they always assigned primacy to science and technology. On the contrary, they often emphasised that the dominant role was a changing one. In the terminology of Lundvall's Introduction in Chapter 2, the approach to NSI was a 'broad' and not a 'narrow' conception.

The classical school of economists had of course already recognised long ago the crucial role of technical change in economic growth, interacting with the division of labour, the expansion of trade, exchange and markets and the profits of entrepreneurship. But it was Friedrich List in his book on *The National System of Political Economy* (1841) who first attempted to identify those institutions which were responsible for the advance of science, technology and education during the tempestuous period of the industrial revolution. He was mainly concerned with how the German states might catch up with England in technology so that his prescription might just as well have been entitled 'The National System of Innovation'.

For this reason, the early chapters in the present book identify Friedrich List as the true originator of the NSI concept, despite the many criticisms which could be made (and have been made) of his work. In particular, his ideas about 'catching up' are highly relevant still today for the less developed countries in the world economy and not only, or even mainly, because of his views on infant industries. Then Chapters 4 and 5 look at some wider social problems, especially employment and structural change in the economy.

Two of the major books on NSI which appeared only in the 1990s, both multi-authored works edited by Lundvall (1992) and by Nelson (1993), already contained numerous comparisons of national systems in various parts of the world and these books demonstrated that much can be learned from such comparisons. In particular, there is a sharp contrast between the 'exploding' economies of Eastern Asia and the so-called 'imploding' economies of Eastern Europe in the closing years of the twentieth century. The chapters in the central part of this book are concerned with the key features of each of these and with the NSI of the strongest power – the United States. Hopefully they help to make clear the wide variety of NSI and the varying role of political coordination, of economic policies and of the science and technology sub-systems. Hopefully too, they indicate some of the enduring strengths of the United States NSI while simultaneously pointing out its vulnerability to the competition of catch-up NSI.

An earlier set of essays *Economics of Hope* (1992) confronted many gloomy forecasts of the 1970s and 1980s and argued that there were still some grounds for a more optimistic view of the future prospects for the human species. Climate change since then means that the prospects are even more daunting as some of the pessimistic forecasts are already being realised. Nevertheless, this present set of essays retains the fundamentally hopeful view of that earlier book.

This is not sheer perversity or stubbornness; nor is it based on viewing the world through rose-tinted glasses. On the contrary, the scale of poverty, of environmental pollution and of authoritarian threats to civil liberty are fully acknowledged. So, too, are the effects of numerous wars and the threat of nuclear war. All of this is more than enough to blunt facile optimism. If, nevertheless, these essays still point to some hopes for a brighter future, this is because of the unique characteristics of the human species in developing science and technology and, simultaneously, a deeper understanding of the social and ethical problems of organising and controlling scientific and technical activities. These are far from simple. Yet, one result of having a 'semi-autonomous' political system is that political leadership is, in Al Gore's immortal phrase, itself a 'renewable resource'. Although he has been one of the foremost politicians in warning of the dangers of climate change and the extent of the changes which have already taken place, he believes there are potential international political solutions for these problems, using new science and technologies.

In searching for and attempting to implement these solutions, hope is itself a vital ingredient of attempts to improve and change the world. Flickering hopes are sustained in part by deeper understanding. It is my hope that these essays will make a small but positive contribution to this deeper understanding of technical and social change. The concluding chapters of the book elaborate this perspective in various ways.

REFERENCES

Dosi, G., C. Freeman, R. Nelson, G. Silverberg and L. Soete (eds) (1988), *Technical Change and Economic Theory*, London: Pinter.

Freeman, C. (1992), *Economics of Hope*, London: Pinter.

Freeman, C. and F. Louçã (2001), *As Time Goes By: From the Industrial Revolutions to the Information Revolution*, Oxford: Oxford University Press.

Freeman, C. and C. Perez (1988), 'Structural Crises of Adjustment, Business Cycles and Investment Behaviour', in G. Dosi et al. (eds), *Technical Change and Economic Theory*, London: Pinter, pp. 38–66.

Giddens, A. (1981, 1995), *A Contemporary Critique of Historical Materialism*, London: Macmillan.

List, F. (1841), *The National System of Political Economy*, London: Longman.

Lundvall, B.-Å. (ed.) (1992), *National Systems of Innovation: Towards a Theory of Innovation and Interactive Learning*, London: Pinter.

Nelson, R.R. (ed.) (1993), *National Systems of Innovation: A Comparative Analysis*, Oxford: Oxford University Press.
Perez, C. (2002), *Technological Revolutions and Financial Capital: The Dynamics of Bubbles and Golden Ages*, Cheltenham, UK and Northampton, MA, USA: Edward Elgar.

2. Technological infrastructure and international competitiveness

The paper is probably the first written paper using the concept of 'the national innovation system' and it analyses how technological infrastructure differs between countries and how such differences are reflected in international competitiveness. It makes a critical review of new (in the 1980s) developments in the theory of international trade and confronts them with recent empirical results. It shows how competitiveness cannot be explained by wage rates/prices/currency rates. Technological leadership gives absolute rather than comparative advantage and technological leadership will reflect institutions supporting coupling, creating, clustering comprehending and coping in connection with technology. The analysis is rooted in historical context through references to Friedrich List and his criticism of Adam Smith and laissez-faire. Special emphasis is put on List's concept of mental capital. Finally, the analytical arguments are illustrated by the catching-up and forging ahead of first Germany and later Japan. The paper concludes that disequilibria in international trade will be persistent and that for laggard economy the free trade doctrine may be unduly restrictive. Another conclusion is that public investment in technological infrastructure and intellectual capital is crucial for successful economic development. It is pointed out that there is a need to couple education, science, trade and industry policy in order to build competitiveness.

B.-Å. Lundvall

1. INTERNATIONAL SPECIALIZATION AND INTERNATIONAL COMPETITIVENESS

Some recent OECD work has drawn a distinction between the study of trade performance on the one hand and studies of the 'evolution of factors affecting trade performance' on the other (OECD, 1981). The former type of study concentrates on factors, which modify 'the structure (volume, product composition, geographical distribution) of trade between countries in a quasi-objective way that is largely independent of the conscious action of individual countries'. Much of the academic literature on the economics of international trade is of this nature. The latter type of study concentrates on 'ways in which competition is waged between firms and the measures taken by governments to help them'. These studies are more characteristic of the literature of business economics and, one might add, of economic history and history more generally. In so far as they deal with technology at all, the first type of study treats it as a quasi-autonomous factor modifying traditional theories of comparative advantage based on relative factor costs. The second type of approach, however, treats technology as one (usually rather important) element in the competitive struggle between firms and nation-states, which may be manipulated by appropriate policies, both at the national level and the level of the firm (OECD, 1978).

In so far as it may be useful to make this conceptual distinction, this paper belongs clearly to the second category. It attempts some very elementary analysis of the influence of science and technology infrastructure on international competitiveness and it is concerned in particular with various ways in which a science-technology system may be organized, and how these have changed over time. It is argued that such changes have been an important element in the changing locus of international technological leadership and that this leadership has been a dominant element in competitiveness. However, it is an important part of the argument which will be developed, that there has in fact been some convergence between the two approaches distinguished above, as the theory of international trade has been going through a period of turmoil which without exaggeration could be described as a paradigm change, involving both a far more explicit recognition of the importance of technology in the explanation of past patterns of trade performance and much greater attention to the role of institutional factors.

2.   INTERNATIONAL TRADE THEORIES AND TECHNOLOGY

During the post-war period the traditional theory of international trade proved incapable of providing a satisfactory explanation of the observed patterns of commodity trade. Following the demonstration in 1953 of the 'Leontief Paradox' (Leontief, 1953), it became difficult to sustain explanations of the trade performance of such countries as the United States and the German Federal Republic in terms of the relative costs of labour and capital. Posner's seminal paper in 1961 opened the way to the development of an alternative paradigm, or at the very least a substantial revision of the established theory. Starting from the self-evident fact that a firm which introduces a new product may enjoy an export monopoly from the country of origin at least until imitators come into the market, he developed a set of concepts which became the basis for various 'technology gap' theories of foreign trade. As long as the 'imitation lag' was longer than the 'demand lag', technology gap trade could persist. Posner identified several mechanisms that might tend to maintain this gap for fairly long periods, including the quality and scale of commitment to R&D, the 'clustering' of technical innovations and dynamic economies of scale.

A few years after the appearance of Posner's paper, Hufbauer (1966) provided an excellent empirical illustration and validation of the theory with his study of international trade in synthetic materials. He measured imitation lags for many countries for some 60 synthetic materials and demonstrated a clear-cut relationship between trade performance and innovative leadership. He recognized that as a product matured, traditional cost elements could become increasingly important, so that 'low wage' trade could take over from 'technology gap' trade in mature technologies. Although he showed convincingly that innovation and early imitation explained the predominant position of the German and US chemical industries in trade performance in the early decades of the new synthetic materials industry, he did not attempt to investigate the source of these innovations other than by identifying the firm of origin.

This question was taken up in a series of studies at the National Institute of Economic and Social Research in the 1960s (Freeman et al., 1963, 1965, 1968). These attempted to relate both the innovative and the comparative trade performance of firms and countries to various factors which Posner (1961) had identified, particularly the scale, location and quality of their R&D and the 'outputs' from that R&D, as measured by various indicators such as patents. The results of this work lent support to the view that the innovative leadership of German chemical firms over a long period was related to their exceptionally heavy investment in R&D and the same point also emerged in relation to the leadership of US firms in the world market for electronic capital goods. Patent statistics showed that technological leadership in these industries was broadly based and did not rest simply on a few chance inventions or discoveries. However, it was never suggested that the innovative successes of leading firms or countries could be explained simply in terms of the quantity of R&D performed. The studies also attempted to take into account firm strategies, institutional factors, such as the role of government research, of the education system and the inter-dependent relationship between various groups of firms, such as for example chemical firms, chemical process plant contractors and machinery suppliers. This paper represents an attempt to extend and generalize this approach, taking into account the results of more recent work.

Both the NIESR studies and Hufbauer's work were important also in underlining the relationship between imitation lags, dynamic economies of scale, process innovation, and a range of scientific and technical activities. Imitation lags could be prolonged if R&D threshold costs were high and the best competitive efforts of would-be imitators could be repeatedly frustrated if the innovators could maintain a flow of process innovations related to scale economies and new generations of products. Such mechanisms were later shown to be extraordinarily important in the semiconductor industry by the studies of Golding (1972), Sciberras (1977) and Dosi (1981a). All of this empirical evidence pointed to the conclusion that technology gaps could be sustained over long periods. However, it related only to a few specific industrial sectors and could thus be dismissed as irrelevant for the greater part of foreign trade.

The first attempts to relate trade performance to some measure of technical innovativeness across a wide range of industries were made by Vernon, Keesing and their colleagues at Harvard in the mid-1960s (Vernon et al., 1967). Their work pointed the way to a resolution of the Leontief Paradox, in as much as it demonstrated that there was a fairly strong statistical association between the ranking of US shares of world export markets by product group, the R&D intensity of those industries and other measures of the participation of highly qualified manpower. World export performance of the United States was exceptionally strong in several industries, which although they were certainly 'labour-intensive' rather than capital-intensive in the traditional sense, were characterized by very large inputs from highly skilled personnel. However, this work related only to the United States and attempts to extend it to a wider range of countries at the OECD in the late 1960s ran into severe difficulties because of the limitations of the R&D data, the problems of reconciliation of the R&D classification with trade classifications, and international comparability problems.

In any case, it was always conceptually unsatisfactory to use an 'input' measure (R&D expenditures or manpower data) as a surrogate for technological innovativeness. In the absence of any direct measures of innovative achievement (except those laboriously constructed for individual industries such as synthetic materials), patent statistics seemed to offer the best available 'output' indicator, as they were universally available for long periods. Some of the main problems associated with their use (lack of comparability of different national systems, reflecting variations in propensity to patent) were ingeniously circumvented by Pavitt and Soete (1980) through their use of the new statistics, which became available through the Office of Technology Assessment and Forecasting of the United States Department of Commerce.

The first systematic attempts to relate international trade performance to some measure of 'technological output' across the board and for a large number of OECD countries were made by Soete (1980, 1981). In his 'General Test of Technological Gap Trade Theory' he regressed variations in export performance across 22 OECD countries on variations in innovativeness for each of 40 industrial sectors. His results demonstrated the crucial role of the technology variable in explaining inter-country variations in export performance in the great majority of industries. Non-significant results were obtained for a few industries such as food, petroleum and stone, clay and glass in which natural resource endowment clearly plays an extremely important role. A second group of industries where results also were sometimes not significant were the typical mature industries of relatively low research intensity, such as textiles and ship-building. But the results were significant for 70% of the product groups at the 5% level and for half of them at the 1% level of significance.

In the face of such evidence and the lack of any comparable support in the empirical work to justify the traditional factor proportions theory of comparative advantage, it has become difficult[1] to ignore the importance of the influence of technology on trade performance. Indeed, already in the 1960s some of the leading traditional trade theories had begun to acknowledge the need for some revision of the mainstream theory, notably Harry Johnson, who developed the concept of 'human capital' within neoclassical trade theory (Johnson, 1968).

This major revision of the theory by its leading exponent meant that, after the Montreal Conference of the International Economics Association, both believers and heretics could agree up to a point in stressing the importance of such factors as investment in education and industrial technical training, as well as R&D and other scientific and technical services. In the 1970s a number of economists provided further strong support for this view (see e.g. Horn, 1976; Wolter, 1977).

This did not necessarily mean that 'technology gap' and 'human capital' trade theories were in agreement about other fundamental issues such as the assumptions of perfect competition, attitudes to government intervention and so forth. In practice, despite Harry Johnson's revisionism a significant body of trade theory continued to neglect or ignore the issues raised by the neo-technology debate and to make somewhat unrealistic assumptions about the role of relative prices and of government in relation to trade competition. All the more importance therefore attaches to the other recent empirical and theoretical work by neo-technology trade theorists.

One stream of such work has concentrated on the relevance of 'non-price factors' in the explanation of trade competitivity and of international trade performance. Almost all such studies, whether based on interviews with buyers and sellers, or on more general statistical analysis, point to the conclusion that price is only one element in effective competition. It is of decisive importance for homogeneous primary commodities traded in internationally competitive markets or subjected to relatively simple processing or refining. But in most capital goods markets and for many consumer goods, empirical research points unambiguously to the conclusion that factors such as real or perceived quality variables related to design, technical service, reputation and marketing play an extremely important role, along with non-technical factors such as credit. Kravis and Lipsey (1971) report that their questionnaires showed that only 28% of US exporters attributed success to lower prices, while 37% suggested that the critical factor was product superiority and a further 10% product uniqueness.

Of German importers, only 7% said they were buying in America because of lower prices, whereas 63% explained their imports by non-availability of products at home. Rothwell's (1980, 1981) results for textile machinery and agricultural machinery showed an even greater emphasis on non-price factors. Only 4% of UK companies importing textile machinery in the 1970s gave lower prices as the reason, whilst over 80% gave reasons such as 'superior overall performance and design' or 'technically more advanced' or 'no suitable UK alternative'. In his study of the success of Japanese exporters in the world colour television industry Sciberras (1981) reported that evidence from consumer organizations in both Europe and the United States in the 1970s stressed superior product quality over a great part of the product range. For example, Juran reported in the *Journal of the Electronics Industry* (March 1979) that US sets failed at least five times as frequently as Japanese sets at that time.

At the aggregate statistical level the evidence is no less decisive. Posner and Steer (1979) sum up the results of their analysis as follows:

> Historically there is no doubt that non-price influences have dominated (in UK trade performance) – the proportion of the total change which they 'explain' is an order of magnitude greater than the explanatory power of price competitiveness.

The OECD secretariat paper on the notion of international competitiveness quotes the results of Kaldor (1978) and of the OECD Balance of Payments Division (OECD, 1981), which show 'perverse' relationships between measures of 'price competitiveness' and development of export shares during the 1960s and 1970s. Japan and Germany in particular managed to combine a deterioration of relative prices and labour costs per unit of output with improved export performance, whilst the UK in particular showed a fall in world export shares when her relative export prices and costs were apparently improving. These very strong long-term tendencies of the entire post-war period were deeply rooted and could only be counteracted by changes in relative prices to a limited extent.

3.   TECHNOLOGICAL LEADERSHIP AND TRADE PERFORMANCE

These last results are of the greatest interest for our present purpose since they demonstrate that long-term shifts in world export shares between the leading manufacturing countries are not primarily explicable in terms of traditional price competition theory, but must be explained in other terms. The studies, which have been discussed so far, have provided fairly conclusive evidence that 'technology' broadly defined has played a very important role. But that evidence relates mainly to competitive performance sector by sector. This applies even to studies, such as those of Soete, which have looked across the board at all sectors of industry. His results and those of similar studies show that firms (and the countries in which they are based) tend to do well in their trade performance if they are relatively more successful than their competitors in developing new products and improving old ones, and in improving the manufacturing technology by which such products are made. They do not show why it is that in certain historical periods particular countries tend to do exceptionally well in export performance not just in one or two industrial sectors, but in many simultaneously, indeed sometimes in almost all of those sectors which are not dominated by natural resource availability or long-term traditional fashion-based factors. It was such general shifts in country performance, which lent credibility to such general explanations as relative prices (sometimes brought about by deliberate exchange rate policies) or low wages.

But if such older general explanations do not stand up to empirical testing or explain only a small part of the observed long-term changes in international trade patterns, then what can technology theories offer which might help to explain shifts in world technological leadership, shifts which are not just randomly distributed across industries or between the various industrial countries or in proportion to their earlier shares of world production or world trade, but occur in waves or long historical periods? What too can they offer to help explain why, when many countries are striving to catch up with the world technology leaders, only a few succeed and then only after a very long period? It is to these and similar questions that we now turn, since they have the greatest interest from the standpoint of international competitiveness as well as the new trends in international trade theory.

What has already been said about Posner's theoretical framework and about the NIESR studies of innovation and trade performance have suggested that 'catching up' and overtaking established technological leaders could pose formidable problems for imitators and aspirants for leadership, since they must aim at a moving target. It is no use simply importing today's technology from the leading countries for, by the time it has been introduced and efficiently assimilated, the leaders have moved on and the relative position of the various countries may be unchanged or even worsened from the standpoint of the followers. It cannot be simply assumed that 'catching-up' is an easy and almost costless process, based on the simplistic assumption that new technology is equally and freely available to all comers. This is one of several very unrealistic assumptions of perfect competition theory, which must be finally discarded if any progress is to be made in understanding the factors affecting international competitiveness. On the contrary, as has already been pointed out much of the empirical work on technology and international competition points to such problems as high R&D entry barriers, major bottlenecks in acquiring requisite skills, very significant dynamic economies of scale, high cost of the most recent and desirable patents, licences and know-how and so forth.

It is for these reasons that 'overtakers' face such difficult policy issues as the scale and direction of investment in technological infrastructure, as well as the infant industry problem which has pre-occupied them since the days of Friedrich List. It is for this reason too that great interest attaches to the achievement of those firms and those countries, which have succeeded in overcoming these entry barriers and overtaking the established leaders. This surely lies behind the great worldwide interest in those factors, which might explain the recent (1960s–1970s) astonishing performance of the Japanese economy or the rather less successful efforts of the Soviet economy, except in the military-space field. Much might be learned also from the earlier experience of Germany and the United States in overtaking and surpassing the one-time technology (and trade) leaders of the nineteenth century. Finally, something also is surely to be learned from the successful (and unsuccessful) attempts of the Newly Industrializing Countries (NICs) to break into the circle of leading industrial countries.

In developing such an analysis it is far less possible to make use of international statistics, whether with respect to trade or technology. This is for several reasons, both practical and analytical. On the purely practical level, the problems of reclassification of the immense volume of international trade statistics to reconcile them with the only available measures of technological output – patent statistics – are so formidable as to virtually preclude any major retrospective extension of the type of work accomplished by Soete, except perhaps in terms of some very broad sectors or over a long period. Pavitt and Soete (1981) have indeed already demonstrated that the type of approach, which they pioneered, can be used at the aggregate level to investigate long-term changes in the relative inventive performance of the leading industrial countries in relation to economic growth perform-ance. However, the problems that we wish to investigate can only to a small degree be illuminated by statistical evidence, since they involve also social, institutional and organizational questions and qualitative rather than quantitative assessment. Moreover, this is a first and rather tentative and speculative attempt to examine a range of problems, which have not hith-erto been the subject of systematic investigation. Consequently the method will be that of 'reasoned history', only occasionally supported by fragments of quantitative evidence.

This need not distress us too much. It was Schumpeter (1939) who, more than any other twentieth-century economist, recognized the fundamental importance of technology for competition between firms, and who in his work on long-term developments in the world economy commented:

> . . . it is absurd to think that we can derive the contour lines of our phenomena from our statistical material only. All we could ever prove from it is that no regular contour lines exist . . . We cannot stress this point sufficiently. General history (social, political and cultural), economic history and more particularly industrial history[2] are not only indispensable, but really the most important contributors to the understanding of our problem. All other materials and methods, statistical and theoretical, are only subservient to them and worse than useless without them.

Clemence and Doody (1950), in their summary of the Schumpeterian system, add further:

> If innovation and qualitative change are the fundamental elements in economic development, then no amount of quantitative analysis can reveal the really significant pattern. As soon as we open the door to qualitative phenomena we admit a degree of human judgment that must largely supplant more objective and mechanical devices.

Whilst not everyone may be entirely happy with this degree of demotion for quantitative techniques of inquiry, we may now proceed to discuss the fol-lowing questions: what changes in the science-technology system of a country might help to explain its rise to technology leadership over a con-siderable period and its corresponding rise in world market leadership? Were such changes the result of deliberate national policies designed to improve competitive performance? Are there any pointers to the type of policies, which might prove more effective for the next wave of new tech-nologies? In attempting what must inevitably be rather sketchy and flimsy preliminary answers to these very fundamental questions, we accept fully the point made by Chesnais (1981) in his critique of some earlier research: the social circumstances surrounding each new long cycle of technological and economic development differ from the preceding cycle.

Nevertheless we may distinguish certain features of the process of technical innovation which are inherent in the very nature of innovation[3] itself. What changes in successive historical periods in the mode of dealing with these basic characteristics, i.e. which social innovations permit and stimulate a particular society to introduce specific new technologies and to achieve technological and economic leadership?

4.   SOME BASIC CHARACTERISTICS OF TECHNICAL INNOVATION

If it is accepted that success in technical innovation is a crucial element in competitiveness and if we wish to place it at the heart of our analysis, instead of relegating it to a peripheral or residual role, then it follows that some basic characteristics of innovation must be taken into account. These may be summarized as:

1.   Coupling (of changing technology, production and markets)
2.   Creating (new products, processes, systems and industries)
3.   Clustering (of groups of related innovations)
4.   Comprehending (new skills, new technologies, new markets)
5.   Coping (with the technical and market uncertainty of innovation)

We shall consider each of these briefly in turn before going on to discuss the ways in which various countries modified and changed the institutional framework in which they dealt with these characteristic features of innovation in successive cycles of economic development.

4.1   Coupling

This aspect of innovation may be considered as definitional or as purely tautological. Nevertheless it is a feature of the process, which is often forgotten in practice (thus leading to failure in attempts at innovation both in market and in planned economies). Its profound implications for theory are often also overlooked. Following Schumpeter, innovation is usually defined as the commercial realization or introduction of a new product, process or system in the economy. This may be contrasted with *invention*, which is simply the bright idea for such a new product, process or system.

Schumpeter pointed out that there is a world of difference between the two. Most inventions never become innovations since there is many a slip between cup and lip, and the process of developing an invention to the point of commercial introduction is often long and sometimes expensive and risky too. It also requires a special type of creative ability, which Schumpeter defined as entrepreneurship, reserving this term for the management of innovation rather than everyday management.

It follows from this definition of innovation that one of the most important roles of the entrepreneur or innovation manager is to match new technical and scientific possibilities with the needs of potential users of the innovation. At the very elementary level this may be quite straightforward, as, for example, in the inventions and innovations described by Adam Smith, where working men recognized the opportunities for improving their own machines and did the job themselves. On the other hand it can often be far more complicated, as, for example, in the introduction of an instrument landing system for aircraft or a new computerized radar system for air traffic control or a new drug. Such innovations require a complex matching process of new technical knowledge with information about, and experience of, many aspects of the potential market. It is the contention of this paper that whilst Adam Smith's incremental innovation is still extremely important and will remain so for the foreseeable future, the 'coupling' process between technology and the market (or simply users where markets are not involved) has tended to become increasingly difficult, because of the growing complexity of both. This means that social innovations in this coupling system have been a crucial factor in achieving and retaining technological leadership.

4.2   Creating

As has already been indicated above, creativity is an essential element of entrepreneurship, since it involves the bringing together of what were previously disparate and scattered pieces of knowledge to create something new. Sometimes the term 'creativity' is reserved for those abilities of the scientist, which lead to new discoveries or of the artist, which lead to new works of art. These kinds of creativity are important for innovation too. But when we are considering national innovation systems (as opposed to global civilization and the world economy) then at least in the past they have not been so central to innovative success as those types of creativity which are characteristic of the engineer in the work of invention and design and of the entrepreneur. In these entrepreneurial/engineering types of creativity the *synthesis* and creative application of information from a variety of different sources (including the arts and sciences) are critical. Another contention of this paper is that the capacity for such creative synthesis has become increasingly related to more effective modes of coupling with the arts and sciences and their creative initiatives.

4.3 Clustering

It was Schumpeter (1939) again, who observed that innovations, like troubles, do not come singly but in battalions. They are 'more like a series of explosions than a gentle though incessant transformation'. They are not distributed at random, but tend to concentrate in certain sectors and those other sectors, which are intimately affected. This clustering is related to the diffusion process, which leads to further innovations as the band-wagon gets rolling. These observations of Schumpeter have been amply confirmed by much empirical research since his day. All statistics of the inputs and outputs of the R&D system illustrate the point. They show heavily skewed distributions of research, inventive and innovative activities. Moreover, the research-intensive industries and activities tend to be the same throughout the world, with certain exceptions related to military R&D and to the small size of many countries. This suggests that the common underlying factors are the progress of world science and technology and new market opportunities related to income growth. There are a number of mechanisms, which might explain the clustering in terms of world technology. A major new material would involve many applications innovations to take advantage of its new properties in various areas of application. A new piece of equipment, such as a computer, would lead both to component innovations and applications innovations, which are an obvious feature of the contemporary industrial scene. Most product innovations lead to further process and product innovations, as their scale of manufacture increases and as competitors strive to gain some cost of production or quality improvement advantage. The expression 'natural trajectory' has been coined to describe this process of the cumulative exploitation of new ideas, and Nelson and Winter (1977) have pointed out that:

> . . . there is no reason to believe (and many reasons to doubt) that the powerful general trajectories of one era are the powerful ones of the next. For example, it seems apparent that in the twentieth century two widely used natural trajectories opened up (and later variegated) that were not available earlier: the exploitation of the understanding of electricity and the resulting creation and improvement of electrical and later electronic components, and similar developments regarding chemical technologies. It is apparent that industries differ significantly in the extent to which they can exploit the prevailing general natural trajectories, and these differences influence the rise and fall of different industries and technologies.

Schumpeter suggested that 'the rise and fall of different industries and technologies' lay behind the 'Kondratiev' long cycles of economic development,
lasting about half a century. He distinguished three such cycles – the first
(1780s to 1840s) based primarily on the steam engine and a cluster of textile
innovations; the second (1840s to 1890s) based on railways and steel; the
third (1890s to 1940s) based on electricity, the internal combustion engine
and chemicals. Had he lived, he might have identified a fourth (1940s to
1990s) based on electronics, synthetics, petrochemicals and nuclear power,
and speculated about a fifth. The controversy about such 'long waves' has
recently given rise to a considerable literature, as the change in the economic climate of the 1970s and 1980s has become a matter of increasing
concern (Freeman, 1981). However, this controversy need not detain us
here. The substantive point for this discussion is the one made by Nelson
and Winter – as it implies that changes in world technological leadership
may be associated with the emergence of 'new technological systems' and
the associated changes in industrial structure. Further, it suggests that some
countries might fall behind through a failure to adapt sufficiently quickly
to the new 'natural trajectories'. If the new technological systems have very
widespread applications – as, for example, electricity or computers – then
they could help to explain the tendency for countries to succeed (or fail) in
many different sectors in the same periods. It is the contention of this paper
that the capacity to exploit a 'natural trajectory' or a 'new technological
system' rapidly and efficiently is strongly related to various types of infrastructural investment, especially education, as well as to the modes of interaction between industrial firms themselves and their own arrangements for
education and training.

4.4   Comprehending

In whatever country and in whatever institutions the original scientific and
technical ideas, which underlie a new technological system, may have
originated, the ability to innovate successfully and continuously depends
upon the number and quality of the people who have assimilated these
ideas and the depth of their understanding. These in turn depend upon
monitoring systems, information systems and education systems as well as
upon the general 'openness' of a society and the movement of people and
ideas.

4.5   Coping

Again this is in part a matter of definition. Innovation inevitably involves
uncertainty with respect to technology and markets. By definition, it is not

possible to make accurate predictions of the costs, duration and consequences of technical innovation. If it is possible, then what is being done is
not innovation. It is possible to speculate, to make informed guesses, and
to anticipate some of the problems and some of the consequences. The
less radical the innovation, the easier this is, and in the case of simply imitating an innovation made elsewhere the uncertainty may be minimal.
Nevertheless, the ability to cope with uncertainty and to live with it is an
essential element in the successful management of innovation. This has
many implications for technological leadership. It puts a premium on
flexibility in ideas and in institutions. It puts a premium on 'management
slack' of some kind or other in innovating organizations. It puts a premium
on long-term patience with radical new ideas and inventions, and long-term
strategies generally as opposed to the apparent near-certainties of short-
term profit maximization.

We now turn to consider some historical examples of major shifts in
world technological and trade leadership in the light of the above discussion. We first consider the way in which Britain, the leading country of the
first two waves of new technology (steam power, textiles and railways), was
overtaken and surpassed by other countries, particularly Germany. We then
consider another case – Japan – a relative latecomer to international technological competition. We also take a sidelong glance at the Soviet Union,
even though this has not been a market economy since 1917.

5.   FRIEDRICH LIST, LAISSEZ-FAIRE AND MENTAL CAPITAL

George Ray, who introduced the discussion on the changing locus of technological leadership in relation to Kondratiev long waves (Ray, 1980), has
pointed out that British dominance of world production and world exports
in the first half of the nineteenth century was so complete that she
accounted for half or more of total output of most of the major industrial
commodities of that time, including coal, iron, steel, metal products and
cotton cloth. Although bought at a high price in working class suffering,
the great success story of the industrial revolution, which made Britain the
'workshop of the world', was regarded at that time in rather the same way
as the contemporary industrial and trade success of Japan. Britain was the
home not only of the industrial revolution but also of classical political
economy, which she recommended to her competitors and would-be imitators as a sure and universal prescription for success. However, although
classical economics did indeed have a powerful worldwide influence, both
as a social science paradigm and as a religion, not all of its propositions

commanded the same allegiance as in Britain. Foreigners were more inclined to ascribe British success to her technology, her institutions and her investment in manufacturing than to any natural comparative advantages or special dispensation from above.

In particular, the most important and influential economic theorist in Germany, Friedrich List, discussed the British economy in terms highly reminiscent of much contemporary discussion on Japan. He was a powerful critic of Adam Smith on a number of key issues, which are relevant to our analysis:

> Commerce is also certainly productive (as the Laissez-Faire school maintains); but it is so in quite a different manner from agriculture and manufactures. These latter actually produce goods, commerce only brings about the exchange of goods . . . From this it follows that commerce must be regulated, according to the interests and wants of agriculture and manufactures, not vice-versa. But the school has exactly reversed this last dictum by adopting as a favourite expression the saying of old Gourney, 'Laissez-faire, laissez-passez', an expression which sounds no less agreeable to cheats and thieves than to the merchant, and is on that account rather doubtful as a maxim. This perversity of surrendering the interests of manufactures and agriculture to the demands of commerce without reservation, is a natural consequence of that theory which everywhere merely takes into account present values, but nowhere the powers that produce them, and regards the whole world as but one indivisible republic of merchants. (List, 1845)

He accompanied this onslaught on the 'school' by another line of attack in which he anticipated by more than a century the 'human capital' theories of the neo-classical school. Adam Smith had condemned the idea of 'artificially' directing capital into new industries, but List replies:

> Adam Smith has merely taken the word capital in that sense in which it is necessarily taken by rentiers or merchants in their book-keeping and their balance sheets . . . He has forgotten that he himself includes (in his definition of capital) the mental and bodily abilities of the producers under this term. He wrongly maintains that the revenues of the nation are dependent only on the sum of its material capital. His own work on the contrary contains a thousand proofs that these revenues are chiefly conditional on the sum of its mental and bodily powers, and on the degree to which they are perfected, in social and political respects, and that although measures of protection require sacrifices of material goods for a time, these sacrifices are made good a hundred-fold in powers, in the ability to acquire values of exchange, and are consequently merely reproductive outlay by the nation.He has forgotten that the ability of the whole nation to increase the sum of its material capital consists mainly in the possibility of converting unused natural powers into material capital, into valuable and income-producing instruments He has not taken into account that by the policy of favouring native manufacture a mass of foreign capital, mental as well as material, is attracted into the country . . . He falsely maintains that these

manufacturers have originated in the natural course of things and of their own accord; notwithstanding that in every nation the political power interferes to give to this so-called natural course an artificial direction for the nation's own special advantage.

He has illustrated his argument, founded on an ambiguous expression and consequently fundamentally wrong, by a fundamentally wrong example, in seeking to prove that because it would be foolish to produce wine in Scotland by artificial methods, therefore it would be foolish to establish manufactures by artificial methods . . . He reduces the process of the formation of capital in the nation to the operation of a private rentier . . . The augmentation of the national material capital is dependent on the augmentation of the national mental capital and vice-versa.

These arguments of List have been quoted at considerable length for several reasons. First, to convey the flavour and the vehemence of List's onslaught. Second, because List is seldom read in the original in these days. Third, and most important, because in these passages are contained the seeds of most of the policies later adopted in Germany (and in other countries trying to overtake established technology and trade leaders). If we are really to understand international competitivity, then it is of no use to go back to Adam Smith and still less to Ricardo and the 'school' of neo-classical comparative advantage theory, and Michalet (1981) has rightly warned against this. We must go to the original source of the national competitivity school. No doubt, if Adam Smith had been writing two hundred years later, he would have been able to find many much better examples of the folly of 'artificial' investment in non-competitive industries than the hypothetical and improbable one of vine-growing in Scotland. No doubt either, as many have observed, that List exaggerated somewhat the extent to which Adam Smith might be criticized for the dogmatism of his followers (the 'school'). Nevertheless, the debate still has a contemporary ring and is echoed today around the whole world, and not only in the industrializing countries of the Third World with their infant and teenage industries.

The fundamental points in List's spirited defence of national competitive strategies were the following:

1. The importance of 'mental capital' ('intellectual capital' might be a better rendering today than the English translation of that time. As with Adam Smith, we must allow also for the changes in terminology over the past 150–200 years. When Adam Smith talked about 'natural philosophers'; we would talk today about scientists). But there can be no doubt whatever what List was talking about in this passage:

The present state of the nations is the result of the accumulation of all discoveries, inventions, improvements, perfections and exertions of all generations which have lived before us; they form the mental capital of the present
human race, and every separate nation is productive only in the proportion
in which it has known how to appropriate these attainments of former generations, and to increase them by its own acquirements.

2. The recognition of the importance of the interaction between 'mental
    capital' and 'material capital' (or as we might put it today 'tangible' and
    'intangible' investment).

List clearly recognized both the importance of new investment embodying
the latest technology and the importance of learning by doing from the
experience of production with this equipment.

3. The importance of importing foreign (especially English) technology
    and of attracting foreign investment and the migration of skilled
    people as a means of acquiring the most recent technology.
4. The importance of skills in the labour force. One of the most telling
    criticisms of Adam Smith is for his failure to develop this aspect of his
    theory. He quotes Smith's famous passage – 'Labour forms the fund
    from which every nation derives its wealth, and the increase of wealth
    depends first on the productive power of labour, namely on the degree
    of Skill, dexterity and judgment with which the labour of the nation is
    generally applied' – but argues that Smith did not follow up this clear
    insight into the importance of 'productive powers', skill, knowledge
    and education, but concentrated only on the division of labour aspect
    of the problem. He ridicules the 'school' for regarding teachers and
    doctors as 'non-productive': 'We now see to what extraordinary mis-
    takes and contradictions the popular school has fallen in making mate-
    rial wealth or value of exchange the sole object of its investigations,
    and by regarding merely bodily labour as the sole productive power . . .
    A Newton, a Watt, or a Kepler is not so productive as a donkey, a horse
    or a draught-ox (a class of labourers who have been recently intro-
    duced by McCulloch into the series of the productive members of
    human society).'
5. The importance of the manufacturing sector for economic progress and
    the necessity for investment in manufacturing as a means of stimulat-
    ing the development of the entire economy and especially agriculture.
6. The importance of taking a very long-term historical view in develop-
    ing and applying economic policies. He clearly regarded the develop-
    ment of the appropriate institutions and 'mental capital' to enable
    manufacturing to flourish as a matter of many decades. He ridiculed

J.B. Say for his acceptance of the infant industry argument exception to free trade only in those cases where a branch of industry would become remunerative after a few years.

7.   The importance of manufacturing industry for national defence and the importance of national defence for national morale, political power and indirectly for economic progress. The nationalistic, not to say chauvinistic, tone of many passages in List's 'National System' and his frank advocacy of colonialism are the least palatable aspects of his entire theory. But it is important to remember again the historical context in which he wrote. Nor should our distaste for his nationalism blind us to the real importance of the issues, which he raised. The military sector is really important in the national economy and especially in the twentieth century its relationship to the accumulation of 'mental capital' is a crucial (although complex) issue. Moreover, it is essential to recognize that the exemption of this sector from the otherwise inexorable rules of laissez-faire provided an escape clause of enormous proportions. In this respect its importance was analogous to the relaxation of the Mediaeval strictures on the rate of interest and usury more generally through the Protestant Reformation.

After Calvin's revision of the traditional doctrine and the general acceptance of the loophole which this provided, God-fearing Christians could sleep peacefully at night whilst allowing the market rather than the scriptures to determine the rate of interest. Similarly, ardent believers in the theory (and the virtues) of free market forces and the undesirability (and the evils) of government intervention did not suffer the pangs of conscience or the agonies of doubt in authorizing or endorsing massive government expenditure on defence R&D or other forms of government intervention which would have horrified them in any other context. It is difficult, however, not to agree with List in his critique of Adam Smith about the significance of this particular one of the three 'special cases' which Smith accepted as providing some justification for protection:

> By the second exception, Adam Smith really justifies not merely the necessity of protecting such manufactures as supply the immediate requirements of war, such as, for instance, manufactories of arms and powder, but the whole system of protection as we understand it; for by the establishment in the nation of a manufacturing power of its own, protection to native industry tends to the augmentation of the nation's population, of its material wealth, of its machine power, of its independence, and of all mental powers, and therefore of its means of national defence, in an infinitely higher degree than it could do by merely manufacturing arms and powder.

As we shall see, this argument about the interdependence of the arms industry and the rest of the national economy is a two-edged one, but it is difficult to deny List's basic contention that the productive power of the economy as a whole is highly relevant to long-term defence capability.

8.   Finally, List stressed very strongly the importance of an active interventionist economic policy in order to promote long-term development, and as we have seen, rejected the philosophy of the 'night-watchman state' decisively.

6.   THE CASE OF GERMANY

We have quoted rather extensively from the original text of Friedrich List not only for the reasons which have already been advanced, but also because of the importance of Keynes's (1936) dictum:

> The ideas of economists and political philosophers, both when they are right and when they are wrong, are more powerful than is commonly supposed. Indeed, the world is ruled by little else. Practical men, who believe themselves to be quite exempt from any intellectual influences, are usually the slaves of some defunct economist. Madmen in authority, who hear voices in the air, are distilling their frenzy from some academic scribbler of a few years back.

It was because he believed that the entrenched authority of a 'school' was such a powerful influence on national economic policies that Keynes in his day launched an attack on the classical school no less vigorous (and some might say no less exaggerated) than that of List. And, at least for a generation, if not longer, both were successful in establishing a new orthodoxy. The 'defunct economists' who influenced most of those rising to authority in Germany in the latter half of the nineteenth century were not the classical school, as in Britain, but the school of Friedrich List. This was of decisive importance for the evolution of German politics, first of all in the various states grouped in the Zollverein (itself a triumph of List's vision) and later in Imperial Germany.

The importance of protecting manufacturing industry by 'regulating commerce' was fully accepted, but it would be a great mistake to see German policy purely in the light of this traditional 'free trade versus protection' argument. One of the legacies of British dominance in academic economics over two centuries has been the very narrow context in which many of these issues were perceived and debated. It is the central argument of this paper that the other aspects of List's heritage were actually more important than his protectionist doctrines in shaping the climate of opinion and the policies that were adopted in Germany and less directly in other nations, particularly Japan, as they strove to overtake the technological leaders.

As we have seen, the central feature of List's doctrine was his belief that economic progress depended on building up the 'mental capital' and productive powers of the nation. This depended in turn on the capacity to assimilate and use all the discoveries, inventions and improvements which had been made in any part of the world and to improve upon them. In practice, this meant that English technology was acquired through three main channels: first, the movement of British inventors, entrepreneurs and mechanics to the rest of Europe – this was particularly important in the early period of the Industrial Revolution; second, through German inventors, and entrepreneurs working in England – this was important for both the metal and the chemical industries in the mid-nineteenth century (Freeman, 1974; Freeman et al., 1982); third, through the development of an education and training system capable of putting the whole process of acquiring and disseminating world technology on a regular and systematic basis.

The last channel was ultimately the most important and its benefits became increasingly apparent to contemporary observers and to historians as the century wore on, and indeed up to the present time (Albu, 1980; Prais, 1981). However, the importance of the other two channels in the early period should not be underrated. Most studies on the transfer of technology are in agreement that the movement of ideas 'on the hoof' is one of the most efficient channels. In the case of the United States, it was of quite exceptional importance for craftsmen and technicians of all kinds, and in the twentieth century especially for scientists and technologists. So much was this so that it may have led the US to neglect the systematic development of industrial technical training and even of science education in schools despite the general expansion of the education system on a scale far surpassing that of any European country.

The advantages which German industry and the German economy acquired through the development of what is by general consent a first-rate system of educating and training craftsmen, technicians and technologists would be difficult to overestimate. This was recognized clearly by the Japanese, who, when they systematically investigated the various national systems of education, chose the German system as the one most worth emulating. It was also recognized, though very belatedly, by the British as they began to realize that the ever increasing effectiveness of German trade competition in the period leading up to the first world war was related to superior technology and quality of products, based on the achievements of the Technische Hochschulen and the other institutions involved in the advance of knowledge and its dissemination.

This belated British recognition, although it was important in various attempts at educational reform in the nineteenth and twentieth centuries (such as the establishment of Imperial College), was never sufficiently widespread as to overturn the dominant influence of the classical school on industrial and economic policy. So much was this so that the majority of British engineers down to the middle of the twentieth century had no professional academic qualifications, but only a part-time qualification based on evening class study. British industry paid the penalty for national complacency related to the early predominance of Britain in the first two Kondratiev waves. In that period, the method of training engineers 'on the job' on a part-time amateur basis was probably rather effective, but it was not capable of coping with the increasingly sophisticated technologies of the third and fourth Kondratiev cycles. The German system, on the other hand, based on the thorough and deliberate professional development of new technology and its application proved far more effective. It was also of the greatest importance for the general 'management culture' in German industry. Since there were rather few professional academically trained engineers in British industry (and for other sociocultural reasons), the dominant management tradition was amateurish and inclined to give weight to accountancy considerations on a short-term basis. The German management tradition was much more heavily influenced by professional engineers, who had both high status and high rewards. The type of long-term strategic thinking necessary for long-term success with new technologies was therefore far more characteristic of German than of British industry, as well as an insistence on high quality on the technical side.

The importance of this long-term way of thinking was by no means confined to industry. It was also extremely important in government (for example in the finance of research and education, as well as in measures to promote strategic industries and in financial institutions). In commenting on the development of the German banking system and its approach to the provision of industrial capital, the historian David Landes (1970) comments:

> Britain's relative lack of skills and knowledge (who could have imagined this eventuality in the first half of the nineteenth century?) was accompanied by, and contributed to, an equally astonishing inadequacy of venture capital. This statement may well strike the reader as inconsistent with our earlier discussion of Britain's plethora of wealth. But savings are not necessarily investment, and there are all kinds of investment – foreign and domestic, speculative and safe, rational and irrational. The British had the capital. But those who channelled and dispensed it were not alert to the opportunities offered by modern technology; and those who used it did not want or know enough to seek it out.

An essential element in List's approach to economic growth was his insistence on the importance of a capacity to improve technology. In the early part of the nineteenth century this was closely related to direct experience of production and this remains an extremely important source of technical change. However, with the newest technologies, the institutionalization of professional research and development became of steadily increasing importance. As Whitehead pointed out, perhaps the most important invention of the nineteenth century was the discovery of the method of invention itself – the professional research laboratory. It was an invention that was made in Germany. The German universities were the first to institutionalize a system of science laboratories and postgraduate training through laboratory research, which later became characteristic of science education generally.

This was especially important for the nascent German chemical industry and it was this industry, which was also the home of a major social innovation – the 'captive' in-house industrial R&D laboratory in the 1870s. The link between these R&D laboratories, especially in Bayer, Hoechst and BASF, and the subsequent astonishing success of the German dye-stuffs industry (and later other branches of chemical production and exports) is a story which has often been told (Freeman, 1974; Freeman et al., 1982) and which will not be repeated here. Suffice it to say that the newer chemical technologies of the third and fourth Kondratiev long waves were based on cumulative scientific advances in the understanding of molecular structure, and the ability 'artificially' to synthesize and manipulate new materials. Such an understanding could not grow from the simple observation and experience of established production processes, as with some mechanical technologies. It required some basic scientific research. The same was true for electrical engineering.

The social invention of the industrial R&D laboratory was thus of central importance for the new technologies emerging in the late nineteenth centuries. It was their leadership in these newer technologies and their innumerable applications throughout the economic system that gave German and United States industry the edge in the long process of catching up with and overtaking Britain. The new technological paradigms and trajectories also gave some advantages to those enterprises which could organize their R&D on a sufficiently large scale to exploit 'clusters' of innovations – as for example in synthetic dye-stuffs drawing on accumulated knowledge and experience to introduce a whole range of products and – in the case of the electrical industry – systems innovations. This applied also to major process innovations, such as the Haber–Bosch process, which combined two or more technologies. The development of professional R&D was thus closely related to the process of industrial concentration, and the scale economies in many types of innovation, which so impressed Schumpeter. Many, but not all; the relationship between technical innovation and size of firm is a complex one. Especially in the early days of a new technology, flexibility, speed of decision-making and imaginative flair in entrepreneurship favour the small innovative enterprise.

As a technology matures, comparative advantages in production and marketing (especially export marketing) and in large-scale process innovation and applications research shifts overwhelmingly to the larger enterprises. It was characteristic of the two new leaders in world technology, that they combined the advantages of large- and small-scale industrial organization in various sectors of their industrial system. British industry lagged well behind in the development and application of the newer technologies and in the growth of industrial R&D. This lag was reflected in the growth of American and German investment in Britain in the newer industries, especially electrical, as well as in Britain's steadily declining share of exports and her chronic imbalance of visible trade.

It has only been possible to sketch, in the briefest and crudest outline, some aspects of the displacement of Britain as the world technology and trade leader. But from what has been said, it is clear that in their international competitive struggle, Germany and the United States relied not simply on tariffs, important though these were, but on technology, and that in gaining that technological lead, the development of the education system was of central importance for almost all industries, whilst the role of professional R&D became of growing importance for many. In sum, the German economy proved capable of assimilating (comprehending) the best available technology of the day, of improving upon it (creating), of organizing the linkages between science, technology and markets (coupling) necessary for the efficient exploitation of new technological trajectories (clustering), and of coping with the long-term strategies of tangible and intangible investment which all of this implied. As we shall now see, Japan in the twentieth century carried all these strategies to the nth degree in pursuing her own competitive advantage.

7.   THE CASE OF JAPAN

When historians describe the intense Japanese efforts to overtake Western Europe and the United States, they usually start with the Meiji Restoration of 1868, which marked the commencement of a sustained and determined modernization policy. Here it is possible only to summarize very briefly some features of Japanese policy since the end of the Second World War, but it is freely acknowledged that the historical roots of the extraordinary

Japanese success go much deeper. Indeed, it is a central part of the entire thesis that policies lasting half a century or more underlie the major shifts in competitiveness. The long-term nature of Japanese education policy has already been mentioned and already in the nineteenth century many policies had been adopted to stimulate the growth of manufacturing industry and to import the best available technologies from wherever in the world they might be available.

The central point of interest from the standpoint of this analysis is that in the immediate post-war period, after an intense debate, Japan specifically rejected a long-term development strategy based on traditional theory of comparative advantage, which was apparently at that time being advocated by economists in the Bank of Japan and elsewhere who subscribed to the free trade doctrines of the classical school. They had advocated a 'natural' path of industrial development, based on Japan's relatively low labour costs and comparative advantage in labour intensive industries such as textiles. One of the central points at issue was whether Japan could hope to compete in the automobile industry and whether special steps should be taken to encourage its growth, but the debate affected industrial and trade policy in its entirety. In the early days, according to G.C. Allen (1981) (one of the few European economists who has consistently attempted to study and learn from Japanese experience), the views of the Bank of Japan had some influence. They blocked loans in 1951 for a large new up-to-date steel works and:

> Sony was obliged to postpone its imports of transistor technology because the officials in charge of foreign exchange licensing were doubtful both about the technology and about Sony's ability to make use of it. But on the whole the bureaucrats and their advisors at the Ministry of International Trade and Industry (MITI) prevailed. They repudiated the view that Japan should be content with a future as an underdeveloped country with low productivity and income per head.

Again, according to Allen (and many other observers):

> Some of these advisers were engineers who had been drawn by the war into the management of public affairs. They were the last people to allow themselves to be guided by the half-light of economic theory. Their instinct was to find a solution for Japan's post-war difficulties on the supply side, in enhanced technical efficiency and innovations in production. They thought in dynamic terms. Their policies were designed to furnish the drive and to raise the finance for an economy that might be created rather than simply to make the best use of the resources it then possessed.

Whether or not they had ever heard of List, and whether or not they were economists or engineers, those who were responsible in government or in industry (and again all observers agree that industry and government worked very closely together) had clearly accepted the central tenets of List's doctrine.[4] Like their German predecessors, they went far beyond tariff protection to a much wider range of infrastructural and interventionist policies.

In the early days of Japanese industrialization it was quite common for foreigners to treat her successes simply as 'imitation' and her very heavy imports of technology and huge deficit in the so-called 'technological balance of payments' were frequently cited as evidence for this proposition. But as time went by it became increasingly evident that Japanese assimilation of foreign technology went far beyond carbon-copy replication and was based on the creative systematic improvement of these technologies, and increasingly on original innovation. One clear piece of evidence for this is that for the technology agreements signed in recent years, Japan has a clear positive technological balance of payments. But even more decisive is the evidence of Japanese technological leadership in industry after industry and the opening up of a 'technology gap' between Japan and her competitors in productivity and in export performance in these industries.

A good example is that of the colour television industry, which has been studied by Sciberras (1981) and by Peck and Wilson (1982). They have shown that the extraordinary Japanese success in dominating world export markets (and world-wide overseas investment as trade barriers were thrown up) was due primarily to innovative leadership in design and in process technology in the 1970s. Sciberras concluded that:

> Japanese firms have been the most successful innovators. By applying advanced automation in assembly, testing and handling to large production volumes, the Japanese have achieved drastically superior performance in terms both of productivity and of quality.

He estimated that Japanese labour productivity was two or three times as high as European or American levels, and attributed this gap mainly to the integrated approach to automation technology and to the associated intensive industrial training and education programmes at all levels which enabled the Japanese labour force to handle and resolve problems of operating advanced technology, but which caused much greater difficulties elsewhere because of lower levels of responsibility, skill and initiative. Peck and Wilson pointed out that the Japanese manufacturers were actually the first to introduce integrated circuit technology into the colour television industry, with all the associated economies in assembly labour. Their success in this was apparently due to a joint research effort sponsored by MITI and involving five television manufacturers, seven semi-conductor manufacturers, four universities and two research institutes. This is an interesting illustration of the extraordinary capacity of the Japanese social system to bring about very close coupling of diverse partners to achieve a specific technological objective, even when their competitive interests might appear superficially to diverge.

Drawing upon these and many other examples, we might attempt to synthesize and summarize some of the ways in which Japan succeeded in pushing still further the competitive policies which had already proved so successful for Germany, the United States and several smaller European countries, such as Sweden.

First of all, we should note that, like the United States, Japan admits to secondary and higher education a higher proportion of young people than any European country (with the possible exception of the USSR). The system is more strongly oriented towards science and technology than most others, and is complemented by an extremely well developed industrial training and education system, which according to many accounts involves almost the whole of the workforce in the larger firms. It seems that this company-level education and training system makes a very big contribution to the remarkable ability of Japanese industry to assimilate new technologies rapidly and efficiently and, more importantly, to improve upon them. Both Germany and the United States showed a capacity to introduce production system innovations (the assembly line, interchangeable standardized parts, flow processes, etc.). But Japan has shown an even more remarkable ability to re-think and redesign production technologies in old as well as new industries.

The examples of ship-building and steel are often cited in this connection and that of colour television has already been mentioned, but the contemporary use of robotics, which is more advanced in Japan than anywhere else, suggests that even more dramatic changes may be ahead. The Japanese system sets great store on the involvement of employees in such system changes, affecting as they do the entire workforce. The 'quality circles' are a social innovation designed to maximize the specific contribution from the lower levels of the workforce and to assign to the lower management levels a responsibility for technical change. We should also note that the Japanese policy of mainly rejecting foreign direct investment as a means of technology transfer automatically places on the enterprise the full responsibility for assimilating imported technology, and is far more likely to lead to total system improvements than the 'turn-key plant' mode of import or the foreign subsidiary mode.

As in Germany and the United States, the greater part of R&D is carried out at the level of the industrial enterprise in Japan, but Japanese management appears to have taken this coupling mechanism a stage further by relating decisions on strategic priorities for R&D both in government and in industry on the one hand to a careful identification of the major growth areas in world markets, and on the other hand to a concerted effort to introduce the most up-to-date process technology and quality improvements. The long-term strategic approach to investment in physical plant is no less characteristic, and Allen particularly emphasizes that government policies and incentives were deliberately designed to encourage this long-term approach to investment.

Finally, as Allen (1981) points out:

> In the United States and Britain defence has absorbed not only a large proportion of total expenditure on R&D, but also the skill and energy of many brilliant scientists and technologists. Japan on the other hand, has been able to direct nearly all her resources, human as well as financial, to civil industry and foreign trade.

This point brings out the complexity of the defence technology relationship, which List discussed. In social systems with a heavy ideological bias against government involvement it permitted a means of promoting some of the most advanced technologies, which otherwise might not have been available. The scale of such involvement since the Second World War has however been so great in some countries that the opportunity costs identified by Allen have been extremely high. He mentions specifically the United States and UK, but probably the highest price for this diversion of scarce resources has been paid in the Soviet Union. The comparison here is particularly instructive because like Japan, the USSR was a large country, which industrialized successfully in the twentieth century but, unlike Japan, failed to close the 'technology gap' with the leaders, except in the military area (Amann and Cooper, 1982). Perhaps in retrospect, List was right here too and that the overall long-term consequences of industrial growth and technical change are the most important source of long-term defence capability. In any case most analysts, including much Soviet comment, are agreed that quite apart from the issue of the scale of the military sector, there are other long-term structural defects in the Soviet science-technology system, which have prevented effective 'coupling' with productive enterprises.

We may conclude this all-too-brief summary therefore by reiterating the conclusion that the success (or otherwise) of the leading countries in international technology and trade competition is heavily related to the long-term policies which they have pursued over many decades, rather than to any short-term manipulation of currency exchange rates, or exploitation of relative factor-cost advantages.

8.   CONCLUSIONS

The implications which flow from this conclusion are many and varied, and it would be quite impossible in a short paper to do more than point to a few of the most important (i) at the international level and (ii) at the national level.

At the international level the analysis points to the conclusion that future reforms in the international trading and financial arrangements must start from the expectation that persistent disequilibria in international trade are likely to be the norm rather than the exception. The tendency for the strong (technical leader) countries to run a surplus is likely to persist over long periods and to re-assert itself repeatedly despite currency adjustments and other measures designed to restore equilibrium. Likewise, the tendency for the weak countries to run into vicious spiral problems is likely to be persistent. This means that there are serious dangers of deflationary pressures in the system arising from competitive national attempts to restore short-term equilibrium, unless (i) international financial arrangements and credit arrangements clearly recognize the very long-term structural (and developmental) nature of the underlying tendencies. The proposals which Keynes originally advanced at Bretton Woods are still relevant in this connection; (ii) surplus countries with the help of the international community, should have the imagination (and sense of history) to recognize that their own long-term interests depend not only on seeking exclusive national competitive advantages, but on the international transfer of technology as well as capital. List has been proved right in his belief that free trade could be an acceptable and desirable framework for countries once they had 'caught up', but unduly restrictive in his view for those who are still in the midst of catching up.

At the national level, the analysis points to the conclusion that long-term infrastructural investment in 'mental capital' and its improvement is crucial for successful economic development, and for competitive trade performance.Whilst this necessity may be mitigated to some extent by fortunate natural resource endowment (OPEC and up to a point such countries as Australia, Canada and even USA), it is an important issue for all. This has been a commonplace of development economics for a long time and it has also been a basic element in the work of the OECD since the 1950s. The DSTI in particular always gave prominence to work on education, training, research, development and technical innovation. But although this conclusion is itself far from novel, what has perhaps not been sufficiently recognized is the extent to which policies for science and technology are intertwined with policies for trade and industry. The 'coupling mechanisms' between the education system, scientific institutions, R&D facilities, production and markets have been an important aspect of the institutional changes introduced in the successful 'overtaking' countries. These qualitative and institutional aspects of the problem have perhaps been underrated by comparison with the quantitative issues of scale of invest- ment, annual expenditures, etc. Such quantitative analysis is essential and comparative studies of this type can certainly be instructive. But as at the enterprise level, the study of effective national competitive strategies must fully take into account those organizational and social factors, which make the difference between success and failure.

The recognition of the importance of this point does not emerge only from the success story of countries such as Japan. It emerges also from studies in smaller countries, such as The Netherlands. One of the most successful sectors of the Dutch economy has been agriculture, in terms of both pro- ductivity and trade performance. A recent study by a group of researchers at the TNO (Bilderbeek et al., 1982) has concluded that its performance has been strongly affected by the close coupling mechanisms set up and system- atically promoted between the research system, the specialized education system, the information dissemination system, the producers and the market. Taking such social-organizational factors as those identified by the Michigan group of Havelock (1973) and his co-workers on innovation, the TNO study found them all to be highly relevant to the experience of the Dutch agricul- tural system – openness, proximity (social and geographical), synergy, cap- acity to absorb external information and so on. The research at Aalborg on the inter-dependencies between various groups of firms in promoting tech- nical progress in key sectors of the Danish economy is also highly relevant here (Andersen et al., 1981). The work of Williamson (1975) and Phillips (1980) also suggests the limitations of formal competition theory in under- standing the interactions of the science–technology system with production. They identify those characteristics of research and development activities which mean that specialist firms simply attempting to develop and sell infor- mation on a commercial market basis are not usually effective for successful innovation and only in-house R&D and other types of 'vertical integration' are typical. The innovation process is one which requires often rather exten- sive networks of information flows and rather free informal contacts over a fairly long period and often of a rather unpredictable kind. National com- petitive strategies, if they are to be relevant to the real problems, must take into account these types of empirical results, rather than rest on the laurels of the 'school' in economics.

NOTES

1. Not impossible, as we know from other cases of paradigm change in the natural as well as the social sciences that 'rationality' counts for less than the emergence of a new young generation of practitioners (Easlea, 1973).

2. A good example of Schumpeter's point with respect to the semi-conductor industry is to be found in Dosi (1981b).
3. These characteristics, which we shall identify may be compared with Dosi's (1981b) list of 'stylised facts' about the economics of technical change (para. 26).
4. In the financial system, too, whatever the views of the Government or the Bank of Japan may have been in the late 1940s, over the next 30 years a very different philosophy clearly prevailed.

REFERENCES

Albu, A. (1980), 'British attitudes in engineering education: a historical perspective,' in K. Pavitt (ed.), *Technical Innovation and British Economic Performance*, pp. 67–87. Macmillan: London.
Allen, G.C. (1981), 'Industrial policy and innovation in Japan,' in C. Carter (ed.), *Industrial Policy and Innovation*, pp. 69 and 77. Heinemann: London.
Amann, R. and J. Cooper (eds) (1982), *Industrial Innovation in the Soviet Union*. Yale University Press: New Haven, CT.
Andersen, E.S., B. Dalum and G. Villumsen (1981), 'International specialisation and national inter-industrial linkages,' mimeo, Aalborg University.
Bilderbeek, R., A. Dekker and P.G. Schipper (1982), 'Infra-struktuur in de Nederlandse land en tuinbouw,' mimeo, TNO, Centre for Study of Technology.
Chesnais, F. (1981), 'Schumpeterian recovery and the Schumpeterian perspective – some unsettled issues and alternative interpretations,' mimeo [published in 1982 in H. Giersch (ed.), *Proceedings of Conference on Emerging Technology, Consequences for Economic Growth, Structural Change and Employment in Advanced Open Economics*. J. Mohr: Tübingen].
Clemence, R.V. and F. Doody (1950), *The Schumpeterian System*. MIT Press: New York.
Dosi, G. (1981a), *Technical Change, Industrial Transformation and Public Policies: The Case of the Semiconductor Industry*. Sussex European Research Centre, University of Sussex: Brighton.
Dosi, G. (1981b), 'Technology, industrial structure and international economic performance,' DSTI/SPR/81.43, mimeo, OECD, Paris.
Easlea, B. (1973), *Liberation and the Aims of Science*. Chatto &Windus.
Freeman, C. (1974), *Economics of Industrial Innovation, Penguin Modern Economics Texts*. Frances Pinter: London. Second edition, MIT Press: New York, 1982.
Freeman, C. (ed.) (1981), 'Technological innovation and long waves in world economic development,' *Futures*, **13** (August and October).
Freeman, C., J. Clark and L.L.G. Soete (1982), *Unemployment and Technical Innovation*. Frances Pinter: London.
Freeman, C., J.K. Fuller and A. Young (1963), 'The plastics industry: a comparative study of research and innovation,' *National Institute Economic Review*, No. 26, 22–60.
Freeman, C., A. Robertson, J. Fuller and R. Curnow (1965), 'Research and development in electronic capital goods,' *National Institute Economic Review*, No. 34, 40–91.
Freeman, C., A. Robertson, R. Curnow, P. Whittaker and J. Fuller (1968), 'Chemical process plant: innovation and the world market,' *National Institute Economic Review*, August, 29–57.

Golding, A.M. (1972), 'The semi-conductor industry in Britain and the United States,' D.Phil. thesis, University of Sussex.

Havelock, R.G. (1973), 'Planning for innovation through dissemination and utilisation of knowledge,' CRUSK, Institute for Social Research, Michigan.

Horn, E.J. (1976), *Technologische Neuerungen und internationale Arbeitsteilung.* J. Mohr: Tübingen.

Hufbauer, G. (1966), *Synthetic Materials in International Trade.* Harvard: Cambridge.

Johnson, H.G. (1968), 'The state of theory in relation to the empirical analysis,' in R. Vernon (ed.), *The Technology Factor in International Trade.* Columbia University Press: New York.

Kaldor, N. (1978), 'The effects of devaluation on trade,' in N. Kaldor, *Further Essays on Applied Economics.* Duckworth: London.

Keynes, J.M. (1936), *General Theory of Employment, Interest and Money.* Harwell Brace: New York.

Kravis, I. and R.E. Lipsey (1971), *Price Competitiveness in World Trade.* Columbia University Press: New York.

Landes, D.S. (1970), *The Unbound Prometheus: Technological Change and Industrial Development in Western Europe from 1750 to the Present.* Cambridge University Press: Cambridge.

Leontief, W. (1953), 'Domestic production and foreign trade: the American capital position re-examined,' Proceedings of the American Philosophical Society, September.

List, F. (1845), *The National System of Political Economy* [English translation by S.S. Lloyd (1904), Longmans].

Michalet, C.-A. (1981), 'Competitiveness and internationalisation,' DSTI/SPR/81.63, OECD, Paris.

Nelson, R.R. and S.G.Winter (1977), 'In search of useful theory of innovation,' *Research Policy*, **6**, 36–76.

OECD (1978), 'The international competitiveness of selected OECD countries,' occasional papers, supplement to OECD Economic Outlook, July.

OECD (1981), 'The notion of international competitiveness: a discussion paper,' DSTI/SPR/81.32, OECD, Paris.

Pavitt, K. and L.L.G. Soete (1980), 'Innovative activities and export shares: some comparisons between industries and countries,' in K. Pavitt (ed.), *Technical Innovation and British Economic Performance*, pp. 38–66. Macmillan: London.

Pavitt, K. and L.L.G. Soete (1981), 'International differences in economic growth and the international location of innovation,' paper presented at the Kiel Conference, June.

Peck, M.J. and R. Wilson (1982), 'Innovation, imitation and comparative advantage: the case of the consumer electronics industry,' in H. Giersch (ed.), *Proceedings of Conference on Emerging Technology, Consequences for Economic Growth, Structural Change and Employment in Advanced Open Economics.* J. Mohr: Tübingen.

Phillips, A. (1980), 'Organisational factors in R&D and technological changes: market failure considerations,' in D. Sahal (ed.), *Research, Development and Technological Innovation.* Lexington, KY.

Posner, M.V. (1961), 'International trade and technical change,' *Oxford Economic Papers*, October.

Posner, M. and A. Steer (1979), 'Price competitiveness and the performance of manufacturing industry,' in F. Blackaby (ed.), *De-industrialisation.* Heinemann: London.

Prais, S.G. (1981), 'Vocational qualifications of the labour force in Britain and Germany,' *National Institute Economic Review*, No. 98, 47–59.

Ray, G.F. (1980), 'Innovation in the long cycle,' *Lloyds Bank Review*, No. 135, 14–28.

Rothwell, R. (1980), 'Innovation in textile machinery,' in K. Pavitt (ed.), *Technical Innovation and British Economic Performance*, pp. 126–41. Macmillan: London.

Rothwell, R. (1981), 'Non-price factors in the export competitiveness of agricultural engineering goods,' *Research Policy*, **10**, 260–88.

Schumpeter, J.A. (1939), *Business Cycles*. McGraw Hill: New York.

Sciberras, E. (1977), *Multi-national Electronic Companies and National Economic Policies*. JAI Press: New York.

Sciberras, E. (1981), 'Technical innovation and international competitiveness in the television industry,' mimeo, SPRU, University of Sussex.

Soete, L.L.G. (1980), 'The impact of technological innovation in international trade performance: the evidence reconsidered,' paper presented at the OECD Science and Technology Output Indicators Conference, Paris, September.

Soete, L.L.G. (1981), 'A general test of technological gap trade theory,' *Weltwirtschaftliches Archiv*, **117**, 638–66.

Vernon, R., R. Gruber and D. Mehta (1967), 'The R&D factor in international trade and international investment of US industries,' *Journal of Political Economy*, February.

Williamson, O.E. (1975), *Markets and Hierarchies: Analysis and Anti-trust Implication: A Study in the Economics of Internal Organisation*. Free Press: London.

Wolter, F. (1977), 'Factor proportions, technology and West German industry's international trade patterns,' *Weltwirtschaftliches Archiv*, **113**, 250–67.

3. Structural crises of adjustment, business cycles and investment behaviour

with Carlota Perez

INTRODUCTION

This chapter discusses the revival of interest in long-term fluctuations in the growth of the world economy and particularly in the Schumpeterian theory of business cycles. After reviewing the common ground in relation to investment behaviour and business cycles, it goes on to discuss the failure of Keynesian economics to come to terms with the influence of technical change. The central theme of the chapter is that certain types of technical change – defined as changes in 'techno-economic paradigm' – have such widespread consequences for all sectors of the economy that their diffusion is accompanied by a major structural crisis of adjustment, in which social and institutional changes are necessary to bring about a better 'match' between the new technology and the system of social management of the economy – or 'regime of regulation'. Once, however, such a good match is achieved a relatively stable pattern of long-term investment behaviour can emerge for two or three decades. This point is illustrated with respect to the rise of information technology. It is argued that this pervasive technology is likely to heighten still further the instability of the system before a new, more stable pattern of growth is attained.

The resurgence of interest in Schumpeter's ideas (e.g. Elliott, 1985) is associated with the slow-down in the growth of the world economy in the last decade. Whereas during the prolonged post-war boom of the 1950s and the 1960s there was some tendency to assume that the general adoption of Keynesian policies would prevent the recurrence of any depression comparable to that of the 1930s and would smooth out smaller fluctuations, this confidence was somewhat undermined by the deeper recessions of the 1970s and 1980s and the return of much higher levels of unemployment. Not surprisingly, this has led to renewed interest in long-cycle or long-wave theories, which make analogies between the 1930s and the 1980s. This chapter concentrates on the explanation of these deeper structural crises of adjustment, without making any assumptions about fixed periodicity or statistical regularity.

We start by looking at the common ground in the analysis of business cycles. We shall quote extensively from Samuelson for several reasons. First of all, he is probably the most authoritative neo-Keynesian economist, and one who commands respect throughout the profession. Secondly, business cycles have always been one of his central professional interests. Thirdly, as the author of the most widely read economics textbook in the Western World, he provides in the successive editions of this book a convenient synthesis of the changing state of the art (Samuelson and Nordhaus in the most recent and thorough revisions, i.e. the 12th edition 1985).

AREAS OF AGREEMENT IN BUSINESS CYCLE THEORY

There are of course many different explanations of business cycles and many explanations for the exceptional severity of the 1930s depression and of the recessions of the 1970s and 1980s. But, as Samuelson has pointed out and most textbooks on the business cycle confirm, there *is* actually a measure of agreement on *some* of the central issues.

Most importantly there is virtually universal agreement that one of the main sources of cyclical fluctuations in the economy is the instability of investment. All empirical studies of business cycles show much greater fluctuations in the capital goods industries than in consumer products, as in the extreme example of the Great Depression of the 1930s, when GNP fell by 30 per cent in the United States but output of producers' durable equipment fell by 75 per cent.

Samuelson (1980) comments:

> Ordinarily, consumption movements seem the *effect* rather than the *cause* of the business cycle. In contrast, there is reason to believe that the movements of *durable* goods represent key causes in a more fundamental sense. [p. 242]

The wording is slightly changed in the 1985 edition but the emphasis on investment remains and indeed virtually all schools of economic theory would accept the empirical evidence on the relative amplitude of fluctuations in different sectors of the economy. Moreover, they would also agree that there are certain aspects of investment in plant and equipment which make some fluctuations almost inevitable: 'postponability' on the one hand and competitive pressures to expand capacity on the other; the uneven development in the relative growth rate and capital intensity of various sectors of the economy; indivisibilities in many large investments ('lumpiness') and the 'accelerator' principle tending to amplify investment in upswings and diminish it in downswings. On a smaller scale some similar considerations apply to inventories and to consumer durables. These 'endogenous' factors are in themselves sufficient to account for fluctuations in the system.

However, Samuelson (1980) points out in his 'synthesis' that 'external' factors also play an important part:

> Most economists today believe in a combination of external and internal theories. To explain major cycles, they place crucial emphasis on fluctuations in *investment* or *capital* goods. Primary causes of these capricious and volatile investment fluctuations are found in such external factors as (1) technological innovation, (2) dynamic growth of population and of territory, and even in some economists' view, (3) fluctuations in business confidence and 'animal spirits'.
>
> With these external factors we must combine the internal factors that cause any initial change in investment to be *amplified* in a cumulative multiplied fashion – as people who are given work in the capital goods industries respond part of their new income on consumption goods, and as an air of optimism begins to pervade the business community, causing firms to go to the banks and the securities market for new credit accommodation.
>
> Also, it is necessary to point out that the general business situation definitely reacts in turn on investment. If high consumption sales make business owners optimistic, they are more likely to embark upon venturesome investment programmes. Inventions or scientific discoveries may occur independently of the business cycle, but their appreciable economic introduction will most certainly depend on business conditions.
>
> Therefore especially in the short run, investment is in part an *effect* as well as a cause of income movements. [p. 246]

As Samuelson points out, essentially similar logic applies, of course, in the reverse direction leading to the danger of a cumulative downward spiral. Temporary over-capacity as a result of bunching of investment, perceived lack of sufficient new markets, the saturation of some existing markets, major instabilities in the international economy, over-restrictive monetary policies, uncertainties about technology, protectionism and general lack of business confidence are among the many influences which may trigger or accelerate a vicious circle of declining investment and national income. All of them have been identified as important influences in the severe depression of the 1930s.

Thus far, then, is an area of general agreement about the causes of business cycles and the problems of 'virtuous' and 'vicious' spirals in economic activity. However, a gulf still remains between those economists who, despite what has been said above, still look to the self-regulating private market mechanism, the rate of interest, capital-labour substitution, and monetary policy as the main stabilising forces governing investment behaviour and consequently the fluctuations in the system as a whole, and those who, like Keynes and Samuelson, lack faith in this mechanism to sustain long-term stable growth. The central issue is the possibility of rational optimising behaviour at the micro level of the firm. It will be argued in Part IV of this book [Dosi et al., 1988] that this model of entrepreneurial behaviour is fundamentally flawed. This means that periods of stable growth depend more on a general climate of confidence, including widespread belief in the future potential benefits from technical change, than on an unbelievable set of assumptions about perfect information and accurate calculations on the future rate of return of a wide variety of investments with uncertain outcomes.

KEYNES

It is often said that Keynes was deeply rooted in the neo-classical tradition of economics and this is no doubt true. Nevertheless, even in his earliest writings, it is possible to trace his awareness of these limitations of the self-regulating market mechanism. Moggridge (1976) points out that already in 1913 in his book on *Indian Currency and Finance* he insisted on '. . . the essential fragility of the economic order which others took to be natural and automatic and emphasized the need for conscious management'.

This already foreshadowed his more general onslaught on *laissez-faire* in the 1920s:

> The world is *not* so governed from above that private and social interest always coincide. It is *not* so managed here below that in practice they coincide. It is *not* a correct deduction from the Principles of economics that enlightened self-interest generally *is* enlightened; more often individuals seeking separately to promote their ends are too ignorant or too weak to attain even these.

In 1934 in one of his broadcasts on the BBC, he was even more explicit (quoted in Eatwell, 1982):

> On the one side are those who believe that the existing economic system is, in the long run, a self-adjusting mechanism, though with creaks and groans and jerks and interrupted by the time lags, outside interference and mistakes . . . on the other side of the gulf are those who reject the idea that the existing economic system is, in any significant sense, self-adjusting . . . The strength of the self-adjusting school depends on its having behind it almost the whole body of organised economic thinking and doctrine of the last hundred years. This is a formidable power . . . For it lies behind the education and the habitual modes of

thought, not only of economists, but of bankers and businessmen and civil ser-
vants and politicians of all parties . . . thus if the heretics on the other side of
the gulf are to demolish the forces of 19th century orthodoxy . . . they must
attack them in their citadel. No successful attack has yet been made . . . I range
myself with the heretics.

This broadcast foreshadowed the publication of his *General Theory of
Employment, Interest and Money*, which at least temporarily was indeed a
fairly successful attack (Keynes, 1936) on the 'citadel', and which argued
that '. . . the duty of ordering the current volume of investment cannot
safely be left in private hands' and advocated the 'socialisation of investment'. By this he meant, of course, not public ownership or socialism, but
public responsibility for the overall level of investment and employment.
He insisted that if private decisions to invest were inadequate to overcome
a depression, then it was the responsibility of government to compensate
for this deficiency. Interest rate policy probably would not be in itself a
sufficient inducement to stimulate the necessary flow.

An inadequate level of private investment might arise from many causes;
in a famous and often-quoted passage Keynes stressed the impossibility of
purely rational calculations about the future rate of return from new investment and compared it with an expedition to the South Pole. He stressed the
crucial importance of a climate of confidence and the role of 'animal
spirits'. He pointed to the problem of excess capacity even in some industries which had grown rapidly in the previous boom and the problem of
temporary saturation of particular markets. He stressed ironically the good
fortune of Ancient Egypt in having pyramids and large-scale investment
which did not 'stale with abundance' and of the Middle Ages in having
cathedrals: 'Two pyramids, two Masses for the dead are twice as good as
one, but not so two railways from London to York.'

From the time of the publication of the *General Theory*, orthodox economics mounted a counter-attack mainly on the issues of monetary policy,
fiscal policy, and wage flexibility. However, there has been no comparable
counter-attack on his theory of private investment behaviour. Indeed,
Siegenthaler (1986), quoting Shackle's (1967) essay on 'Keynes' Ultimate
Meaning', argues that this is Keynes' most lasting and fundamental contribution to economic theory.

According to Shackle:

Keynes' whole theory of unemployment is ultimately the simple statement that,
rational expectation being unattainable, we substitute for it first one and then
another kind of irrational expectation; and the shift from one arbitrary basis to
another gives us from time to time a moment of truth, when our artificial
confidence is for the time being dissolved, and we, as business men, are afraid to

invest and so fail to provide enough demand to match our society's desire to produce.

Siegenthaler comments on this passage:

> This interpretation of Keynes calls for interpretation itself, but at least three things are made very clear by Shackle. First, confidence enters the scene in a context in which rational expectations cannot be formed on the basis of adequate knowledge, so that confidence must be 'artificial'; subjective certainty which encourages an actor to invest is grounded not in a true model of economic reality, but in an arbitrary one for which sufficient evidence fails to be available; in very particular situations confidence gets dissolved and actors become aware of objective uncertainty, of their inability to know the future and it is only in those 'moments of truth' that subjective uncertainty governs the behaviour of the actor . . . Actors get confident not on the basis of adequate knowledge, not as a result of procedures leading to objectively superior forecasting methods, not as an outcome of individual optimising strategies of selecting and handling information . . . But they do get confident despite uncertainty . . . Confidence, albeit an artificial one, prevails except on rare occasions.

Solow (Klamer, 1984) has scornfully dismissed the attempt of the new school of 'rational expectations' to argue that actors, whether consumers, wage earners or entrepreneurs, can indeed form rational, long-term expectations about such future events as the impact of electronic technology on the economy. And indeed few would attempt to deny the force of Solow's argument or that of Keynes, with respect to major technical innovations.

Nevertheless, because of the crucial importance of technical change for investment behaviour, which is acknowledged by all schools of economic thought, it is essential to examine in more depth the question of the influence of technical change, on the state of confidence and vice versa. At certain times technical change appears to undermine confidence and stability, while at others it has the opposite effect. At the level of the individual innovative investment, the findings of empirical studies of investment and evaluation in R&D are clear-cut and virtually unanimous: they strongly support the view of Shackle and Schumpeter that investment in new products and processes has an element of true uncertainty: by definition the outcome cannot be known (Freeman, 1982, Chapter 7).

However, the analysis cannot be restricted to the level of the individual innovation or to counting innovations; the qualitative aspects and the systems interrelatedness of innovations must be taken into account. Under favourable conditions, the Schumpeterian bandwagons roll and business confidence improves, leading to an atmosphere of 'boom' in which, although there are still risks and uncertainties attached to all investment decisions, animal spirits rise. Such favourable conditions include complementarities between innovations and the emergence of an appropriate infrastructure as well as some degree of political stability and institutions which do not hinder too much the diffusion of new technologies. In these favourable circumstances the growth of new markets and the profitability of new investments appear to offer a fairly stable prospect of future growth, despite the uncertainties.

But there are also circumstances when technical change could have the opposite effect and could destabilise investment by undermining confidence in the future prospects for the growth of some firms, industries or economies. Moreover, as technologies and industries mature over a long period, diminishing returns and declining profitability may set in, leading to sluggish investment behaviour. If this is at all widespread it may take major social and political changes to restore confidence in the future growth of the system on the basis of new technologies. In the section on 'Diffusion of new techno-economic paradigms and institutional changes' we shall discuss the circumstances in which this can occur.

Here we wish only to make the point that in the early stages of radical technical innovation uncertainty prevails, so that Schumpeterian entrepreneurship and Keynesian animal spirits are necessary for the first steps. Once diffusion is under way, even though diffusion itself involves further innovation, the excitement generated by rapid growth of markets and/or exceptional profits of innovations may generate rising confidence and waves of imitation, provided the social and institutional framework and the infrastructure favour these developments.

Keynes himself once acknowledged the dominant influence of technical change on investment behaviour in his *Treatise on Money* (1930):

> In the case of fixed capital, it is easy to understand why fluctuations should occur in the rate of investment. Entrepreneurs are induced to embark on the production of fixed capital or deterred from doing so by their expectations of the profit to be made. Apart from the many minor reasons why these should fluctuate in a changing world, Professor Schumpeter's explanation of the major movements may be unreservedly accepted . . .
>
> It is only necessary to add to this that the pace at which the innovating entrepreneurs will be able to carry their projects into execution at a cost in interest which is not deterrent to them will depend on the degree of complaisance of those responsible for the banking system. Thus while the stimulus to a credit inflation comes from outside the banking system, it remains a monetary phenomenon in the sense that it only occurs if the monetary machine is allowed to respond to the stimulus. [Vol. 2, p. 86].

This passage is remarkable not only for its unequivocal acceptance of Schumpeter's explanation of the major surges of investment in capitalist societies but also its emphasis on the enabling role of monetary policy. It is all the more surprising that neither Keynes nor the Keynesians followed up this recognition of the crucial role of technical innovation. In fact, in the *General Theory* Keynes regressed to a position of neglect of technology when he introduced the largely artificial concept of a secular decline in the marginal efficiency of capital unrelated to the actual changes in techniques or in the capital stock. Schumpeter was therefore justified in one of the main points of his critique of the *General Theory*:

> it limits applicability of this analysis to a few years at most – perhaps the duration of the '40 months cycle' – and in terms of phenomena, to the factors that *would* govern the greater or the smaller utilisation of an industrial apparatus *if* the latter remains unchanged. *All* the phenomena incident to the creation and change in this apparatus, that is to say the phenomena that dominate the capitalist process, are thus excluded from consideration. [1952, p. 282]

For the Keynesians it became a matter of relative indifference *which* were the new technologies and the fast-growing industries. We shall argue that it does matter very much *which* are the important new technological systems, because they are unique and their effects on private and public R&D and investment strategies, and the government policies, and institutional changes, which are required to advance them, may be very different. We shall argue that Keynesian analysis and policies were and are deficient with respect to long-term changes in technology, their effects on business confidence and structural change in the economy and the specifics of infrastructural investment. Almost all neo-Keynesian (and much other) macro-economic analysis and modelling is restricted to purely *quantitative* aspects of investment and employment, whereas Schumpeter rightly insisted on the crucial importance of *qualitative* aspects.

Clearly, this criticism of Keynesian theory rests on a particular view of the relationship between technical change and business cycles which is usually associated with Schumpeter's long-wave theory. It sees the major booms, such as those of the 1950s and 1960s or the 1850s and 1860s as based on the diffusion of major new 'techno-economic paradigms' into the world economy and the deeper depressions as periods of structural adjustment, when the social and institutional framework is adapting to the rise of major new technologies.

Interestingly enough, even though Samuelson (1981) has dismissed the likelihood of another major depression, he did stress the probability of a prolonged downturn in the rate of economic growth:

> It is my considered guess that the final quarter of the 20th century will fall far short of the third quarter in its achieved rate of economic progress. The dark horoscope of my old teacher Joseph Schumpeter may have particular relevance here.

Samuelson's reference to Schumpeter clearly implies that the major long-term fluctuations in economic development cannot be explained simply in terms of conventional short- and medium-term business-cycle theory but require an additional dimension of analysis. This involves the rise of new technologies, the rise and decline of entire industries, major infrastructural investments, changes in the international location of industry and techno-logical leadership and other related structural changes, for example, in the skills and composition of the labour force and the management structure of enterprises.

A TAXONOMY OF INNOVATIONS

It has been argued that a weakness of most neo-classical and Keynesian theories of technical change and economic growth is that they fail to take account of the *specifics* of changing technology in each historical period.

One reason that economists do not attempt this daunting task is, of course, the sheer complexity of technical change. How can the thousands of inventions and innovations which are introduced every month and every year be reduced to some kind of pattern amenable to generalisation and analysis? In this section we shall suggest a taxonomy of innovation, based on empirical work at the Science Policy Research Unit. We shall distinguish between (1) Incremental innovation; (2) Radical innovation; (3) New technology systems; (4) Changes of techno-economic paradigms. (See also the introductory dis-cussion on paradigms and trajectories in Chapter 2 [Dosi et al., 1988]).

1. *Incremental innovations*: These types of innovation occur more or less continuously in any industry or service activity although at differing rates in different industries and different countries, depending upon a combination of demand pressures, socio-cultural factors, technologi-cal opportunities and trajectories. They may often occur, not so much as the result of any deliberate research and development activity, but as the outcome of inventions and improvements suggested by engi-neers and others directly engaged in the production process, or as a result of initiatives and proposals by users ('learning by doing' and 'learning by using'). Many empirical studies have confirmed their great importance in improving the efficiency in use of all factors of pro-duction, for example, Hollander's (1965) study of productivity gains in Du Pont rayon plants or Townsend's (1976) study of the Anderton shearer-loader in the British coal-mining industry. They are frequently associated with the scaling-up of plant and equipment and quality improvements to products and services for a variety of specific

applications. Although their combined effect is extremely important in the growth of productivity, no single incremental innovation has dramatic effects, and they may sometimes pass unnoticed and unrecorded. However, their effects are apparent in the steady growth of productivity, which is reflected in input–output tables over time by changes in the coefficients for the existing array of products and services.

2. *Radical innovations*: These are discontinuous events and in recent times are usually the result of a deliberate research and development activity in enterprises and/or in university and government laboratories. There is no way in which nylon could have emerged from improving the production process in rayon plants or the woollen industry. Nor could nuclear power have emerged from incremental improvements to coal or oil-fired power stations. Radical innovations are unevenly distributed over sectors and over time, but our research did not support the view of Mensch (1975) that their appearance is concentrated particularly in periods of deep recessions in response to the collapse or decline of established markets (Freeman et al., 1982). But we would agree with Mensch that, whenever they may occur, they are important as the potential springboard for the growth of new markets, and for the surges of new investment associated with booms. They may often involve a combined product, process and organisational innovation. Over a period of decades radical innovations, such as nylon or 'the pill', may have fairly dramatic effects, i.e., they *do* bring about structural change but in terms of their aggregate economic impact they are relatively small and localised, unless a whole cluster of radical innovations are linked together in the rise of new industries and services, such as the synthetic materials industry or the semiconductor industry.

3. *Changes of 'technology system'*: These are far-reaching changes in technology, affecting several branches of the economy, as well as giving rise to entirely new sectors. They are based on a combination of radical and incremental innovations, together with *organisational* and *managerial* innovations affecting more than one or a few firms. Keirstead (1948), in his exposition of a Schumpeterian theory of economic development, introduced the concept of 'constellations' of innovations, which were technically and economically interrelated. An obvious example is the cluster of synthetic materials innovations, petro-chemical innovations, machinery innovations in injection moulding and extrusion, and innumerable application innovations introduced in the 1920s, 1930s, 1940s and 1950s (Freeman et al., 1982).

4. *Changes in 'techno-economic paradigm' ('technological revolutions')*: Some changes in technology systems are so far-reaching in their effects that they have a major influence on the behaviour of the entire economy.

A change of this kind carries with it many clusters of radical and incremental innovations, and may eventually embody a number of new technology systems. A vital characteristic of this fourth type of technical change is that it has *pervasive* effects throughout the economy, i.e. it not only leads to the emergence of a new range of products, services, systems and industries in its own right; it also affects directly or indirectly almost every other branch of the economy, i.e. it is a 'meta-paradigm'. We use the expression 'techno-economic' (Perez, 1983) rather than 'technological paradigm' (Dosi, 1982) because the changes involved go beyond engineering trajectories for specific product or process technologies and affect the input cost structure and conditions of production and distribution throughout the system. This fourth category corresponds to Nelson and Winter's concept of 'general natural trajectories' and, once established as the dominant influence on engineers, designers and managers, becomes a 'technological regime' for several decades. From this it is evident that we view Schumpeter's long cycles and 'creative gales of destruction' as a succession of 'techno-economic paradigms' associated with a characteristic institutional framework, which, however, only emerges after a painful process of structural change.

We now turn to an elaboration of the main characteristics of 'techno-economic' paradigms and their patterns of diffusion through long waves of economic development. As the following sections will attempt to show, a new techno-economic paradigm develops initially within the old, showing its decisive advantages during the 'downswing' phase of the previous Kondratiev cycle. However, it becomes established as a dominant technological regime only after a crisis of structural adjustment, involving deep social and institutional changes, as well as the replacement of the motive branches of the economy (Table 3.1).

'KEY FACTOR' INPUTS AND CHANGE OF TECHNO-ECONOMIC PARADIGM

As the last section has made clear, our conception of 'techno-economic paradigm' is much wider than 'clusters' of innovations or even of 'technology systems'. We are referring to a combination of interrelated product and process, technical, organisational and managerial innovations, embodying a quantum jump in potential productivity for all or most of the economy and opening up an unusually wide range of investment and profit opportunities. Such a paradigm change implies a unique new combination of decisive technical *and* economic advantages.

Clearly one major characteristic of the diffusion pattern of a new techno-economic paradigm is its spread from the initial industries or areas of application to a much wider range of industries and services and the economy as a whole (Table 3.1). By 'paradigm' change we mean precisely a radical transformation of the prevailing engineering and managerial *common sense* for best productivity and most profitable practice, which is applicable in almost any industry (i.e. we are talking about a 'meta-paradigm').

The organising principle of each successive paradigm and the justification for the expression 'techno-economic paradigm' is to be found not only in a new range of products and systems, but most of all in the dynamics of the relative *cost* structure of all possible inputs to production. In each new techno-economic paradigm, a particular input or set of inputs, which may be described as the 'key factor' of that paradigm, fulfils the following conditions:

1. Clearly perceived low and rapidly falling relative cost. As Rosenberg (1975) and other economists have pointed out, small changes in the relative input cost structure have little or no effect on the behaviour of engineers, designers and researchers. Only major and persistent changes have the power to transform the decision rules and 'common sense' procedures for engineers and managers (Perez, 1985; Freeman and Soete, 1987).
2. Apparently almost unlimited availability of supply over long periods. Temporary shortages may of course occur in a period of rapid buildup in demand for the new key factor, but the prospect must be clear that there are no major barriers to an enormous long-term increase in supply. This is an essential condition for the confidence to take major investment decisions which depend on this long-term availability.
3. Clear potential for the use or incorporation of the new key factor or factors in many products and processes throughout the economic system; either directly or (more commonly) through a set of related innovations, which both reduce the cost and change the quality of capital equipment, labour inputs, and other inputs to the system.

We would maintain that this combination of characteristics holds today for microelectronics and we discuss this further in the section below on the 'information technology paradigm'. It held until recently for oil, which underlay the post-war boom (the 'fourth Kondratiev' upswing). Before that, and more tentatively, we would suggest that the role of key factor was played by low-cost steel in the third Kondratiev wave, by low-cost and steam-powered transport in the 'Victorian' boom of the nineteenth century (Table 3.1, column 5 – 'Key factor industries . . .').

Table 3.1 A tentative sketch of some of the main characteristics of successive long waves (modes of growth)

1 Number	2 Approx. periodisation Upswing Downswing	3 Description	4 Main 'carrier branches' and induced growth sectors infrastructure	5 Key factor industries offering abundant supply at descending price	6 Other sectors growing rapidly from small base	7 Limitations of previous techno-economic paradigm and ways in which new paradigm offers some solutions	8 Organisation of firms and forms of cooperation and competition
First	1770s & 1780s to 1830s & 1840s 'Industrial revolution' 'Hard times'	Early mechanisation Kondratieff	Textiles Textile chemicals Textile machinery Iron-working and iron castings Water Power Potteries Trunk canals Turnpike roads	Cotton Pig iron	Steam engines Machinery	Limitations of scale, process control and mechanisation in domestic 'putting out' system. Limitations of hand-operated tools and processes. Solutions offering prospects of greater productivity and profitability through mechanisation	Individual entrepreneurs and small firms (< 100 employees) competition. Partnership structure facilitates co-operation of technical innovators and financial managers. Local capital and individual wealth.

50

Wave	Period / name	Kondratieff	Industries	Key factors	New leading sectors	Constraints	Business organisation
							and factory organisation in leading industries.
Second	1830s & 1840s to 1880s & 1890s Victorian prosperity 'Great depression'	Steam power and railway Kondratieff	Steam engines Steamships Machine tools Iron Railway equipment Railways World Shipping	Coal Transport	Steel Electricity Gas Synthetic dyestuffs Heavy engineering	Limitations of water power in terms of inflexibility of location, scale of production, reliability and range of applications, restricting further development of mechanisation and factory production to the economy as a whole. Largely overcome by steam engine and new transport system.	High noon of small-firm competition, but larger firms now employing thousands, rather than hundreds. As firms and markets grow, limited liability and joint stock companies permit new pattern of investment, risk-taking and ownership.
Third	1880s & 1890s to 1930s & 1940s 'Belle epoque'	Electrical and heavy engineering Kondratieff	Electrical engineering Electrical machinery	Steel	Automobiles Aircraft Telecommunications Radio	Limitations of iron as an engineering material in terms	Emergence of giant firms, cartels, trusts and

Table 3.1 (continued)

1 Number	2 Approx. periodisation Upswing Downswing	3 Description	4 Main 'carrier branches' and induced growth sectors infrastructure	5 Key factor industries offering abundant supply at descending price	6 Other sectors growing rapidly from small base	7 Limitations of previous techno-economic paradigm and ways in which new paradigm offers some solutions	8 Organisation of firms and forms of cooperation and competition
	'Great depression'		Cable and wire Heavy engineering Heavy armaments Steel ships Heavy chemicals Synthetic dyestuffs Electricity supply and distribution		Aluminium Consumer durables Oil Plastics	of strength, durability, precision, etc., partly overcome by universal availability of cheap steel and of alloys. Limitations of inflexible belts, pulleys, etc., driven by one large steam engine overcome by unit and group	mergers. Monopoly and oligopoly became typical. 'Regulation' or state ownership of 'natural' monopolies and 'public utilities'. Concentration of banking and 'finance-capital'. Emergence of specialised 'middle

Fourth	1930s & 1940s to 1980s & 1990s Golden age of growth and Keynesian full employment Crisis of structural adjustment	Fordist mass production Kondratieff	Automobiles Trucks Tractors Tanks Armaments for motorised warfare Aircraft Consumer durables Process plant Synthetic materials Petro-chemicals Highways Airports	Energy (especially oil) Computers Radar NC machine tools Drugs Nuclear weapons and power Missiles Micro-electronics Software	drive for electrical machinery, overhead cranes, power tools permitting vastly improved layout and capital saving. Standardisation facilitating world-wide operations. Limitations of scale of batch production overcome by flow processes and assembly-line production techniques, full standardisation of components and materials and abundant cheap energy. New patterns of industrial location and urban	management' in large firms. Oligopolistic competition. Multinational corporations based on direct foreign investment and multiplant locations. Competitive subcontracting on 'arms length' basis or vertical integration. Increasing concentration, divisionalisation and hierarchical

53

Table 3.1 (continued)

1 Number	2 Approx. periodisation Upswing Downswing	3 Description	4 Main 'carrier branches' and induced growth sectors infrastructure	5 Key factor industries offering abundant supply at descending price	6 Other sectors growing rapidly from small base	7 Limitations of previous techno-economic paradigm and ways in which new paradigm offers some solutions	8 Organisation of firms and forms of cooperation and competition
			Airlines			development through speed and flexibility of automobile and air transport. Further cheapening of mass consumption products.	control. 'Techno-structure' in large corporations.
Fifth*	1980s & 1990s to?	Information and com-munication Kondratieff	Computers Electronic capital goods Software	'Chips' (micro-elecronics)	'Third generation' biotechnology products and processes	Diseconomies of scale and inflexibility of dedicated assembly-line	'Networks' of large and small firms based increasingly on computer

Tele-
communi-
cations
equipment
Optical
fibres
Robotics
FMS
Ceramics
Data banks
Information
services
Digital tele-
communi-
cations
network
Satellites

Space activities
Fine chemicals
SDI

and process
plant partly
overcome by
flexible
manufacturing
systems,
'networking' and
'economies of
scope'.
Limitations of
energy intensity
and materials
intensity partly
overcome by
electronic control
systems and
components.
Limitations of
hierarchical
departmentalisation
overcome by
'systemation',
'networking' and
integration of
design, production
and marketing.

networks and
close co-operation
in technology,
quality control,
training,
investment
planning
and production
planning
('just-in-time')
etc. 'Keiretsu' and
similar structures
offering internal
capital markets.

Table 3.1 (continued)

9 Number	10 Techno-logical leaders	11 Other industrial and newly industrialising countries	12 Some features of national regimes of regulation	13 Aspects of the international regulatory regime	14 Main features of the national system of innovation	15 Some features of tertiary sector development	16 Representative innovative entrepreneurs and engineers	17 Political economists and philosophers
First	Britain France Belgium	German states Netherlands	Breakdown and dissolution of feudal and medieval monopolies, guilds, tolls, privileges and restrictions on trade, industry and competition. Repression of unions. Laissez-faire established as dominant principle.	Emergence of British supremacy in trade and international finance with the defeat of Napoleon.	Encouragement of science through National Academies, Royal Society, etc. Engineer and inventor-entrepreneurs and partner-ships. Local scientific and engineering societies. Part-time training and	Rapid expansion of retail and wholesale trade in new urban centres. Very small state apparatus. Merchants as source of capital.	Arkwright Boulton Wedgwood Owen Bramah Maudslay	Smith Say Owen

Second	Britain France Belgium Germany USA	Italy Netherlands Switzerland Austria–Hungary	High noon of laissez-faire. 'Nightwatch-man state' with minimal regulatory functions except protection of property and legal framework	'Pax Britannica'. British naval, financial and trade dominance. International free trade. Gold standard.	on-the-job training. Reform and strengthening of national patent systems. Transfer of technology by migration of skilled workers. British Institution of Civil Engineers. Learning by doing, using and interacting.	Establishment of Institution of Mechanical Engineers and development of UK Mechanics' Institutes. More rapid development of professional education and	Rapid growth of domestic service for new middle class to largest service occupation. Continued rapid growth of transport and distribution.	Stephenson Whitworth Brunel Armstrong Whitney Singer	Ricardo List Marx

Table 3.1 (continued)

9 Number	10 Techno-logical leaders	11 Other industrial and newly industrialising countries	12 Some features of national regimes of regulation	13 Aspects of the international regulatory regime	14 Main features of the national system of innovation	15 Some features of tertiary sector development	16 Representative innovative entrepreneurs and engineers	17 Political economists and philosophers
			for production and trade. Acceptance of craft unions. Early social legislation and pollution control.		training of engineers and skilled workers elsewhere in Europe. Growing specialisation. Internationalisation of patent system. Learning by doing, using and interacting.	Universal postal and communication services. Growth of financial services.		
Third	Germany USA Britain France Belgium Switzerland Netherlands	Italy Austria–Hungary Canada Sweden Denmark Japan Russia	Nationalist and imperialist state regulation or state ownership of basic intrastructure (public utilities).	Imperialism and colonisation. 'Pax Britannica' comes to an end with First World War. Destabilisation	'In-house' R&D departments established in German and US chemical and electrical engineering	Peak of domestic service industry. Rapid growth of state and local bureaucracies. Department stores and chain	Siemens Carnegie Nobel Edison Krupp Bosch	Marshall Pareto Lenin Veblen

Fourth						
USA Germany Other EEC Japan Sweden Switzerland USSR Other EFTA Other Eastern European Korea Brazil Mexico Venezuela Argentina	'Welfare state' and 'warfare state'. Attempted state regulation of investment, growth and Arms race. Much social legislation. Rapid growth of state bureaucracy.	'Pax Americana' US economic and military dominance. Decolonisation. Arms race and cold war with of international financial and trade system leading to world crisis and Second World.War.	Spread of specialised R&D departments to most industries. Large-scale state involvement in military R&D through Recruitment of university scientists and engineers and graduates of the new Technische Hochschulen and equivalent Institutes of Technology. National Standard Institutions and national laboratories. Universal elementary education. Learning by doing, using and interacting.	Sharp decline of domestic service. Self-service fast food and growth of supermarkets and stores. Education, tourism and entertainment expanding rapidly. Corresponding take-off of white-collar employment pyramid. London as centre for major world commodity markets.	Sloan McNamara Ford Agnelli Nordhoff Matsushita	Keynes Schumpeter Kalecki

Table 3.1 (continued)

9 Number	10 Techno-logical leaders	11 Other industrial and newly industrialising countries	12 Some features of national regimes of regulation	13 Aspects of the international regulatory regime	14 Main features of the national system of innovation	15 Some features of tertiary sector development	16 Representative innovative entrepreneurs and engineers	17 Political economists and philosophers
	Canada Australia	China India Taiwan	employment by Keynesian techniques. High levels of state expenditure and involvement. 'Social partnership' with unions after collapse of fascism. 'Roll-back' of welfare state de-regulation and privatisation during crisis of adjustment.	USSR. US-dominated international financial and trade regime (GATT, IMF, World Bank) Destabilisation of Bretton Woods regime in 1970s.	contracts and national laboratories. Increasing state involvement in civil science and technology. Rapid expansion of secondary and higher education and of industrial training. Transfer of technology through extensive licensing and know-how agreements and investment	hypermarkets, petrol service stations. Continued growth of state bureaucracy, armed forces and social services. Rapid growth of research and professions and financial services, packaged tourism and air travel on very large scale.		

Fifth*	Japan USA Germany Sweden Other EEC EFTA USSR and other Eastern European Taiwan Korea Canada Australia	Brazil Mexico Argentina Venezuela China India Indonesia Turkey Egypt Pakistan Nigeria Algeria Tunisia Other Latin American	'Regulation' of strategic ICT infra-structure. 'Big Brother' or 'Big Sister' state. Deregulation and reregulation of national financial institutions and capital markets. Possible emergence of new-style participatory decentralised welfare state based on ICT and red-green alliance.	'Multi-polarity'. Regional blocs. Problems of developing appropriate international institutions capable of regulating global finance, capital, ICT and transnational companies.	by multinational corporations. Learning by doing, using and interacting. Horizontal integration of R&D, design, production and process engineering and marketing. Integration of process design with multi-skill training. Computer networking and collaborative research. State support for generic technologies and university–industry collaboration. New types of proprietary regime for	Rapid growth of new information services, data banks and software industries Integration of services and manufacturing in such industries as printing and publishing. Rapid growth of professional consultancy. New forms of craft production linked to distribution.	Kobayashi Uenohara Barron Benneton Noyce	Schumacher Aoki Bertalanffy

Table 3.1 (continued)

9 Number	10 Techno-logical leaders	11 Other industrial and newly industrialising countries	12 Some features of national regimes of regulation	13 Aspects of the international regulatory regime	14 Main features of the national system of innovation	15 Some features of tertiary sector development	16 Representative innovative entrepreneurs and engineers	17 Political economists and philosophers
					software and biotechnology 'Factory as laboratory'.			

Note: * All columns dealing with the 'fifth Kondratieff' are necessarily speculative.

Source: Based on Freeman (1987).

Clearly, every one of these inputs identified as 'key factors' existed (and was in use) long before the new paradigm developed. However, its full potential is only recognised and made capable of fulfilling the above conditions when the previous key factor and its related constellation of technologies give strong signals of diminishing returns and of approaching limits to their potential for further increasing productivity or for new profitable investment. (In quite different types of society and different historical circumstances, archaeologists have also recognised the crucial importance of 'key factors' in economic development in their classification of the 'Stone Age', 'Bronze Age' and 'Iron Age'.)

From a purely technical point of view, the explosive surge of interrelated innovations involved in a technological revolution could probably have occurred earlier and in a more gradual manner. But, there are strong economic and social factors at play that serve as prolonged containment first and as unleashing forces later. The massive externalities created to favour the diffusion and generalisation of the prevailing paradigm act as a powerful deterrent to change for a prolonged period (see Chapter 26 by Brian Arthur [Dosi et al., 1988]). It is only when productivity along the old trajectories shows persistent limits to growth and future profits are seriously threatened that the high risks and costs of trying the new technologies appear as clearly justified. And it is only after many of these trials have been obviously successful that further applications become easier and less risky investment choices.

The new key factor does not appear as an isolated input, but rather at the core of a rapidly growing system of technical, social and managerial innovations, some related to the production of the key factor itself and others to its utilisation. At first these innovations may appear (and may be in fact pursued) as a means for overcoming the specific bottlenecks of the old technologies, but the new key factor soon acquires its own dynamics and successive innovations take place through an intensive interactive process, spurred by the limits to growth which are increasingly apparent under the old paradigm (Table 3.1, column 7 – 'Limitations of previous techno-economic paradigm . . .'). In this way the most successful new technology systems gradually crystallise as a new 'ideal' type of production organisation which becomes the common sense of management and design, embodying new 'rules of thumb' and restoring confidence to investment decision-makers after a long period of hesitation.

Clearly, this approach differs radically from the dominant conceptualisation of changing factor costs in neo-classical economic theory, although it has points of contact, such as the persistent search for least-cost combinations of factor inputs to sustain or increase profitability. Most formulations of neo-classical theory put the main emphasis on varying combinations of labour and capital and on substitution between them, and implicitly or explicitly assume responsiveness even to small changes in these relative factor prices in either direction, i.e. 'reversibility'. Our approach stresses the system's response to *major* changes in the price of *new* inputs, and *new* technologies which exploit their potential to reduce costs of both labour and capital, as a result of new total factor input combinations and organisational–managerial innovations. Such major changes are the result of an active and prolonged search in response to perceived limits, not on the basis of perfect information but on the basis of trial and error, i.e. the historical learning process stressed by Hahn (see Chapter 1 [Dosi et al., 1988]). Once the new technology is widely adopted, the change is generally irreversible (i.e. the principal actors became 'locked in' by the pervasive economic and technical advantages and complementarities; (see Chapter 26 [Dosi et al., 1988]).

We have stressed the role of a key factor or factors in creating widening investment opportunities and creating the potential for big increases in productivity and profits. We turn now to consider the wider societal problems involved in the transition from one 'techno-economic paradigm' to another.

DIFFUSION OF NEW TECHNO-ECONOMIC PARADIGMS AND INSTITUTIONAL CHANGE

It is a clear implication of our mode of conceptualising successive 'techno-economic paradigms' that a new paradigm emerges in a world still dominated by an old paradigm and begins to demonstrate its comparative advantages at first only in one or a few sectors. The fastest-growing new sectors are thus *not* those which are the motive branches of an established, technological regime (Table 3.1, columns 4 – 'Main "carrier branches"' and 6 – 'Other sectors growing rapidly'). There is no possibility of a new paradigm displacing an old one until it has first clearly demonstrated such advantages and until the supply of the new key factor or factors already satisfies the three conditions described above: falling costs, rapidly increasing supply, and pervasive applications. Thus a period of rapid growth in the supply of the key factor(s) occurs already *before* the new paradigm is established as the dominant one, and continues when it is the prevailing regime.

A new techno-economic paradigm emerges only gradually as a new 'ideal type' of productive organisation, to take full advantage of the key factor(s) which are becoming more and more visible in the relative cost structure. The new paradigm discloses the potential for a quantum jump in total

factor productivity and opens up an unprecedented range of new investment opportunities. It is for these reasons that it brings about a radical shift
in engineering and managerial 'common sense' and that it tends to diffuse
as rapidly as conditions allow, replacing the investment pattern of the old
paradigm.

The full constellation – once crystallised – goes far beyond the key
factor(s) and beyond technical change itself. It brings with it a restructuring of the whole productive system.

Among other things as it crystallises, the new techno-economic paradigm involves:

(a)   a new 'best-practice' form of organisation in the firm and at the plant
      level;
(b)   a new skill profile in the labour force, affecting both quality and quan-
      tity of labour and corresponding patterns of income distribution;
(c)   a new product mix in the sense that those products which make inten-
      sive use of the low-cost key factor will be the preferred choice for
      investment and will represent therefore a growing proportion of
      GNP;
(d)   new trends in both radical and incremental innovation geared to
      substituting more intensive use of the new key factor(s) for other rela-
      tively high-cost elements;
(e)   a new pattern in the location of investment both nationally and inter-
      nationally as the change in the relative cost structure transforms
      comparative advantages;
(f)   a particular wave of infrastructural investment designed to provide
      appropriate externalities throughout the system and facilitate the use
      of the new products and processes everywhere;
(g)   a tendency for new innovator-entrepreneur-type small firms also to
      enter the new rapidly expanding branches of the economy and in
      some cases to initiate entirely new sectors of production;
(h)   a tendency for large firms to concentrate, whether by growth or
      diversification, in those branches of the economy where the key factor
      is produced and most intensively used, which results in there being dis-
      tinctly different branches acting as the engines of growth in each suc-
      cessive Kondratiev upswing;
(i)   a new pattern of consumption of goods and services and new types of
      distribution and consumer behaviour.

From this it is evident that the period of transition – the downswing and
depression of the long wave – is characterised by deep structural change in
the economy and such changes require an equally profound transformation

of the institutional and social framework. The onset of prolonged reces-
sionary trends indicates the increasing degree of mismatch between the
techno-economic sub-system and the old socio-institutional framework. It
shows the need for a full-scale reaccommodation of social behaviour and
institutions to suit the requirements and the potential of a shift which has
already taken place to a considerable extent in some areas of the techno-
economic sphere. This reaccommodation occurs as a result of a process of
political search, experimentation and adaptation, but when it has been
achieved, by a variety of social and political changes at the national and
international level, the resulting good 'match' facilitates the upswing phase
of the long wave. A climate of confidence for a surge of new investment is
created through an appropriate combination of regulatory mechanisms
which foster the full deployment of the new paradigm. Since the achievement of a 'good match' is a conflict-ridden process and proceeds very
unevenly in differing national political and cultural contexts, this may exert
a considerable influence on the changing pattern of international technological leadership and international patterns of diffusion (Table 3.1 and
Chapter 23 [Dosi et al., 1988]).

Schumpeter's (1939) theory of depression was rather narrowly 'economic' and strangely, for someone who was so much aware of social and
organisational aspects of technical innovation, tended to ignore the institutional aspects of recovery policies. This was one of the main reasons for
the relative neglect of his ideas compared with those of Keynes.

THE INFORMATION TECHNOLOGY PARADIGM

The technological regime, which predominated in the post-war boom, was
one based on low-cost oil and energy-intensive materials (especially petrochemicals and synthetics), and was led by giant oil, chemical, automobile
and other mass durable goods producers. Its 'ideal' type of productive
organisation at the plant level was the continuous-flow assembly-line
turning out massive quantities of identical units. The 'ideal' type of firm was
the 'corporation' with a separate and complex hierarchical managerial and
administrative structure, including in-house R&D and operating in oligopolistic markets in which advertising and marketing activities played a
major role. It required large numbers of middle-range skills in both the blue-
and white-collar areas, leading to a characteristic pattern of occupations
and income distribution. The massive expansion of the market for consumer durables was facilitated by this pattern, as well as by social changes
and adaptation of the financial system, which permitted the growth of 'hire
purchase' and other types of consumer credit. The paradigm required a vast

infrastructural network of motorways, service stations, airports, oil and petrol distribution systems, which was promoted by public investment on a large scale already in the 1930s, but more massively in the post-war period. At various times in different countries both civil and military expenditures of governments played a very important part in stimulating aggregate demand, and a specific pattern of demand for automobiles, weapons, consumer durables, synthetic materials and petroleum products.

Today, with cheap microelectronics widely available, with prices expected to fall still further and with related new developments in computers and telecommunications, it is no longer 'common sense' to continue along the (now expensive) path of energy and materials-intensive inflexible mass production.

The 'ideal' information-intensive productive organisation now increasingly links design, management, production and marketing into one integrated system – a process which may be described as 'systemation' and which goes far beyond the earlier concepts of mechanisation and automation. Firms organised on this new basis, whether in the computer industry such as IBM, or in the clothing industry such as Benetton, can produce a flexible and rapidly changing mix of products and services. Growth tends increasingly to be led by the electronics and information sectors, taking advantage of the growing externalities provided by an all-encompassing telecommunications infrastructure, which will ultimately bring down to extremely low levels the costs of access to the system for both producers and users of information.

The skill profile associated with the new techno-economic paradigm appears to change from the concentration on middle-range craft and supervisory skills to increasingly high- and low-range qualifications, and from narrow specialisation to broader, multi-purpose basic skills for information handling. Diversity and flexibility at all levels substitute for homogeneity and dedicated systems.

The transformation of the profile of capital equipment is no less radical. Computers are increasingly associated with all types of productive equipment as in CNC machine tools, robotics, and process control instruments as well as with the design process through CAD, and with administrative functions through data processing systems, all linked by data transmission equipment. According to some estimates computer-based capital equipment already accounts for nearly half of all new fixed investment in plant and equipment in the United States.

The deep structural problems involved in this change of paradigm are now evident in all parts of the world. Among the manifestations are the acute and persistent shortage of the high-level skills associated with the new paradigm, even in countries with high levels of general unemployment, and the persistent surplus capacity in the older 'smokestack', energy-intensive industries such as steel, oil and petrochemicals.

As a result there is a growing search for new social and political solutions in such areas as flexible working time, shorter working hours, re-education and retraining systems, regional policies based on creating favourable conditions for information technology (rather than tax incentives to capital-intensive mass production industries), new financial systems, possible decentralisation of management and government, and access to data banks and networks at all levels and new telecommunication systems. But so far, these seem still to be partial and relatively minor changes. If the Keynesian revolution and the profound transformation of social institutions in the Second World War and its aftermath were required to unleash the fourth Kondratiev upswing, then social innovations on an equally significant scale are likely to be needed now. This applies especially to the international dimension of world economic development.

THE STRUCTURAL CRISIS OF THE 1980s

From this brief summary of some of the characteristics of the new paradigm it will have become apparent that the widespread diffusion of the new technology throughout the economic system is not just a matter of incremental improvements, nor just a question of the extension of existing capacity in a few new industries. It involves a major upheaval in *all* sectors of the economy and changes in the skill profile and capital stock throughout the system. It is for this reason that periods like the 1930s and the 1980s cannot be treated in the same way as the minor recessions of the 1950s and 1960s.

The structural crisis involved in the transition from one technological regime to another increases the instability of investment behaviour for a number of reasons. The leading-edge industries of the new paradigm are growing so rapidly that they constantly tend to outstrip the supply of skilled labour. However, the headlong rush to increase capacity as band-wagons get rolling also leads to periodic crises of over-capacity, as there is no way in which the supply can precisely anticipate and match smoothly the growth of market demand (in Hahn's terminology, the 'true' demand function cannot be known). Moreover the technology is still changing so rapidly that successive generations of equipment and products rapidly become obsolete. The tempestuous growth of the chip industry and the computer industry in the 1970s and 1980s has also been marked by periodic, though short-lived, crises of over-supply (Ernst, 1983, 1987). There were similar problems with the leading-edge industries of the 1920s and the 1930s – automobiles, consumer durables and organic chemicals.

The problems in the other sectors of the economy are even more severe. Some industries which have previously been at the heart of the (now super-seded) paradigms now experience much slower rates of growth or absolute decline. They may also have problems of over-capacity and rationalisation which are prolonged, as has been the case in some of the energy-intensive industries in the 1970s and 1980s, such as steel, petrochemicals and synthetic fibres. Similar problems were encountered by the railways and railway equipment industries as well as by coal and textiles in previous structural crises.

There are also severe problems in those manufacturing and service sectors which still have ample growth potential but are confronted with the need to change their production processes, their product mix, their management systems, their skill profiles and their marketing to accomplish the shift to an entirely new technological paradigm. This is a painful and difficult process of adjustment, involving, as we have seen, a kind of cultural revolution as well as the need for major re-equipment. These problems can be seen very clearly today in such industries as printing, vehicles and machine tools, as well as in services such as insurance, distribution and transport. They were equally apparent in many industrial sectors adapting in the 1920s and 1930s to the new energy-intensive mass and flow production systems which at that time represented the leading edge of the new techno-economic paradigm.

The depression of the 1930s was certainly one of extraordinary severity, especially in the leading industrialised countries – the United States and Germany. Between 1929 and 1933 GNP fell by 30 per cent in the United States, industrial production by nearly 50 per cent, output of durable producers' equipment by 75 per cent and new construction by 85 per cent. It is hardly surprising that Keynesian economists, such as Samuelson (1980), discount the likelihood of the recurrence of such a catastrophe:

> Although nothing is impossible in an inexact science like economics, the probability of a great depression – a prolonged cumulative chronic slump like that of the 1930s, 1890s or 1870s – has been reduced to a negligible figure. No one should pay an appreciable insurance premium to be protected against the risk of a total breakdown in our banking system and of massive unemployment in which 25 per cent of workers are jobless. The reason for the virtual disappearance of great depressions is the new attitude of the electorate . . . The electorate in a mixed economy insists that any political party which is in power – be it Republican or Democratic, the Tory or Labour Party – take the expansionary actions that can prevent lasting depressions. [p. 251]

This may be an over-optimistic view. Whilst not dissenting from Samuelson's description of economics as an inexact science, this chapter suggests that it is quite possible for the world economy to experience a depression, which, even if not so severe in all respects as that of the 1930s, could be more severe than the earlier recessions of the 1870s and the 1890s.

This somewhat pessimistic view is based on the observation that the main sources of instability which gave rise to the depression of the 1930s are also present today, albeit in a somewhat different form: the international debt situation, extreme imbalances in international payments, weakness in agricultural prices, instability in exchange rates, creeping protectionism, the absence of an adequate system of regulating the international economy and in particular the absence of an adequate international lender of last resort, disarray in the economics profession, and lack of long-term vision in policy-making. The present wave of technical change sweeping through the world economy is likely to exacerbate the problems of instability in investment, and of structural change at the national and international level and the associated disequilibria in the international economy.

It is notable that Samuelson's argument that severe depressions can be averted rests not on any faith in the self-regulating powers of the market, but unequivocally on the belief that *political* factors, principally the level of unemployment, will put pressure on governments to adopt expansionary policies, which are assumed to be available and applicable. We share with him and other Keynesians their scepticism that the rate of interest and monetary policy are in themselves sufficient to achieve an equilibrium growth path.

But for his argument to carry conviction it would be necessary not only for governments to adopt *national* policies to counteract tendencies toward depression, but also at least for the leading countries to act in a coordinated manner at the *international* level. Recent experience must cast some doubt on both these assumptions. It is no doubt true that the experience of recession and stagnation does induce a search for expansionary policies at the political level. But, as in the 1930s, this search may lead to nationalistic, protectionist and even militaristic policies as well as to neo-Keynesian policies and other as yet untried solutions. It may also be hindered by the extreme divergence of views from the economics profession on such questions as the feasibility and desirability of a return to fixed exchange rates.

The uneven and varied response of governments, firms and industries to the threats and opportunities posed by information technology tends to accentuate the uneven process of development. Typically in the past, major changes in techno-economic paradigm have been associated with shifts in the international division of labour and international technological leadership. Newcomers are sometimes more able to make the necessary social and institutional innovations than the more arthritic social structures of established leaders. Erstwhile leading countries such as the United Kingdom or the United States may become the victims of their own earlier success. On the other hand, countries lacking the necessary minimal educational, managerial, R&D and design capability may be even more seriously disadvantaged in international competition.

This means that changes of paradigm are likely to be associated with the temporary aggravation of instability problems in relation to the flow of international investment, trade and payments. The enormous Japanese trade surplus and the US trade deficit reflect not merely exchange rate problems, but also the more successful Japanese exploitation and application of IT outside the leading-edge industries, and the introduction of many institutional innovations facilitating this process (Chapter 23 [Dosi et al., 1988]). The US economy leads in military applications of IT but lags in other areas. There is thus a major 'structural' component in the international trade imbalances, as there was in the 'technological gap' which the United States opened up between the 1920s and the 1950s (Freeman, 1987).

The same is even more true of the problems of Third World countries. A report of the Inter-American Development Bank has highlighted these critical problems confronting the world economy and has warned that the IMF measures to deal with the crisis have been short-term palliatives, not long-term solutions. Albert Fishlow (1985) points out that Latin America faces a burden of debt service repayments greater than the level of reparations that Germany found impossible after the First World War. Only a widespread recovery of productive investment and technical innovation in Latin America could sustain the growth needed to finance even a much lower level of debt repayment and interest payments. It is not without interest that Samuelson and Nordhaus in the 12th edition of *Economics* (1985) do introduce a sentence or two suggesting that 'default of major heavily indebted countries' could lead to a Great Depression.

The Third World countries are experiencing difficulties in developing the new information technology industries to sustain their competitive power, but the new technologies do actually offer some major advantages to them, provided they modify their trade, industrial and technology policies, as indicated in Chapter 21 by Perez and Soete [Dosi et al., 1988].

However, these 'catching up' efforts of Third World countries also require some resolution of the basic structural problems confronting the entire world economy. This implies new measures to facilitate the international transfer of technology as well as a resolution of the debt problem. Thus the greatest problem of institutional adaptation lies in the sphere of international financial and economic institutions, to take account of these long-term structural adaptation difficulties. The development of new national and international 'regimes of regulation' is discussed in the following chapter by Boyer [Dosi et al., 1988].

BIBLIOGRAPHY

Dosi, G (1982), 'Technological paradigms and technological trajectories', *Research Policy*, vol. II, no. 3, June, pp. 147–162.

Dosi, G., Freeman, C., Nelson, R.R., Silverberg, G. and Soete, L.L.G. (eds) (1988), *Technical Change and Economic Theory*, London and New York, Pinter Publishers.

Eatwell, J. (1982), *Whatever Happened to Britain?*, London, Duckworth.

Elliott, J.E. (1985), 'Schumpeter's theory of economic development and social change: exposition and 'assessment', *International Journal of Social Economics*, vol. 12, Parts 6 and 7, pp. 6–33.

Ernst, D. (1983), 'The global race in microelectronics: innovation and corporate strategies in a period of crisis', MIT.

Ernst, D. (1987), 'Programmable automation in the semiconductor industry: reflections on current diffusion patterns', GERTTD Conference on Automisation Programmable, Paris, 12–14 April 1987.

Fishlow, A. (1985), 'The state of Latin American economics', in *Economic and Social Progress in Latin America, External Debt: Crisis and Adjustment*, Washington, DC: Inter-American Development Bank, pp. 139–40.

Freeman, C. (1982), *The Economics of Industrial Innovation*, 2nd edn, London: Frances Pinter.

Freeman, C. (1987), *Technology Policy and Economic Performance: Lessons from Japan*, London, Pinter.

Freeman, C., Clark, J. and Soete, L.L.G. (1982), *Unemployment and Technical Innovation: A Study of Long Waves in Economic Development*, London, Frances Pinter.

Freeman, C. and Soete, L.L.G. (eds) (1987), *Technical Change and Full Employment*, Oxford, Blackwell.

Galbraith, J.K. (1961), *The Great Crash, 1929*, Harmondsworth, Pelican.

Hollander, S.G. (1965), *The Sources of Increased Efficiency: A Study of DuPont Rayon Plants*, Cambridge, MA, MIT Press.

Jewkes, J., Sawers, D. and Stillerman, J. (1956), *The Sources of Invention*, London, Macmillan.

Keirstead, B.S. (1948), *The Theory of Economic Change*, Toronto, Macmillan.

Keynes, J.M. (1930), *A Treatise on Money*, vol. 2, London, Macmillan.

Keynes, J.M. (1936), *General Theory of Employment, Interest and Money*, New York, Harcourt-Brace.

Klamer, A. (1984), *The New Classical Macroeconomics*, Brighton, Wheatsheaf.

Kuznets, S. (1940), 'Schumpeter's business cycles', *American Economic Review*, vol. 30, no. 2, pp. 257–71.

Mensch, G. (1975), *Das Technologische Patt: Innovationen Uberwinden die Depression*, Frankfurt, Umschau; English edn (1979): *Stalemate in Technology: Innovations Overcome Depression*, New York, Ballinger.

Moggridge, D.E. (1976), *Keynes*, London, Fontana.

Nelson, R.R. and Winter, S.G. (1977), 'In search of a useful theory of innovation', *Research Policy*, vol. 6, no. 1, pp. 36–76.

Perez, C. (1983), 'Structural change and the assimilation of new technologies in the economic and social system', *Futures*, vol. 15, no. 5, October, pp. 357–75.

Perez, C. (1985), 'Microelectronics, long waves and world structural change', *World Development*, vol. 13, no. 3, pp. 441–63.

Perez, C. (1986), 'The new technologies: an integrated view'; original Spanish in C. Ominami (ed.), *La Tercera Revolución Industrial*, Buenos Aires.

Rosenberg, N. (1975), *Perspectives on Technology*, Cambridge, Cambridge University Press.

Samuelson, P. (1980), *Economics*, 11th edn, New York, McGraw-Hill.

Samuelson, P. (1981), 'The world's economy at century's end', *Japan Economic Journal*, 10 March, p. 20.

Samuelson, P. and Nordhaus, W. (1985), *Economics*, 12th edn, New York, McGraw-Hill.

Schumpeter, J.A. (1939), *Business Cycles: A Theoretical, Historical and Statistical Analysis of the Capitalist Process*, 2 vols, New York, McGraw-Hill.

Schumpeter, J.A. (1952), *Ten Great Economists*, Allen & Unwin, London.

Shackle, G.L.S. (1967), 'To the *QJE* from Chapter 12 of the General Theory: Keynes' "Ultimate Meaning" ', in G.L.S. Shackle (ed.), *The Years of High Theory: Invention and Tradition in Economic Thought 1926–1939*, Cambridge, Cambridge University Press. (Shackle refers to the article of J.M. Keynes on 'The general theory of employment' in the *QJE* (1937), February, pp. 209–23.)

Siegenthaler, H. (1986), 'The state of confidence and economic behaviour in the 30s and 70s: theoretical framework – historical evidence', in I.T. Berend and K. Borchardt (eds) (1986), *The Impact of the Depression of the 1930s and its Relevance for the Contemporary World*, papers of Section 5 of the International Economic History Congress, Berne, pp. 409–37.

Soete, L. and Dosi, G. (1983), *Technology and Employment in the Electronics Industry*, London, Frances Pinter.

Townsend, J. (1976), *Innovations in Coal-Mining Machinery: The Anderton Shearer-Loader and the Role of the NCB and Supply Industry in its Development*, SPRU Occasional Paper No. 3.

4. Innovation and growth

INTRODUCTION: MARX AND SCHUMPETER

There is actually very little disagreement among economists about the importance of innovations for long-term economic growth. From Adam Smith to Robert Solow via Ricardo, Marx, Marshall, Schumpeter and Keynes there is virtual unanimity that the long-term growth of productivity is intimately related to the introduction and diffusion of technical and organizational innovations. Although, as we shall see, there are certainly difficulties about measuring the precise contribution of technical change (or any other factor) to the growth of industries or countries, no one doubts that innovation is essential to this process. Fagerberg (1987) provides recent strong evidence of this association for twenty-seven countries and many other studies have also shown its importance, albeit with varying techniques and models. Yet only Marx in the 19th century and Schumpeter in the 20th could be said to place innovation at the very centre of their growth theory.

Paradoxically, Karl Marx, although the most powerful and consistent critic of capitalist society, was also its most ardent admirer so far as innovation was concerned. He devoted more attention to innovation than any of the other classical economists and Schumpeter was indebted to him for much of his own analysis (Swedberg, 1991). Marx and Engels recognized already in *The Communist Manifesto* (1848) that capitalism depended for its very existence on a constant drive to introduce both new processes and new products. The competitive process itself drove firms to innovate: 'the bourgeoisie cannot exist without constantly revolutionizing the means of production'. Moreover, new products were the weapons with which capitalism overcame and swept aside all older social and economic formations. Ironically, a hundred years after Marx's death, they were still the weapons with which capitalism swept aside the would-be socialist economies created in his name. Both Marx's followers and Schumpeter (1942) underestimated the continuing innovative vitality of mature capitalist economies.

Schumpeter, of course, did not accept many features of Marx's theory; he did not believe, as Marx did, that profits were a surplus based on exploitation and maintained by the social and political power of the capitalist class as well as by innovations. For Schumpeter profits were defined as arising exclusively from entrepreneurship.

In Schumpeter's theory, the ability and initiative of entrepreneurs, drawing upon the discoveries of scientists and inventors, create entirely new opportunities for investment, growth and employment. The profits made from these innovations are then the decisive impulse for new surges of growth, acting as a signal to swarms of imitators. The fact that one or a few innovators can make exceptionally large profits, which they sometimes do, does not of course mean that all the imitators necessarily do so. Nobody else made such profits from nylon as Du Pont, or from main-frame computers as IBM; indeed, many would-be imitators made losses. This is an essential part of the Schumpeterian analysis. The present difficulties of IBM and some other computer firms fit well within his theory. When the bandwagon starts rolling some people fall off, profits are gradually 'competed away' until recession sets in, and the whole process may be followed by depression before high growth starts again with a new wave of technical innovation and organizational and social change.

Whereas in the Keynesian growth theory the emphasis is on the management of demand, and in neo-classical theory on removing market imperfections and price flexibility, with Schumpeter it is on autonomous investment, embodying new technical innovation which is the basis of economic development. In such a framework economic growth must be viewed primarily as a process of reallocation of resources between industries and firms. That process necessarily leads to structural changes and disequilibrium if only because of the uneven rate of technical change between different industries. Economic growth is not merely accompanied by fast-growing new industries and the expansion of such industries; it primarily *depends* on that expansion.

Schumpeter justified on three grounds his view that growth based on technical innovation was more like a series of explosions than a gentle and incessant transformation. First, he argued that innovations are not at any time distributed randomly over the whole economic system, but tend to be concentrated in certain key sectors and their surroundings, and that consequently they are by nature lopsided and disharmonious.

Secondly, he argued that the diffusion process is also inherently an uneven one because first a few and then many firms follow in the wake of successful pioneers. Kuznets (1930) had already emphasized the cyclical pattern underlying the growth of new industries. Product life-cycle theory and international trade theory have since confirmed many of these insights: a normal life-cycle would comprise a hesitant start, then take-off and fast growth and subsequent saturation or maturation, followed by slower growth, decline or stagnation – a typical sigmoid pattern.

There is, of course, enormous variety but inevitably for any new product, as new capacity is expanded, at some point (varying with the product in question) growth will begin to slow down. Market saturation and the tendency for technical advance to approach limits (Wolf's Law), as well as the competitive effects of swarming and changing costs of inputs, all tend to reduce the level of profitability and with it the attractions of further investment. Exceptionally, this process of maturation may take only a few years, but more typically it will take several decades and sometimes even longer. Schumpeter maintained that these characteristics of innovation imply that the disturbances engendered could be sufficient to disrupt the existing system and enforce a cyclical pattern of growth.

Hardly anyone would deny the first of Schumpeter's propositions: it is confirmed by a great deal of empirical observation and research as well as everyday commonsense. The differences between rates of growth in different branches of production are well-known and obvious, as is the fact that some industries decline while others grow rapidly. Moreover, it is now universally agreed that these structural changes are related to the flow of technical innovations. The most R&D-intensive industries are by and large the fastest growing. Most of them did not exist at all before this century. In industries such as electronics, aerospace, drugs, scientific instruments, synthetic materials, it is fairly clear that extremely high growth rates were closely related to clusters of technical innovations.

However, as Kuznets (1940) pointed out, whether or not the very rapid growth of new leading sectors of the economy and new technologies offers a plausible explanation of long-term cycles in economic development depends crucially on whether some of these innovations are so large in their impact as to cause major perturbations in the entire system – as, for example, could plausibly be argued in the case of the railways – or on whether such innovations are bunched together systematically in such a way as to generate exceptional booms and spurts of growth alternating with periods of recession.

The very rapid growth of the world economy in the 1950s and 1960s, followed by the slow-down in the 1970s and 1980s and the resurgence of structural unemployment, might reasonably be held to vindicate at least some of Kondratiev's and Schumpeter's ideas about long waves in the growth of capitalism. If the test of a theory in the social sciences is held to be predictive power, then long-wave theories come out better than most others in considering the development of the world economy in the 20th century. Nevertheless, Schumpeter's theory of long waves is still far from gaining general acceptance, whereas most economists would probably now accept many of his other ideas on the role of innovation in competition.

NEO-SCHUMPETERIAN RESEARCH ON INNOVATION IN FIRMS

Whilst Schumpeter deserves the credit for restoring innovation to a central place in the theory of economic growth, he actually had very little to say about the origin of innovations or about the management of innovations at the micro-level. Ruttan (1959) put it rather strongly when he said:

> Neither in *Business Cycles* nor in Schumpeter's other work is there anything that can be identified as a theory of innovation. The business cycle in Schumpeter's system is a direct consequence of the appearance of clusters of innovations. But no real explanation is provided as to why the clusters possess the particular types of periodicity which Schumpeter identified.

A more moderate criticism would be that in describing innovation as an act of will rather than an act of intellect, Schumpeter substituted a theory of entrepreneurship for a theory of innovation. Whilst there is certainly an element of truth in Schumpeter's perception of the exceptional difficulties facing many innovators and the exceptional persistence which is often needed to see an innovation through from the invention stage to commercial success, his conceptualization is lacking in depth and, more surprisingly, in historical perspective (Freeman, 1990).

To be fair to Schumpeter, he looked upon his theories as a first approximation and called upon his followers to criticize and develop his ideas by further research. This request has led to considerable response. From the pioneering studies of Mansfield (1968), Mansfield et al. (1971), Nelson (1962a), Nelson et al. (1967), Rosenberg (1963, 1976) and Scherer (1965), a wave of neo-Schumpeterian research gathered force in the 1970s and 1980s, so that it is no longer possible in the 1990s to speak of innovation as a neglected area of research. Whilst it is difficult to summarize the results of such an enormous literature (see Dosi, 1988; Freeman 1994, for recent attempts; see also, of course, the other chapters in this book [Dodgson and Rothwell, 1994]), it is possible to point to some of the main conclusions so far as they affect theories of the growth of firms. Among the most important results are the following:

First of all, the research points strongly to the cumulative aspects of technology, the great importance of incremental as well as radical innovations, the multiple inputs to innovation from diverse sources within and outside the firm and the changes made to innovations by numerous adopters during diffusion, both within and between countries. Schumpeter's emphasis on the original entrepreneurs had tended to overstate the importance of original innovation and understate the role of diffusion in economic growth. It is true that the empirical research does often confirm the importance of individuals variously described as 'product champions' (Schon, 1973), 'business innovators' (Project Sappho), or 'network coordinators', but they are sometimes hard to identify within a more anonymous process in which pygmies play an essential part as well as giants. The fastest growing firms are distinguished by their capacity for a flow of incremental innovations as well as (more rarely) outstanding success with a radical innovation.

Secondly, the emphasis in much neo-Schumpeterian research on firm-specific technological knowledge accumulation (e.g. Teece, 1988; Amendola and Gaffard, 1988; Pavitt, 1986, 1987; Teubal, 1987; Teubal et al., 1991; Gaffard, 1990; Granstrand, 1982; Eliasson, 1990, 1992; Dosi, 1984; Achilladelis et al., 1987, 1990) should not be taken to mean that exogenously generated scientific discoveries and advances play no part in technical innovation and growth at firm level. On the contrary, much of the recent empirical work, like the earlier studies of Carter and Williams (1957, 1958, 1959) points to the importance of contacts with the world of science and to the increasing interdependence of science and technology (Nelson, 1962a and b; Freeman, 1974; Price, 1984).

A particularly important point made by Pavitt (1993) in his paper 'What do firms learn from basic research?' is that the contribution made by basic science to industry is mainly indirect, in the form of young recruits with new and valuable skills and knowledge, rather than direct, in the form of published papers, (though these too, of course, can be very useful). The Yale University Survey of 650 US industrial research executives showed that basic scientific skills and techniques in all disciplines were valued more highly and rated as more relevant than academic research results in most industries. The capability to assimilate the results of recent scientific research, whether directly or indirectly is now essential for innovation and growth in many industries.

Thirdly, most recent research on success and failure in innovation (see Rothwell, 1992) and on growth based on that success, has generally confirmed these conclusions whilst also demonstrating the role of corporate strategy and government policy in developing *networking* relationships with external sources of information, knowledge and advice (Dodgson, 1993a and b; Teubal, 1987; Teubal et al., 1991; Coombs et al., 1990; Carlsson and Jacobsson, 1993; Steele, 1991). The new generic technologies diffusing rapidly in the 1970s and 1980s – ICT (information and communication technology), biotechnology, and new materials technology – have been shown in numerous studies to intensify the science-technology interface and to enhance the importance of external networks for innovative success (see, for example, Orsenigo, 1989, 1993; Dodgson, 1991, 1993a and b; Faulkner, 1986, for bio-technology: Lastres, 1992, and Cohendet, 1988, for new materials technology: Nelson, 1962b, Gazis, 1979; Dosi, 1984;

Antonelli, 1992; Lundgren, 1991, and Freeman, 1991, for information and communication technology). The intensity of the interaction between science and technology has also been demonstrated in the 'scientometric' literature using citation analysis and similar techniques, notably in the work of the Leiden Science Studies Unit (Narin and Noma, 1985; Narin and Olivastro, 1992; Van Vianen et al., 1990).

Fourthly, empirical research (see, for example, Lundvall, 1988, 1992) has also shown that another major determinant of innovative success lies in the nature and intensity of the interaction with contemporary and future *users* of an innovation. In the case of incremental innovations especially, but also for radical innovations, this has often been shown to be a decisive factor. It was one of the main findings of the Sappho project (Rothwell et al., 1974) and the Manchester project 'Wealth from Knowledge' (Langrish et al., 1972). Von Hippel (1978, 1980, 1988) and Slaughter (1993) have shown that users may often take the lead in stimulating and organizing innovation.

Finally, the *integration* of R&D and design activities with production and marketing functions has been repeatedly shown to be essential for innovative success, for shorter lead times and for simultaneous product and process improvement.

The picture which thus emerges from numerous studies of innovation and growth in firms is one of continuous interactive learning (Lundvall, 1992). Firms learn both from their own experience of design, development, production and marketing *and* from a wide variety of external sources at home and abroad – customers, suppliers, contractors (a particularly important aspect of Japanese firm behaviour – see Imai, 1989; Sako, 1992; Dodgson, 1993a and b) and from many other organizations – universities, government laboratories and agencies, consultants, licensors, licensees and others. The precise pattern of external and internal learning networks varies with industry and size of firm, but *all* firms make use of external sources (Foray, 1991, 1993; Kleinknecht and Reijnen, 1992).

From these results it follows that simple statistical correlations between R&D-intensity of firms and their rate of growth could not be expected to be very strong. Success with innovation depends on many other factors as well as R&D – external relationships, training, integration of design, development, production and marketing functions within the firm, general management quality, the selection environment and so forth. In some industries such as clothing and footwear, fashion design, which is hardly measured in R&D statistics, may be more important than technical innovation. Moreover, R&D statistics do not measure organizational innovations at all, although Schumpeter rightly insisted on their importance and recent research has completely vindicated his view.

R&D-intensity varies greatly between *industries*. Nevertheless, in many industries R&D-intensity may often be a surrogate measure which reflects the importance of many of those activities which *do* contribute to innovative success and growth. Empirical research within each industry tends to show that very high R&D intensity *is* positively related to rapid growth, whilst at the opposite extreme lack of any R&D or very low R&D intensity is often associated with stagnation or decline of firms. In between these extremes there is little clear association between the growth of most firms and their R&D intensity. This reflects the enormous variety of circumstances, of modes of learning, of management and entrepreneurial ability and of marketing and technical uncertainties.

When it comes to the growth of *industries* however, there is a much stronger statistical association between their R&D-intensity and their long-term growth rates (Freeman, 1962; Freeman et al., 1982). This reflects the fact that the advance of science and technology is worldwide and presents similar opportunities to many firms. If one firm does not succeed, others may. Moreover, the very success of some firms may deny that success to others. Thus the competitive process leads generally to the predictably rapid growth of the same industries in most countries but *within* those industries to the unpredictable success or failure of firms. Otherwise, anyone could make a fortune on the stock exchange. When it comes to the growth of *national* economies, the problem is even more complex and it is to these problems of macro-economic growth that we now turn. The innovative success of individual firms and their rate of growth depend not only on their own efforts but on the national environment in which they operate.

UNEVEN GROWTH RATES OF NATIONS AND OF THE WORLD ECONOMY

As we have seen, classical economists, neo-classical economists, Keynesians and others have all accepted in a general way that technical innovations have been extremely important for economic growth. Until recently, however, relatively few economists followed up this general proposition with more detailed study of the origins and diffusion of these innovations, their contribution to the performance of *national* economies and the role of public policy in promoting innovation; the others relegated innovations to a 'black box' to be opened up by engineers and historians but not by economists.

When it came to formal neo-classical mathematical models of growth the black box took the form of a 'residual factor' (sometimes called the Third Factor) in an aggregate production function. This residual comprised all those awkward hard-to-measure elements other than labour and capital, such as technical and institutional change. From Solow's (1957) original study onwards, most of these formal models showed that the 'residual' apparently accounted for a larger part of the growth than the simple accumulation of capital and growth of the labour force (sometimes as much as 90 per cent of the total).

A considerable effort went into the improvement of growth models in the 1960s and 1970s. One line of development was the attempt to 'disaggregate' the residual into various components of institutional and technical change (Denison, 1962, 1967) and to measure the 'contribution' of each component even to two decimal places. However, none of these efforts succeeded in answering the main point of critics of these models such as Nelson (1973) on the *complementarities* and interdependence of the various factors involved. The *quality* of the labour force and of the capital stock are changing all the time as new skills and technologies are acquired; technical, institutional changes and investment are all interdependent.

The so-called 'new growth theory' (Romer, 1986; Lucas, 1988; Grossman and Helpman, 1991) has attempted to respond to some of these criticisms by recognizing the central role of technical change and incorporating measures of R&D and/or education and training. Whilst this somewhat belated recognition of the central importance of part of the contents of the black box is certainly to be welcomed, most of these models still suffer from some of the same unrealistic assumptions and the same measurement problems as the 'old' growth models. In particular, they take little or no account of organizational innovations and of the interplay between institutional change, technical change and investment (Verspagen, 1992a and 1992b; Fagerberg, 1992).

It may be that future generations of growth modellers will succeed in overcoming the main problems with formal growth models and they are useful in any case for heuristic purposes. In the meantime, however, greater depth of understanding and more insights for policy have emerged from the work of historians such as Landes (1970), Hughes (1982, 1989), Hobsbawm, (1968), Abramovitz (1986) and those economists who have recognized the importance of path-dependence, institutional variety and public policies for industry and technology. Perhaps the main conclusion which emerges from the work of neo-Schumpeterian economists described earlier is that history matters. Both the internal accumulation of knowledge within the firm and the external networks are strongly affected by the national environment and national policies, as well as by worldwide developments in science and technology and international flows of capital, trade and migration.

Whereas the assumptions of neo-classical growth theory would lead one to expect *convergence* in the growth rates of nations, the central historical experience is actually of increasing *divergence* between a few industrialized countries and the under-developed Third World (Dosi et al., 1992). At various times in the last three centuries, particular countries have 'forged ahead' (to use the expression of Abramovitz, 1986), whilst others have fallen far behind. The leaders have been followed by a group of 'catching-up' countries that have sometimes succeeded in overtaking the leaders: Britain overtaking the Netherlands and forging ahead in the 18th century; the United States and Germany overtaking Britain in the 19th and 20th centuries; Japan overtaking the United States in the late 20th century.

It is notable that it was in catching-up countries that the most pro-active policies for innovation and growth were developed. People in countries which had fallen behind could see that the leaders had introduced technologies and developed industries and institutions which barely existed in their own countries and they were concerned to emulate them. Hamilton (1791) in his *Report on Manufactures* already advocated a variety of measures to strengthen manufacturing industry in the United States but it was List (1841) in Germany who was the most systematic advocate of industrial and technology policies designed to strengthen the innovative capabilities of German industry, even though the various German states were at that time still not one united country.

Contemporary economists such as Lundvall (1992) and Nelson (1993) have coined the expression 'national systems of innovation' to describe the complex mixture of institutions and policies which influence the innovative process at micro-level in any particular national economy. List's (1841) book was entitled *The National System of Political Economy* but it might just as well have been called 'The National System of Innovation' since it covered many of those topics such as technology accumulation, transfer of technology, education and training, strategic industries and trade policies which are at the heart of more recent analysis.

List criticized the free trade and *laissez-faire* policies of the classical economists, maintaining that Germany and other countries could only catch up with England if they protected and nurtured their 'infant' industries: hence his advocacy of a strong Customs Union for the German states. The neo-classical economists in their turn attacked protectionism and state intervention as a hindrance to the free movement of goods, ideas, capital and labour, which were in their view the recipe for rapid growth in any economy. This debate finds its contemporary reflection in the analysis of the astonishing post-Second World War growth performance of Japan and more recently of the so-called Asian 'tigers' or 'dragons' (South Korea, Taiwan, Singapore, Hong Kong and now China and others).

Neo-liberal theorists attempt to explain this rapid growth in terms of opening up these countries to foreign investment and to freer trade. Their performance in competitive export markets is particularly underlined. As against this neo-Schumpeterians and other development economists such as Amsden (1989), Wade (1990), Johnson (1982), and Freeman (1987) point to the pro-active policies for education, R&D, technology import and strategic industries pursued with determination over several decades in the 'tigers' as well as in Japan.

Even greater controversy surrounds the cyclical fluctuations in growth rates which have affected these economies as well as the more mature industrialized economies and the less fortunate Third World countries of Latin America and Africa. Whilst it is true that some Asian countries have continued to grow rapidly through the recessions of the 1980s and 1990s, Japan has been deeply affected in 1992–93 and the other Asian countries have also been affected to some degree. The former socialist countries, which experienced some very rapid growth in the 1950s and 1960s, stagnated or collapsed in the 1980s and 1990s, with the major exception of China.

In attempting to explain the high growth boom of the *belle époque* before 1913 or the even greater boom of the 1950s and 1960s, neo-Schumpeterians point to the rapidly growing industries of each epoch but, as we have seen, the critics of Schumpeter's long-wave theory argue that there is no special reason why innovations should conveniently cluster together just before the take-off of a long-wave boom. Mensch (1975) and Kleinknecht (1987, 1990) have suggested as a possible explanation that depressions stimulate radical innovations in the long-wave troughs and they have argued in support of this theory that the empirical evidence demonstrates a clustering of major innovations in the 1830s, 1880s and 1930s. The depressions themselves occur because a group of formerly fast-growing industries have passed their peak and slow down.

As against this, Freeman et al. (1982) maintained that clusters of radical innovations could and did appear at any time in the economic cycle based on breakthroughs in science and technology and that strong demand, whether military or civil, was as likely or more likely to stimulate radical innovations as deep depressions. They argued that in any case a radical innovation had hardly any perceptible effect on the macro-economy. Only the widespread *diffusion* of clusters of radical and incremental innovations (new technological systems) could lead to the huge upswings of investment characteristic of long-wave booms. Perez (1983, 1985, 1989) pointed out that the diffusion of new technologies was strongly inhibited by the institutional framework surrounding older, now mature and obsolescent technologies.

She suggested that each wave is characterized by a dominant technological style or 'techno-economic paradigm' which transforms almost all branches of the economy to some extent as well as creating new dynamic industries. Thus her explanation is not just based on a few major innovations occurring in a particular decade, nor yet on a few leading sectors, but on a pervasive technological style embracing a whole constellation of technically and economically interrelated innovations and influencing an entire phase of economic development. These constellations of innovations, including managerial and organizational innovations, do not emerge suddenly just before a new Kondratiev upswing but crystallize over several decades. They rejuvenate old industries at the same time as creating new ones, thus providing a double impetus to a new upswing after appropriate institutional changes have been made.

A number of economists had pointed to the importance of 'technological trajectories' (Nelson and Winter, 1977) and of 'constellations of innovations' (Keirstead, 1948) which are both technically and economically interrelated. Several also extended Kuhn's notion of scientific paradigms to the concept of 'technological paradigms' (Dosi, 1982). Nelson and Winter (1977) suggested that some trajectories could be so powerful and influential that they could be regarded as 'generalised natural trajectories'. Freeman et al. (1982) and other economists had stressed the interdependence of technical innovations in 'new technology systems'. Perez, however, goes much further. Her idea of 'techno-economic paradigms' relates not just to a particular branch of industry but to the broad tendencies in the economy as a whole. Her model may be described as a 'meta-paradigm' or a 'pervasive technology' theory.

It is of particular interest for growth theory as it provides a link between national systems of innovation and business cycle theory. Those nations which prove most adept in making institutional innovations which match the emerging new techno-economic paradigm are likely to prove the most successful in growing fast, catching up or forging ahead. Those, on the other hand, which suffer from institutional 'drag' or inertia may experience a prolonged mis-match between their institutions (including management systems at firm level as well as government structures), and the growth potential of new technologies.

From all this it is evident that economic growth, whether at micro- or at macro-level, offers one of the most exciting, challenging and controversial areas in the whole field of innovation research.

BIBLIOGRAPHY

Abramovitz, M. (1986) 'Catching Up, Forging Ahead and Falling Behind', *Journal of Economic History*, Vol. 66, pp. 385–406.
Achilladelis, B.G., Schwarzkopf, A. and Lines, M. (1987) 'A Study of Innovation in the Pesticide Industry', *Research Policy*, Vol. 16, No. 2, pp. 175–212.

Achilladelis, B.G., Schwarzkopf, A. and Lines, M. (1990) 'The Dynamics of Technological Innovation: the Case of the Chemical Industry', *Research Policy*, Vol. 19, No. 1, pp. 1–35.

Amendola, M. and Gaffard, J.L. (1988) *The Innovation Choice: An Economic Analysis of the Dynamics of Technology*, Blackwell, Oxford.

Amsden, A. (1989) *Asia's Next Giant: South Korea and Late Industrialisation*, Oxford University Press, New York.

Antonelli, C. (1992) *The Economics of Localised Technological Change: The Evidence from Information and Communication Technologies*, University of Turin, Department of Economics.

Carlsson, B. and Jacobsson, S. (1993) 'Technological Systems and Economic Performance: the Diffusion of Factory Automation in Sweden', Chapter 4 in Foray, D. and Freeman, C. (eds) *Technology and the Wealth of Nations*, Pinter, London.

Carter, C.F. and Williams, B.R. (1957) *Industry and Technical Progress*, Oxford University Press, Oxford.

Carter, C.F. and Williams, B.R. (1958) *Investment in Innovation*, Oxford University Press, Oxford.

Carter, C.F. and Williams, B.R. (1959) 'The Characteristics of Technically Progressive Firms', *Journal of Industrial Economics*, Vol. 7, No. 2, pp. 87–104.

Cohendet, P.M. et al. (1988) *New Advanced Materials: Economic Dynamics and European Strategy*, Springer-Verlag, New York (English edition edited by M. Ledoux).

Coombs, R., Saviotti, P. and Walsh, V. (1990) *Technological Change and Company Strategies*, Harcourt Brace, London.

Denison, E.F. (1962) *The Sources of Economic Growth in the United States*, Committee for Economic Development, New York.

Denison, E.F. (1967) *Why Growth Rates Differ: Post-War Experience in Nine Western Countries*, Brookings Institution, Washington DC.

Dodgson, M. (1991) *The Management of Technological Learning: Lessons from a Biotechnology Company*, De Gruyter, Berlin.

Dodgson, M. (1993a) *Technological Collaboration in Industry*, Routledge, London.

Dodgson, M. (1993b) 'Organisational Learning: A Review of Some Literature', *Organisation Studies*, Vol. 14, No. 3, pp. 375–93.

Dodgson, M. and Rothwell, R. (eds) (1994) *Handbook of Industrial Innovation*, Edward Elgar, Aldershot, UK and Brookfield, USA.

Dosi, G. (1982) 'Technological Paradigms and Technological Trajectories: a Suggested Interpretation of the Determinants and Directions of Technical Change', *Research Policy*, Vol. 11, No. 3, June, pp. 147–62.

Dosi, G. (1984) *Technical Change and Industrial Transformation*, Macmillan, London.

Dosi, G. (1988) 'Sources, Procedures and Microeconomic Effects of Innovation', *Journal of Economic Literature*, Vol. 36, pp. 1126–71.

Dosi, G., Freeman, C., Nelson, R., Silverberg, G. and Soete, L. (eds) (1988) *Technical Change and Economic Theory*, Pinter, London; Columbia University Press, New York.

Dosi, G. et al. (1992) 'Convergence and Divergence in the Long-Term Growth of Open Economies', paper at MERIT Conference, Maastricht, December.

Eliasson, G. (1990) 'The Firm as a Competent Team', *Journal of Economic Behavior and Organization*, Vol. 13, No. 3.

Eliasson, G. (1992) 'Business Competence, Organizational Learning and Economic Growth: Establishing the Smith–Schumpeter–Wicksell (SSW) Connection', in

Scherer, F. and Perlman, M. (eds) *Entrepreneurship, Technological Innovation and Economic Growth*, University of Michigan Press, Ann Arbor, MI.

Fagerberg, J. (1987) 'A Technology Gap Approach to Why Growth Rates Differ', *Research Policy*, Vol. 16, No. 2–4, pp. 87–101.

Fagerberg, J. (1991) 'Innovation, Catching Up and Growth', in *Technology and Productivity: the Challenge for Economic Policy*, OECD, Paris.

Fagerberg, J. (1992) 'Technology and Economic Growth: a Review of the Theoretical and Empirical Literature', NUPI, Paper No. 457, Oslo.

Faulkner, W. (1986) *Linkage between Academic and Industrial Research: the Case of Biotechnological Research in the Pharmaceutical Industry*, D.Phil. thesis, University of Sussex, Brighton.

Foray, D. (1991) 'The Secrets of Industry are in the Air: Industrial Cooperation and the Organisational Dynamics of the Innovative Firm', *Research Policy*, Vol. 20, No. 5, pp. 393–405.

Foray, D. (1993) 'General Introduction', in Foray, D. and Freeman, C. (eds) *Technology and the Wealth of Nations*, Pinter, London.

Freeman, C. (1962) 'Research and Development: a Comparison between British and American Industry', *National Institute Economic Review*, Vol. 20, pp. 21–39.

Freeman, C. (1974) *The Economics of Industrial Innovation*, first edition Penguin, Harmondsworth; second edition Frances Pinter, London (1982).

Freeman, C. (1987) *Technology Policy and Economic Performance: Lessons from Japan*, Frances Pinter, London.

Freeman, C. (1990) 'Schumpeter's Business Cycles Revisited', in Heertje, A. and Perlman, M. (eds) *Evolving Technology and Market Structure*, University of Michigan Press, Ann Arbor, MI.

Freeman, C. (1991) 'Networks of Innovators: a Synthesis of Research Issues', *Research Policy*, Vol. 20, No. 5, pp. 499–514.

Freeman, C. (1994) 'The Economics of Technical Change: a Critical Survey Article', *Cambridge Journal of Economics*, Vol. 18, No. 5, 463–514.

Freeman, C., Clark, J. and Soete, L. (1982) *Unemployment and Technical Innovation*, Frances Pinter, London.

Gaffard, J.-L. (1990) *Economie Industrielle de l'Innovation*, Dalloz, Paris.

Gazis, D.L. (1979) 'The Influence of Technology on Science: a Comment on Some Experiences of IBM Research', *Research Policy*, Vol. 8, No. 4, pp. 244–59.

Granstrand, O. (1982) *Technology, Management and Markets*, Frances Pinter, London.

Grossman, G.M. and Helpman, E. (1991), *Innovation and Growth in the Global Economy*, MIT Press, Cambridge, MA.

Hamilton, A. (1791) *Report on the Subject of Manufactures*, Reprinted US GPO (1913), Washington, DC.

Hobday, M. (1992) *Foreign Investment, Exports and Technology Development in the Four Dragons*, UN TNC Division, Campinas Conference, Brazil, November.

Hobsbawm, E. (1968) *Industry and Empire*, Weidenfeld and Nicolson, London.

Hughes, T.P. (1982) *Networks of Power: Electrification in Western Society 1800–1930*, Johns Hopkins University Press, Baltimore, MD.

Hughes, T.P. (1989) *American Genesis*, Viking, New York.

Imai, K. (1989) 'Evolution of Japan's Corporate and Industrial Networks', in Carlsson, B. (ed.) *Industrial Dynamics*, Kluwer Academic Publishers, Boston, MA.

Johnson, C. (1982) *MITI and the Japanese Miracle: the Growth of Industry Policy 1925–1975*, Stanford University Press, Stanford, CA.

Keirstead, B.S. (1948) *The Theory of Economic Change*, Macmillan, Toronto.

Kleinknecht, A. (1987) *Innovation Patterns in Crisis and Prosperity: Schumpeter's Long Cycle Reconsidered*, Macmillan, London.

Kleinknecht, A. (1990) 'Are There Schumpeterian Waves of Innovation?' *Cambridge Journal of Economics*, Vol. 14, No. 1, pp. 81–92.

Kleinknecht, A. and Reijnen, J.O.N. (1992) 'Why do Firms Cooperate on R&D? An Empirical Study', *Research Policy*, Vol. 21, No. 4, pp. 347–60.

Kuznets, S. (1930) *Secular Movements in Production and Prices*, Houghton Mifflin, Boston, MA.

Kuznets, S. (1940) 'Schumpeter's Business Cycles', *American Economic Review*, Vol. 30, No. 2, pp. 257–71.

Landes, D.S. (1970) *The Unbound Prometheus: Technological and Industrial Development in Western Europe from 1750 to the Present*, Cambridge University Press, Cambridge.

Langrish, J., Gibbons, M., Evans, P. and Jevons, F. (1972), *Wealth from Knowledge*, Macmillan, London.

Lastres, H. (1992) *Advanced Materials and the Japanese National System of Innovation*, D.Phil. thesis, University of Sussex, SPRU, Brighton.

List, F. (1841) *The National System of Political Economy*, English translation, Longman (1904).

Lucas, R.E. (1988) 'On the Mechanisms of Economic Development', *Journal of Monetary Economics*, Vol. 22, pp. 3–42.

Lundgren, A. (1991) *Technological Innovation and Industrial Evolution: The Emergence of Industrial Networks*, D.Phil. dissertation, Stockholm School of Economics.

Lundvall, B-Å. (1988) 'Innovation as an Interactive Process: from User-Producer Interaction to the National System of Innovation', in Dosi, G. et al. (eds) *Technical Change and Economic Theory*, Pinter, London.

Lundvall, B-Å. (ed.) (1992) *National Systems of Innovation*, Pinter, London.

Maddison, A. (1991) *Dynamic Forces in Capitalist Development*, Oxford University Press, New York.

Mansfield, E. (1961) 'Technical Change and the Rate of Imitation', *Econometrica*, Vol. 29, No. 4, October, pp. 741–66; and NSF *Reviews of Data in R&D*.

Mansfield, E. (1968) *The Economics of Technological Change*, Norton, New York.

Mansfield, E. et al. (1971) *Research and Innovation in the Modern Corporation*, Norton, New York; Macmillan, London.

Marx, K. and Engels, F. (1848) *The Communist Manifesto*, English translation, Karl Marx Selected Works, Vol. 1, Marx–Engels–Lenin Institute, Moscow, 1935.

Mensch, G. (1975) *Das technologische Patt*, Umschau, Frankfurt, English translation, *Technological Stalemate: Innovations Overcome Depression*, Ballinger, New York.

Narin, F. and Noma, E. (1985) 'Is Technology Becoming Science?', *Scientometrics*, Vol. 7, No. 3, pp. 369–81.

Narin, F. and Olivastro, D. (1992) 'Status Report: Linkage Between Technology and Science', *Research Policy*, Vol. 21, pp. 237–51.

Nelson, R.R. (1962a) 'The Link Between Science and Invention: the Case of the Transistor', in NBER, *The Rate and Direction of Inventive Activity*, Princeton University Press, Princeton, NJ.

Nelson, R.R. (ed.) (1962b) *The Rate and Direction of Inventive Activity*, National Bureau of Economic Research, Princeton University Press, Princeton, NJ.

Nelson, R.R. (1973) 'Recent Exercises in Growth Accounting: New Understanding or Dead End?', *American Economic Review*, Vol. 63, pp. 462–68.

Nelson, R.R. (ed.) (1993) *National Innovation Systems*, Oxford University Press, New York.

Nelson, R.R. and Winter, S.G. (1977) 'In Search of a Useful Theory of Innovation', *Research Policy*, Vol. 6, No. 1, pp. 36–76.

Nelson, R.R., Peck, M.J. and Kalachek, E.D. (1967) *Technology, Economic Growth and Public Policy*, Allen and Unwin, London.

Orsenigo, L. (1989) *The Emergence of Biotechnology: Institutions and Markets in Industrial Innovation*, Pinter, London.

Orsenigo, L. (1993) 'The Dynamics of Competition in a Science-based Technology: the Case of Biotechnology', Chapter 2 in Foray, D. and Freeman, C. (eds) *Technology and the Wealth of Nations*, Pinter, London.

Pavitt, K. (1984) 'Patterns of Technical Change: Towards a Taxonomy and a Theory', *Research Policy*, Vol. 13, No. 6, pp. 343–73.

Pavitt, K. (1986) 'International Patterns of Technological Accumulation', in Hood, N. (ed.) *Strategies in Global Competition*, Wiley, New York.

Pavitt, K. (1987) 'On the Nature of Technology', Inaugural Lecture, University of Sussex, 23 June.

Pavitt, K. (1993) 'What do Firms Learn from Basic Research?', Chapter 1 in Foray, D. and Freeman, C. (eds) *Technology and the Wealth of Nations*, Pinter, London.

Perez, C. (1983) 'Structural Change and the Assimilation of New Technologies in the Economic and Social System', *Futures*, Vol. 15, No. 5, pp. 357–75.

Perez, C. (1985) 'Microelectronics, Long Waves and the World Structural Change: New Perspectives for Developing Countries', *World Development*, Vol. 13, No. 3, 13 March, pp. 441–63.

Perez, C. (1989) 'Technical Change, Competitive Restructuring and Institutional Reform in Developing Countries', *World Bank Strategic Planning and Review*, Discussion Paper 4, World Bank, Washington, DC, December.

Price, D. de S. (1984) 'The Science/Technology Relationship, the Craft of Experimental Science and Policy for the Improvement of High Technology Innovation', *Research Policy*, Vol. 13, No. 1, February, pp. 3–20.

Romer, P. (1986) 'Increasing Returns and Long-Run Growth', *Journal of Political Economy*, Vol. 94, No. 5, pp. 1002–37.

Rosenberg, N. (1963) 'Technological Change in the Machine Tool Industry: 1840–1910', *Journal of Economic History*, Vol. 23, pp. 414–43.

Rosenberg, N. (1976) *Perspectives on Technology*, Cambridge University Press, Cambridge.

Rothwell, R. (1992) 'Successful Industrial Innovation: Critical Factors for the 1990s', *R&D Management*, Vol. 22, No. 3, pp. 221–39.

Rothwell, R. et al. (1974) 'SAPPHO Updated', *Research Policy*, Vol. 3, No. 3, pp. 258–91.

Ruttan, V. (1959) 'Usher and Schumpeter on Innovation, Invention and Technological Change', *Quarterly Journal of Economics*, Vol. 73, No. 4, pp. 596–606.

Sako, M. (1992) *Contracts, Prices and Trust: How the Japanese and British Manage Their Subcontracting Relationships*, Oxford University Press, Oxford.

Scherer, F.M. (1965) 'Firm Size, Market Structure, Opportunity and the Output of Patented Inventions', *American Economic Review*, Vol. 55, No. 5, pp. 1097–1123.

Scherer, F.M. (1973) *Industrial Market Structure and Economic Performance*, Rand McNally, Chicago, IL.

Schon, D.A. (1973) 'Product Champions for Radical New Innovations', *Harvard Business Review*, March–April, pp. 77–86.

Schumpeter, J.A. (1928) 'The Instability of Capitalism', *Economic Journal*, Vol. 38, pp. 361–86.

Schumpeter, J.A. (1934) *The Theory of Economic Development*, Harvard University Press, Cambridge, MA (English translation from 1913 German edition).

Schumpeter, J.A. (1939) *Business Cycles: A Theoretical, Historical and Statistical Analysis of the Capitalist Process*, 2 vols, McGraw-Hill, New York.

Schumpeter, J.A. (1942) *Capitalism, Socialism and Democracy*, McGraw-Hill, New York.

Science Policy Research Unit (1972) *Success and Failure in Industrial Innovation*, London Centre for the Study of Industrial Innovation.

Slaughter, S. (1993) 'Innovation and Learning during Implementation: A Comparison of User and Manufacturer Innovation', *Research Policy*, Vol. 22, No. 1, pp. 81–97.

Solow, R. (1957) 'Technical Change and the Aggregate Production Function', *Review of Economics and Statistics*, Vol. 39, pp. 312–20.

Steele, L. (1991) *Managing Technology: A Strategic View*, McGraw-Hill, New York.

Swedberg, R. (1991) *Joseph A. Schumpeter: His Life and Work*, Polity Press (Blackwell), Oxford.

Teece, D.J. (1986) 'Profiting from Technological Innovation: Implications for Integration, Collaboration, Licensing and Public Policy', *Research Policy*, Vol. 15, No. 6, pp. 285–305.

Teece, D.J. (1988) 'The Nature and the Structure of Firms', in Dosi et al. (eds) *Technical Change and Economic Theory*, Pinter, London.

Teubal, M. (1987) *Innovation, Performance, Learning and Government Policy: Selected Essays*, University of Wisconsin Press, Madison, WI.

Teubal, M., Yinnon, T. and Zuscovitch, E. (1991) 'Networks and Market Creation', *Research Policy*, Vol. 20, No. 5, pp. 381–92.

Van Vianen, B.G., Moed, H.F. and Van Raan, A.J.F. (1990) 'An Exploration of the Science Base of Recent Technology', *Research Policy*, Vol. 19, No. 1, pp. 61–81.

Verspagen, B. (1992a) 'Endogenous Innovation in Neo-Classical Growth Models: A Survey', *Journal of Macro-Economics*, Vol. 14, No. 4, pp. 631–62.

Verspagen, B. (1992b) *Uneven Growth between Interdependent Economies: An Evolutionary View on Technology Gaps, Trade and Growth*, Dissertation 92-10, University of Limburg.

von Hippel, E. (1978) 'A Customer–Active Paradigm for Industrial Product Idea Generation', *Research Policy*, Vol. 7, pp. 240–66.

von Hippel, E. (1980) 'The User's Role in Industrial Innovation', in Burton, D. and Goldhar, J. (eds) *Management of Research and Innovation*, North Holland, Amsterdam.

von Hippel, E. (1988) *The Sources of Innovation*, Oxford University Press, Oxford.

Wade, R. (1990) *Governing the Market: Economic Theory and the Rise of Government in East Asian Industrialisation*, Princeton University Press, Princeton, NJ.

5. Family allowances, technical change, inequality and social policy

FAMILY ALLOWANCES

Eleanor Rathbone was probably the most truly independent MP who ever sat in the House of Commons. The peculiar constituency which she represented from 1929 until her death on 2nd January 1946 – the 'Combined Universities' – favoured her unique reforming zeal and forthright political style. Few MPs have been so devoted to the principle of thorough research as the basis for social reform as Eleanor Rathbone and few have been so determined to follow through the results of that research.

She is best known as the MP who, almost single-handedly in the early days, led the campaign for Family Allowances. In fact, she began this work long before she became an MP. It was in the '1917 Club' in Gerard Street, Soho (so-called after the February Revolution against the Czar of Russia) that she convened the first meeting of the 'Family Endowment Committee'. She had already contributed an article on the subject to the leading academic journal in Economics – the *Economic Journal* – and she invited two young economics students, Emile Burns and Elinor Burns, to join her Committee, together with colleagues who had worked with her in her social research and in the campaign for Women's Suffrage, and Mr. HN Brailsford, a journalist sympathetic to feminism.

They produced a one shilling pamphlet entitled *Equal Pay and the Family: a Proposal for the National Endowment of Motherhood* in 1918, using the example of the allowances paid to the wives of servicemen to reinforce their argument based on the statistics of poverty and income distribution. She was familiar with these statistics, having worked for many years in the tradition of Charles Booth, making detailed observations and collecting facts on the scale and nature of poverty in Liverpool in the decade before the First World War. This work had demonstrated the peculiar adverse effects of casual labour in the docks, at that time the biggest single source of employment in Liverpool. Her report (*How the Casual Labourer Lives*) was published in 1909 and was based on an investigation of family budgets collected and tabulated by a small committee (Stocks, 1949, p. 62).

It was followed by a similar painstaking study on *The Condition of Widows under the Poor Law in Liverpool*, published in 1913.

It was this tradition of thorough social and economic research which made it possible for Eleanor Rathbone and her colleagues to produce such effective arguments for the reforms advocated in the booklet on *National Endowment of Motherhood*. However, Sidney Webb warned her that for any great social reform there was a time lag of about nineteen years between the dawn of an idea and its acceptance by public opinion (Stocks, 1949, p. 86). In the case of Family Allowances the time lag from this first pamphlet to the Family Allowance Act of 1945 was 27 years. All through this long period it was her main, although certainly not her only preoccupation. Her biographer, Mary Stocks (1949, p. 102), observed that one reason for her extraordinary persistence was that this particular cause could offer perpetually renewed exhilaration. She contrasted this with the more straightforward arguments for Women's Suffrage (for which Eleanor Rathbone had also campaigned) and in which

> a simple cause sweetened by a cheerful sense of comradeship kept feminist propagandists on their feet.

> Family allowances, on the other hand, could be approached from so many directions, with such an infinite variety of emphasis and application. It could be handled as a problem of vital statistics, housing administration, minimum wage legislation, child nutrition, national insurance, teachers' salary scales, coal-mining economies, feminism, social philosophy or pure finance. That is perhaps one reason why Eleanor's handling of it never became, as far as her audiences were concerned, tedious by repetition.

Opposition to Family Allowances came from many different sources and from both the major parties in the 1920s and 1930s. Conservative opposition was based on traditional *laissez-faire* market economics and of course on resistance to any increase in government expenditure. Labour opposition was based on the fear that family allowances would undermine the case for a living wage, sufficient to provide for a male wage-earner and his family and would weaken the traditional machinery of collective bargaining. However, undeterred by this formidable opposition, Eleanor Rathbone continued to win over individual converts in both parties and among independents. One of her most important successes was to win the support of William Beveridge, who had become Director of the London School of Economics in 1919 and in 1925 began the system of child allowances for the staff of LSE. He became a member of Eleanor's Family Endowment Society, the successor to the old Family Endowment Committee of 1917. But whereas the Committee which produced the first pamphlet was predominantly left-wing (the Secretary, Emile Burns, later became a leading publicist for the Communist Party and HN Brailsford became a prominent left-wing journalist) its successor was middle of the road and included people of all parties or of none.

Eleanor Rathbone herself was never a Socialist and was indeed in 1931 briefly committed to the support of the 'National Government'. However, even in that year on 18th September, when the Government proposed a 10 per cent cut in the unemployment benefits, her immediate reaction was to query whether it would not be better to increase taxation on higher incomes or luxury spending. Mary Stocks comments that she always 'looked sympathetically on proposals which involved the redistribution of wealth through taxation and the elimination of wide discrepancies of material well-being between rich and poor' (1949, p. 188). This passion for social justice led her into increasingly bitter conflict with the Conservative-dominated government of the mid-1930s, especially in relation to their treatment of the unemployed and their rejection of her arguments on child nutrition. She used the new findings of medical research on calories and vitamins to support the results of her earlier research on family budgets and cost of living.

It was of course mainly the Second World War which changed the climate of opinion on this and many other social reforms. Social justice and social cohesion, neglected or rejected as wishy-washy liberal ideals before the war, now became an essential element in sustaining civilian morale. Reformers like Keynes and Beveridge were once more invited to participate in the highest levels of policy-making. The 1940 Cambridge lectures of Keynes on 'How to pay for the War' became the basis for one of the most egalitarian fiscal regimes and rationing systems ever seen in Western Europe, which also succeeded in containing inflation at levels far below those experienced in the First World War. In June 1941, the government appointed an inter-departmental Committee under the chairmanship of Sir William Beveridge to report on the whole problem of social insurance and allied services. The famous 'Beveridge Report' appeared in November 1942 and was based on three key assumptions:

1. The acceptance of family allowances.
2. A comprehensive health service.
3. Full employment.

These were the three foundations of the post-war welfare state. Largely due to the persistent advocacy of Eleanor Rathbone, the first of these principles now proved relatively uncontroversial and the Family Allowance Act went through in 1945. It was not all that she had campaigned for. It started only with the second child. The first draft had provided for payment to the *father* and she threatened to vote against the Bill if this was not changed to payment direct to the *mother*. The Ministry of National Insurance produced legalistic arguments to show that this was impossible, but she won this last campaign by a personal visit to the Ministry. No minute of the meeting exists but a senior civil servant who was present recorded that the Ministry 'was impressed by her vehemence' (Stocks, 1949, p. 310).

She did not live to see the Welfare State flourish in the 1950s and 1960s in Britain and other countries, nor the beginnings of its decline in the 1980s and 1990s. Nor did she witness the widening gap between rich and poor which has reversed the egalitarian trends of the 1940s and 1950s in Eastern as well as in Western Europe, in North as well as in South America, in China as well as in Japan. If she had seen it, it is unlikely in the extreme that she would have seen any connection between these trends and changes in technology, but that is the theme to which I now turn.

UNEMPLOYMENT AND TECHNOLOGY

Eleanor Rathbone, like her two great fellow reformers, Beveridge and Keynes, had little or nothing to say about technology or technical change and it may therefore seem odd to the point of eccentricity to link their great reforming achievements to this topic. Not only did they and many other economists ignore technical change but most engineers and scientists also would not see any connection between technology, inequality and social justice. However, this lecture will attempt to show that there is indeed a profound connection, a connection which if ignored will not only bring down the whole edifice of the welfare state in this and other countries, but will imperil also the very future of science itself.

At the simplest level, it is of course obvious that the standard of living for all of us depends on the achievements of science and technology. Since Adam Smith's *Wealth of Nations* and Marshall's comments on *Knowledge as the Chief Engine of Production* the role of technical change in economic growth has been universally accepted by all schools of economists. The so-called 'New Growth Theory' gives to research, development and education a more central role than earlier growth models but no economist of repute had ever denied their importance.

However, it is one thing to pay lip-service to the importance of science and technology in economic and social change but quite another thing to study this interdependent relationship in depth, i.e. to deploy the patient skills which Eleanor Rathbone deployed in her studies of household budgets and apply them to the empirical study of the actual process of

technical change in firms, in industries, in nations and in the world
economy. In the first half of the twentieth century, almost the only economist to attempt this was Joseph Schumpeter and for this reason, research
on the economics and sociology of technical change is usually described as
'neo-Schumpeterian'. Its relevance to the problems of income distribution
and social cohesion is especially evident in relation to unemployment and
to cycles of investment behaviour. Schumpeter suggested in his *magnum
opus* on *Business Cycles* (1939) that waves of new investment were generated by the diffusion of new technologies. Following the Russian economist, Nikolai Kondratieff, he argued that successive industrial revolutions
led to long cycles of about 50 years' duration (Table 5.1). In Schumpeter's
theory, the ability and initiative of entrepreneurs, drawing upon the discoveries and ideas of scientists and inventors, create entirely new opportunities for investment, growth and employment. The exceptional profits
made from these innovations are then the decisive signal to swarms of imitators generating band-wagon and multiplier effects throughout the
system. Schumpeter studied the extraordinarily rapid growth of the cotton
and iron industries in the first industrial revolution, of steam power and
railways in the second and of electrification in the third.

In a passage which is seldom referred to Keynes (1930) fully acknowledged the significance of these influences on investment behaviour:

> In the case of fixed capital it is easy to understand why fluctuations should occur
> in the rate of investment. Entrepreneurs are induced to embark on the produc-
> tion of fixed capital or deterred from doing so by their expectations of the profits
> to be made. Apart from the many minor reasons why these should fluctuate in a
> changing world, Professor Schumpeter's explanation of the major movements
> may be unreservedly accepted.

The big investment booms of the 1850s and 1860s, or of the 'Belle
Epoque' before the First World War, or of the 'Golden Age' of the 1950s
and 1960s were followed by fairly prolonged periods of recession, depression and high unemployment. In Schumpeter's scheme, these recessions
were the result of the erosion of profits from the previous wave of technology and the necessity for a new infrastructure to unleash the next wave.
His theory is still controversial; opposition has come both from more
orthodox mainstream economists, including Keynesians who have been
preoccupied with the shorter business cycles, and from orthodox
Marxists, who drove Kondratieff to an early death in Siberian labour
camps in the 1930s.

However, if the test of a theory in the social sciences, as in the natural sciences, is its predictive power, then the ideas of Kondratieff and Schumpeter
come out of this test in the twentieth century extremely well. At a time when

Table 5.1 Long waves

Kondratiev Wave	Cycle	Recession Trough	Key Factor(s)	Carrier Branches	Infrastructures
1st	1780s–1840s	1820s 1830s	Cotton yarn Iron	Cotton Textiles Ship Building	Ports Canals Water Power Roads Ships, Barges
2nd	1840s–1890s	1880s 1890s	Coal Coal gas	Steam Engines Railways Mechanisation Gas Machine Tools	Iron – Rail Networks Telegraphy Steam Ships Gas Light & Heat
3rd	1890s–1940s	1920s 1930s	Steel	Electrification Electrical and Heavy Engineering Non-Ferrous metals	Electric Power Steel Ships Global Steel Rail Networks Telephones
4th	1940s–1990s	1980s 1990s	Oil Natural gas	Automobiles Consumer Durables Refineries Automation	Motor Highways Airlines Tankers Roll-on, Roll-off
5th	1990s?–?	?	Micro-Electronics	Computers Video, Telephone Equipment Software, Info Services	'Information Highways' E-Mail Air Freight

more orthodox Marxists were predicting the collapse of capitalism and the final crisis in the 1930s, Kondratieff had pointed to the possibility of a new capitalist growth boom. When the biggest ever boom materialised in the 1950s and 1960s, long wave theorists such as Mandel, pointed to the probability of a new deep recession. This was at a time when many economists and government advisors, such as those at the OECD, assumed that the problem of mass unemployment would never return. Even in the 1970s, they continued to believe this despite the mounting evidence of structural unemployment (see, for example, the McCracken Report, OECD, 1977). In the 1930s, however, many economists had believed the opposite: that unemployment would remain at a permanently high level. Even Beveridge and Keynes in the early 1940s were pessimistic about the possibilities of achieving a 3 per cent level of unemployment and thought 8 per cent a more realistic target. The definition of 'full employment' as 3 per cent or less came relatively late in the deliberations of Beveridge and his colleagues. Mainstream economics thus showed a persistent inability to understand or cope with the problems of structural change related to new technologies.

In what was to become the accepted definition of 'full employment', it was assumed that about 1 per cent would be 'frictional unemployment' – the simple gaps in the movement of people between one job and the next, which would occur in any changing economy; a further 1 per cent would be 'regional' unemployment caused by delays in movement of people between regions and 1 per cent 'structural' – longer lasting unemployment associated with changes in technology, skills and industrial organisation.

In fact, unemployment in the 1950s and 1960s, as in the 1850s and 1860s, fell well below 3 per cent over almost the whole of Europe (Table 5.2). It is still well below 3 per cent in the East Asian 'Tigers' but almost everywhere else and especially in Europe, it has reached levels in the 1980s and 1990s described by the Secretary General of the OECD as 'disturbing, perhaps alarming' (OECD, 1993). The relatively low levels of employment in the 'Tigers' are clearly related to their high overall growth rate, averaging 7 per cent or more over long periods in the 1970s, 1980s and 1990s, but also to the high rate of structural change, as shown in the output and exports of their ICT industries (Table 5.3). Europe has suffered from the reverse problem of low rates of growth and relatively poor performance of the ICT industries (Figure 5.1) and other 'high tech' industries and an inadequate level of aggregate investment.

The social consequences of these failures in economic policy and in structural adjustment are very severe indeed. It is the continuing high levels of unemployment which have undermined all the social services since the payment of unemployment benefits and many other benefits indirectly associated with unemployment, leads to budget deficits of a scale and

Table 5.2   Unemployment 1990s

	1959–67 average	1990	1992	Est. 1995
USA	5.3	5.5	7.4	6.2
Canada	4.9	8.1	11.3	10.5
Germany	1.2	6.0	7.7	10.3
France	0.7	8.9	10.4	12.3
Italy	6.2	11.5	11.6	11.6
UK	1.8	5.9	10.0	9.2
Japan	1.5	2.1	2.2	2.9
Belgium	2.4	8.7	10.3	13.2
Denmark	1.4	9.5	11.1	11.3
Finland	1.7	3.5	13.1	19.3
Ireland	4.6	13.7	16.7	17.8
Netherlands	0.9	7.6	6.8	9.7
Spain	2.3	16.3	18.4	23.5
Sweden	1.3	1.6	5.3	7.9
S. Korea	n.a.	n.a.	2.4	2.3
Singapore	n.a.	n.a.	2.7	2.6

Source: OECD (1993, 1994), *Employment Outlook.*

*Table 5.3   Share of office machinery and Telecom equipment in total
merchandise exports (ranked by value of 1989 exports)*

		1980	1989
1.	Japan	14	28
2.	USA	8	13
3.	FRG	5	5
4.	UK	5	9
5.	Singapore	14	34
6.	South Korea	10	22
7.	Taiwan	14	25
8.	Hong Kong	12	16
9.	France	4	7
10.	Netherlands	5	7
11.	Canada	2.5	4
15.	Sweden	6	8
	Brazil	2*	3*

Note: * Estimated.

Source: GATT (1992), Table IV.40.Vol II.

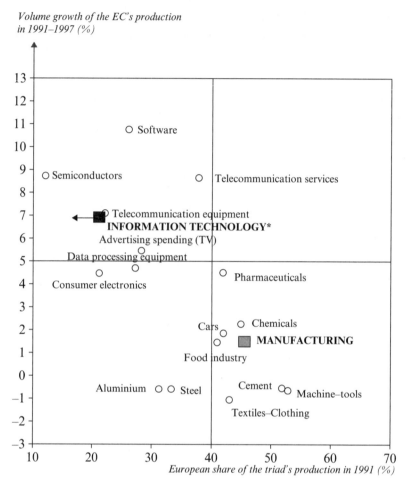

Figure 5.1   The European portfolio

duration which are hard to sustain. Beveridge (1946) (and Eleanor Rathbone) were absolutely right to assume that the welfare state depended on full employment. In her earliest social research in Liverpool, Eleanor Rathbone had demonstrated the close relationship between casual part-time employment, unemployment, poverty and malnutrition.

Persistent mass unemployment confronts society with even greater dangers. It is an unmitigated *social* disaster, as well as a loss of output and the OECD was right to urge that the restoration of full employment in Europe should be a high priority for both economic and social reasons.

Table 5.4   Occupational employment forecasts USA, 1990–2005 (total percentage growth of fastest growing occupations)

Systems analysts	79
Computer programmers	56
Information clerks	47
Home health aides	92
Child care	49
Nurses	44
Nursing aides	43
Cooks	42
Gardeners	40
Food counter	34
Food preparation	32
School teachers	34
Educational assistants	34

Source: US Bureau of Labour (1993).

Policies for the new telecommunications infrastructure and for education and training are an essential part of any strategy to achieve this objective. If we look at the projections for future employment for the United States (Table 5.4) or other leading industrial countries, then it is clear that the areas of future growth fall into three main categories:

1. Occupations related to the computerisation of all industries and services – software engineering, design and programming and new telecommunication-based networking services.
2. Personal and public service occupations in health care, care for the elderly, child care, improvement of the urban and rural environment, and leisure activities.
3. Education, training and related professional occupations. These are closely related to the first category since the education and training system will itself make massive use of multi-media.

All three of these areas offer enormous scope for future growth of employment but the third category is of exceptional importance, since the entire economy will depend increasingly on the efficiency and scope of education, training and retraining. The US figures probably underestimate the potential growth of educational products and services and the associated growth of employment in publishing, multi-media and other 'cultural industries' closely related to the first category.

Whether for nursery schools, primary or secondary education, it is essential for education policy to play an active role in developing new ICT products in cooperation with industry. To develop new modules for new courses in every discipline and combination of disciplines and to keep them up-to-date is an enormous educational undertaking. It will require the active participation of the teaching profession at all levels. A regular part of in-service teacher training and post-experience training should be participation in design and development teams for new course CD-Roms and other materials in cooperation with publishers, video companies, information services and other related industries.

So far from leading to unemployment amongst teachers, the widespread use of ICT will enhance their importance although changing their role to that of guides and counsellors rather than instructors. Home learning will complement rather than replace schools for many social, economic and cultural reasons. Children learn from each other and direct interaction with other children and teachers is essential if they are to develop the social skills and communication skills which are so important in our economic, social and political life. Scale economics and indivisibilities are just as important for experience, equipment and materials in education as in other sectors of the economy (Freeman and Soete, 1994). There is already a tendency for society to divide into 'information rich' and 'information poor' households and any move towards 'de-schooling' would exacerbate these divisions. Schools provide the best opportunity for children from deprived households to obtain education and skills.

TECHNICAL CHANGE AND INCOME DISTRIBUTION

So far, this discussion has focussed on long waves of technical change and their effects on *employment*. It points to the conclusion that to cope with structural change and to return to high levels of employment, it is essential to overcome the mismatch of skills and qualifications, which is an inevitable feature of technical change.

However, as the case of 'information rich' and 'information poor' households suggests, social inequality is not only a question of employment and unemployment. Each new wave of technical change brings with it many social benefits in the form of new more skilled occupations and professions, and higher standards of living for many people based on the growth of new industries and services. But each wave also brings high social costs in the form of erosion of old skills and occupations, the decline of some older industries, services and industrial areas. This uneven distribution of social costs and benefits occurs also on an international scale with some nations taking full advantage of the new technologies and others unable to do so.

The effects of this uneven distribution of social costs and benefits are clearly visible in the statistics of income distribution for the 1980s and 1990s (Table 5.5). Twelve out of seventeen OECD countries showed an increased dispersion of earnings in the 1980s, four showed no change and only one

Table 5.5   General pattern of changes in the dispersion of earnings in the 1970s and 1980s (hourly earnings or earnings of fulltime workers)

	1970s	1980s	Comments on extent and type of changes in dispersion
Australia	−	+	Increase in the dispersion from 1979 onwards
Austria	−	+	Increase from 1980 to 1989
Belgium		+	Slight increase due to gains at top over 1983–88
Canada	0	+	Increase mainly due to gains at top
Denmark		0	Slight gains at top and bottom
Finland	−	0	Slight gains at top and bottom
France	−	−/+	Decrease in dispersion ended in 1983
Germany	0	−	Decrease mainly due to gains at bottom
Italy	−	0	Gains at top and bottom
Japan		+	Increase due to gains at top
Netherlands	0	−/+	Slight decrease to 1984, then slight increase
Norway		0	Gains at top and bottom
Portugal		+	Increase between 1985 and 1990
Spain	−−/0	+	Sharp decrease in mid-1970s, rise in 1980s
Sweden	0	0/+	Increase after 1986, except for low-paid women
United Kingdom	−	++	Increase from 1979 onwards
United States	+	++	Increase for men only in 1970s; strong gains at top in 1980s

Notes: +   Increase in dispersion.
　　　　++   Strong increase.
　　　　−   Decrease.
　　　　−−   Strong decrease.
　　　　0   No clear change (perhaps changes at top and bottom working in opposite directions).
　　　　+/−   Increase followed by decrease (etc.).
　　　　Blank No information available.

Source: OECD (1993), *Employment Outlook*.

(Germany) showed a decrease. In the 1970s the reverse was true. In that decade only one country showed an increase in inequality – the United States – while most others showed a decrease in dispersion. These statistics are for income *before* tax. Taking into account that fiscal changes in the UK and many other countries have been regressive in this period, the increase of inequality in incomes has been substantial for those in employment.

Similar changes took place in previous waves of technical change: the earnings of engine drivers and fitters in the nineteenth century, of electricians in the 1890s, of assembly line workers in the 1940s and 1950s, and of software engineers and programmers in the 1980s, were all above the average earnings of the time. It is obvious that in any well-functioning market system, the shortage of workers in rapidly expanding industries will have these effects. The Japanese electronic employers in the 1980s combined together to agree not to poach each other's workers and so to try and avoid the wage-push effects of the extremely rapid growth of that industry and this was a fairly typical response to this problem, even though it has rarely been effective outside Japan. Consequently, periods of rapid structural change and high unemployment have generally been associated with increased inequality of incomes.

The combined effect of prolonged periods of high unemployment together with this increased dispersion of earnings and increasing regressive taxation has been to create or to enlarge an 'underclass' in the United States, Britain, Russia, France, Spain and many other countries. A huge underclass already existed in Mexico, Brazil and most other countries of Latin America and Africa and this is growing even faster. A rise in social tensions, crime and ethnic hostility is evident almost everywhere and clearly associated with the loss of social cohesion and increasing insecurity of employment.

The Secretary-General of the OECD, M. Paye, described these changes as 'disturbing, perhaps alarming' and in the past the alarm bells which were ringing whether in the 1830s, the 1880s or 1930s, ultimately led in this country and in others to programmes of social reform, educational reform, employment policies, and fiscal changes designed to mitigate the worst effects of these problems of structural change and to share the burdens more equally.

In his highly original and thorough analysis of long waves in the world economy, Andrew Tylecote (1992) studied two aspects of inequality which he designated as inequality in the North and in the South respectively. He suggested that in the North, the dispersion of incomes which widened in the downswing of each long wave was superimposed on a long-term secular trend towards greater equality in income distribution. No such tendency was however yet apparent in the South with the exception of a few countries in East Asia. Moreover, the inequality gap between average per capita incomes in most of the under-developed countries of the South and those in the North has widened enormously in the last century. He argues that deep inequality is actually harmful for long-term growth, whether in the South or the North, and a similar point is made in the World Bank Report on the *The East Asian Miracle* (1993) and by Persson and Tabellini (1994).

Kuznets (1955) in his classic paper on 'Economic Growth and Income Inequality', argued that

> one might assume a long swing in the inequality characterizing the secular income structure: widening in the early phases of economic growth . . .; becoming stabilized for a while; and then narrowing in the later phases.

> . . . The long swing in income inequality is also probably closely associated with the swing in capital formation proportions – in so far as wider inequality makes for higher, and narrower inequality for lower, country-wide savings proportions. (p. 20)

An American economist, Brian Berry (Berry et al., 1994), following in the tradition of Simon Kuznets, suggested that income dispersion increased in four different periods of American history since 1776. Whereas Kuznets suggested that wide dispersion of incomes was characteristic of the early stages of industrialisation and economic growth, diminishing with maturity, Berry proposes that alternating periods of wider and lesser dispersion correspond to long (Kondratieff) cycles of economic development. Like Tylecote, Berry maintains that 'It is in the immediate post stagflation decade that inequality surges'. (1994, p. 10). These surges of inequality in the 1820s, the 1870s, the 1920s and the 1980s were associated with the downturn of the long wave, with major structural changes, with demand for new skills (Williamson and Lindert, 1980) and with exceptionally high profits in new industries.

Initially, strongly pro-business governments tend to aggravate the growing inequality, believing that a dose of strong medicine is needed to set the economy right, but ultimately according to Berry's analysis, this leads to a political revulsion against the hardships which these policies incur (Jackson and the Homestead Act, etc. in the 1830s, the Anti-Trust Legislation and other reforms in the 1890s, and the New Deal etc., in the 1930s and 1940s). Williamson and Lindert (1980) concluded from their study of inequality in America 'In contrast with the previous periods of wealth levelling, the twentieth century levelling has not been reversed' (p. 33).

As Berry points out, this conclusion was too hasty. The United States and the United Kingdom have led the way in the reversal of that trend in the 1980s and 1990s. In the UK, the share of the lowest quintile (20 per cent) of household disposable incomes fell from 10 per cent of the total in 1979 to 6 per cent in 1992, while the share of the top quintile rose from 35 to 43 per cent over the same period (Table 5.19 in 'Social Trends', CSO, 1995).

If Eleanor Rathbone were alive today we do not know what policies she would have favoured to deal with this situation, although she would certainly have been worried by the scale of unemployment, by the growth of involuntary part-time employment, by the resurgence of casual work and by the growing inequality of incomes. We can only speculate about two policy changes which have been proposed by a group which reported early this year to the Directorate of Social Affairs within the European Union (European Commission, 1996). We proposed first of all that the EU and all its member countries should examine the potential of a new tax, the so-called 'Bit Tax', to re-dress the gulf between the 'information rich' and the 'information poor'. Fiscal policy must always change with the changing structure of the economy and political realities. Principles of public finance dictate that any tax should justify three basic criteria:

1. Enlargement of the revenue base.
2. Economy in collection.
3. Social equity.

At the first sight, the Bit Tax would satisfy all these requirements and offer the possibility of significant redistribution, both nationally and internationally. It has been attacked as a 'Luddite Tax', but the rate of growth of ICT transactions is so rapid and the lock-in effects are so strong that a low rate of levy would have only marginal effects and might indeed improve efficiency in the IT industries.

A second proposal which we have made relates to the measurement of inflation and the argument has also been advanced by a recent report to the Senate Finance Committee. The indexing of price inflation depends on the selection of a 'basket' of commodities and services and measuring the changes in the prices of this selection. The Chairman of our Group, Luc Soete, has argued that this selection is far out of date as it omits most of the information services which are now commonplace. The prices of ICT goods and services have generally been falling in the last decade [1986–96] in contrast to the general inflationary trends. Yet the inflation index still reflects to some extent the old structure of the economy. The very use of the word 'basket' reflects the old goods-based structure of the economy when these indices were first introduced. They have of course been revised since then, but the Report to the Senate Finance Committee maintained that US inflation has been over-estimated by between 1 and 2 per cent. Luc Soete has calculated that inflation in the EU has been over-estimated by between 2 and 3 per cent, because hedonic price indexing is less widely used in Europe.

This has major implications for macro-economic policy and social policy as the over-estimation of inflation has led to unnecessarily restrictive policies and higher rates of interest in Germany, France and other European countries. This has slowed down growth and raised unemployment.

The understanding of structural change and technical change is thus fundamentally linked to the great social problems which confront us. We do not know and cannot know what Eleanor Rathbone would have proposed to deal with these problems today, but we do know that she would have tackled them with infinite courage, originality and determination.

REFERENCES

Beveridge, W.H. (1946), *Full Employment in a Free Society*, London, Allen and Unwin.

Berry, B.J.L., Harpham, E.J. and Elliott (1994), 'Long Swings in American Inequality, the Kuznets conjecture revisited', University of Texas at Dallas.

Central Statistical Office (1995), *Social Trends*, London, CSO.

European Commission, (1996), *Building the European Information Society for Us All, (First Reflections of the High Level Group of Experts)*, Interim Report, January, Brussels, EC, DGV.

Freeman, C. and Soete, L. (1994), *Work for All or Mass Unemployment*, London, Pinter.

GATT (1992), *Statistical Tables*, Geneva, GATT.

Keynes, J.M. (1930), *A Treatise on Money*, London, Macmillan.

Kuznets, S. (1955), 'Economic Growth and Income Inequality', *American Economic Review*, Vol. XLV, pp. 1–28.

OECD (McCracken Report), (1977), *Towards Full Employment and Price Stability*, Paris, OECD.

OECD (1993, 1994), *Employment Outlook*, Paris, OECD.

Persson, T. and Tabellini, G. (1994), 'Is Inequality Harmful to Growth?', *American Economic Review*, Vol. 84, No. 3, pp. 600–621.

Schumpeter, J.A. (1939), *Business Cycles*, (2 Vols), New York, McGraw Hill.

Stocks, M. (1949), *Eleanor Rathbone, a Biography*, London, Gollancz.

Tylecote, A. (1992), *The Long Wave in the World Economy*, London, Routledge.

US Bureau of Labour (1993), *Statistics*, Washington, DC, US Bureau of Labour.

Williamson, I. and Lindert, P.H. (1980), *American Inequality: a Micro-economic History*, New York, Academic Press.

World Bank (1993), *The East Asian Miracle*, Washington, DC, World Bank.

6. Continental, national and sub-national innovation systems – complementarity and economic growth*

1. INTRODUCTION

This paper discusses variations over time in rates of growth of various economic regions and the extent to which these variations may be attributed to 'innovation systems'. There has been a rapidly growing literature on this topic during the 1990s (see, for example, Lundvall, 1992; Nelson, 1993; Mjøset, 1992; Villaschi, 1993; Humbert, 1993; Freeman, 1995; Reinert, 1997).

Much of this literature (see especially Hu, 1992; Porter, 1990; Patel, 1995) insists on the central importance of *national* systems but a number of authors have argued that 'globalisation' has greatly diminished or even eliminated the importance of the nation-state (notably Ohmae, 1990). Other critics have stressed alternatively (or in addition) that sub-national entities, such as provinces, industrial districts, cities or 'Silicon Valleys' are becoming, or have already become, more important than the nation-state (see, for example DeBresson, 1989; DeBresson and Amesse, 1991).

Unfortunately, at least in the English language, the same word 'Regional' is often used to describe two entirely different phenomena, viz.

1. Geographical areas embracing several nation-states and even entire sub-continents – the 'Pacific region', 'East Asia', Eastern Europe, Central America, etc.
2. Geographical areas which are smaller sub-divisions of nation-states, e.g. 'states', urban areas, counties, rural areas, etc.

This can be a source of confusion, so for this reason, this paper refers to the wider areas as 'continental' or 'sub-continental' and the smaller areas as 'subnational'. The inter-continental variations in growth rates are indeed very wide, as illustrated in Table 6.1, but the variations between countries have of course been even wider. In particular, a group of countries, today referred to as 'developed' or 'industrialised' drew far ahead of the rest of

Table 6.1   Comparative growth rates sub-continental regions 1965–1999[a]

	1965–1980	1980–1989	1990–1999 (estimate)
GDP % p.a.			
East Asia	7.5	7.9	7.2
South Asia	3.9	5.1	5.5
Africa (sub-Sahara)	4.0	2.1	2.7
Latin America	5.8	1.6	3.1
GDP per capital % p.a.			
East Asia	5.0	6.3	5.7
South Asia	1.5	2.9	3.4
Africa (sub-Sahara)	1.1	−1.2	0.2
Latin America	3.5	−0.5	1.2

Note: [a] Own estimates in 1990s.

Source: World Bank Development Report (1991).

Table 6.2   Estimates of trends in per capita GNP (1960 US$ and prices, 1750–1977)

Year	Developed countries		Third World		Gaps	
	(1) Total (billion of US$)	(2) Per capita, US$	(3) Total (billion of US$)	(4) Per capita, US$	(5) = (2)/(4)	(6) Ratio of the most developed to the least developed
1750	35	182	112	188	1.0	1.8
1800	47	198	137	188	1.1	1.8
1830	67	237	150	183	1.3	2.8
1860	118	324	159	174	1.9	4.5
1913	430	662	217	192	3.4	10.4
1950	889	1054	335	203	5.2	17.9
1960	1394	1453	514	250	5.8	20.0
1970	2386	2229	800	380	7.2	25.7
1977	2108	2737	1082	355	7.7	29.1

Source: Bairoch and Levy-Leboyer (1981), pp. 7–8.

the world (later known as 'under-developed') during the last two centuries (Table 6.2, columns 5 and 6).

Abramovitz (1986) coined the expression 'social capability' to describe that capacity to make institutional changes which led to this divergence in growth rates. He was himself one of the pioneers of 'growth accounting' but, as he cogently pointed out, the accumulation of capital and increase in the labour force are not in themselves sufficient to explain these varying rates of economic growth. The huge divergence in growth rates which is so obvious a feature of long-term economic growth over the past two centuries must be attributed in large measure to the presence or absence of social capability for institutional change, and especially for those types of institutional change which facilitate and stimulate a high rate of technical change, i.e. innovation systems. As we shall see, attempts by Krugman (1994) and others to go back to the quantitative accumulation of capital and labour as the main explanation of the 'East Asian Miracle' are very unconvincing. Institutional changes were essential for the accumulation of capital itself.

Many historians and economists had of course always emphasised the importance of technical and institutional change, as for example, Landes (1970) or Supple (1963). Indeed, going back to the early development of economic theory, List (1841) had strongly criticised Adam Smith and other classical economists for what he perceived as their neglect of technology and skills. In fact, Adam Smith *did* recognise the great importance of science and technology but did not consistently give it the prominence which List thought that it merited.

The main concern of List was with the problem of Germany catching up with England and for under-developed countries (as the German states then were in relation to England), he advocated not only protection of infant industries but a broad range of policies designed to make possible or to accelerate industrialisation and economic growth. Most of these policies were concerned with learning about new technology and applying it and many of them were applied in catching-up countries over the next century and a half (see Section 5).

After reviewing the changing ideas of economists about development in the years since the Second World War, the World Bank (1991) concluded that it is intangible investment in knowledge accumulation, which is decisive rather than physical capital investment, as was at one time believed (pp. 33–35). The Report cited the 'New Growth Theory' (Romer, 1986; Grossman and Helpman, 1991) in support of this view but the so-called 'New Growth Theory' has in fact only belatedly incorporated into neo-classical models the realistic assumptions which had become commonplace among economic historians and neo-Schumpeterian economists. Indeed, it could just as well have cited List (1841), who in criticising a passage from Adam Smith said:

> . . . Adam Smith has . . . forgotten that he himself includes (in his definition of capital) the intellectual and bodily abilities of the producers under this term. He wrongly maintains that the revenues of the nation are dependent only on the sum of its material capital (p. 183).

and further:

> The present state of the nations is the result of the accumulation of all discov-
> eries, inventions, improvements, perfections and exertions of all generations
> which have lived before us: they form the intellectual capital of the present
> human race, and every separate nation is productive only in the proportion in
> which it has known how to appropriate those attainments of former generations
> and to increase them by its own acquirements (p. 113).

List's clear recognition of the interdependence of domestic and imported
technology and of tangible and intangible investment has a decidedly
modern ring. He saw too that industry should be linked to the formal institutions of science and of education:

> There scarcely exists a manufacturing business which has not relation to physics,
> mechanics, chemistry, mathematics or to the art of design, etc. No progress, no
> new discoveries and inventions can be made in these sciences by which a hundred
> industries and processes could not be improved or altered. In the manufacturing
> State, therefore, sciences and arts must necessarily become popular (p. 162).

The recent literature on 'national systems of innovation' could be described
as an attempt to come to terms more systematically with these problems of
social capability for technical change. List's book on *The National System
of Political Economy* might just as well have been entitled 'The National
System of Innovation' since he anticipated many of the concerns of this
contemporary literature. The main purpose of this paper is to discuss the
relevance of systems of innovation to economic growth rate over the last
two centuries. A long-term historical approach is essential for this purpose
because of the very nature of technical and institutional change. The
enormous gaps between different parts of the world took decades or even
centuries to open up and the efforts to close them have also taken many
decades.

The analysis starts with the case of Britain in the 18th century because
Britain was the first country to open up a major gap in productivity, in technology and in *per capita* incomes, compared with all other nations and city
states. The British case is discussed at some length both because it was the
first and also because it serves to introduce some basic problems in the
theory of innovation systems – notably the complementarity (or lack of it)
between various sub-systems of society: science, technology, economy, politics and culture, and the complementarity between national and sub-
national systems. The British slow-down and 'falling behind' in the 20th
century also illustrates the relative rigidity of some *organisational* structures compared with informal institutions, a point emphasised by Edqvist
(1997a, b) in his thorough review of national systems theory.

Following this discussion Section 4 then takes up the second major example of a national system forging ahead of the rest of the world – the case of the United States in the second half of the 19th and first half of the 20th century. The remainder of the paper then discusses the innovation systems of *catching up* countries, which have been described by Viotti (1997) in an excellent dissertation as *learning systems*. He makes an interesting distinction between *active* and *passive* learning systems and applies this distinction to the example of South Korea and Brazil, an example which is reviewed in Section 5.

Finally, Section 6 of this paper speculates about the possible course of events in the next century, taking up the question of globalisation and convergence and drawing some conclusions about the role of innovation systems in future economic growth.

2.   THE CONCEPT OF NATIONAL SYSTEMS

The capacity for technical and social innovations did of course strongly influence economic life *before* nation-states became the dominant form of political organisation. Although Adam Smith's book was entitled *The Wealth of Nations* and his main concern was to explain 'the different progress of opulence in different *nations*', he nevertheless included a long discussion of 'The rise and progress of *cities* and *towns* since the fall of the Roman Empire'. The contemporary discussion is therefore certainly not entirely new: changing forms of political organisation and territorial boundaries necessarily changed the nature of the debate. For Adam Smith, it was the widening gap in living standards and in manufacturing industry between Britain and other political units in Europe which most intrigued him. Some of these were powerful nation-states, such as France and Spain, others were still city states or small principalities and still others were Empires.

Adam Smith's discussion marked the transition from policies which were mainly concerned with the promotion and protection of *trade*, with the finance of shipping, trading posts and cargoes, with the ship-building industry and naval power to policies which were mainly concerned with *manufacturing industry*.

The city-state innovation systems of the Renaissance had many remarkable achievements in craft industries as well as in financial systems, shipping, the arts, medicine and science. We have nevertheless, started this account with 18th century Britain because this was the time when Britain diverged from its great trading competitors in Spain, Portugal and The Netherlands and when the embryonic innovation systems which had grown

Table 6.3   National systems: 'narrow' institutions (sources of innovations)

17th century	Academies of Science, Royal Society 1662, 'Proceedings' and Journals, Internationalism of Science, Science Education
18th century	'Industrial revolution' (factories), Technical Education, Nationalism of Technology, Consulting Engineers
19th century	Growth of Universities, Ph.D. and Science Faculties, Technische Hochschulen, Institutes of Technology, Government Laboratories, Industrial R&D in-house, Standards Institutes
20th century	Industrial in-house R&D in all industries, 'Big Science and Technology', Research Councils, NSF, etc., Ministries of Science and Technology, Service Industries R&D, Networks

up in the period of the Renaissance developed into something new, associated with the predominance of capitalist *industry*.

A distinction has been made (Lundvall, 1992) between 'narrow' definitions of national systems of innovation (Table 6.3) and a broad definition (illustrated in Table 6.4). The narrow approach concentrates on those institutions which deliberately promote the acquisition and dissemination of knowledge and are the main sources of innovation. The 'broad' approach recognises that these 'narrow' institutions are embedded in a much wider socio-economic system in which political and cultural influences as well as economic policies help to determine the scale, direction and relative success of all innovative activities. The decisive changes which came about in 17th and 18th century Britain and later in the United States and other European countries, were the elevation of science in the national culture, the multiplication of links between science and technology and the systematic widespread embodiment of both in industrial processes in the new workshops and factories (Table 6.4). The cultural changes associated with the Renaissance were pushed even further in the direction of secular instrumental rationality and its application to industrial investment.

3.   THE BRITISH NATIONAL SYSTEM

The decisive differences between the city-state innovation systems of the Mediterranean and the British national system were in the role of science and the role of industry. The role of science is still disputed by historians. Some accounts argue that science in Britain in the 18th century lagged behind other European countries, especially France and that it was not particularly important for the success of the industrial revolution. What

Table 6.4   Some characteristics of British national system of innovation during 18–19th century (broad definition)

Strong links between scientists and entrepreneurs

Science has become a national institution, encouraged by the state and popularised by local clubs

Strong local investment by *landlords* in transport infrastructure (canals and roads, later railways)

Partnership form of organisation enables inventors to raise capital and collaborate with entrepreneurs (e.g. Arkwright/Strutt or Watt/Boulton)

Profits from trade and services available through national and local capital markets to invest in *factory* production and in infrastructure

Economic policy strongly influenced by classical economics and in the interests of industrialisation

Strong efforts to protect national technology and delay catching up by competitors

British productivity per person about twice as high as European average by 1850

Consulting engineers develop and diffuse best practice technology in waterwheels, canals, machine-making and railways

Part-time training, night school, and apprenticeship training for new factory technicians and engineers

Gradual extension of primary, secondary and tertiary education

---

these accounts tend to misconstrue is that it was not the location of a particular scientific discovery which mattered. These may have been more frequent outside Britain. What mattered for the industrial revolution was the prevalence of a scientific culture. The treatment of Newton in Britain compared with the treatment of Galileo in Italy exemplifies this point. Newton was revered in Britain by both state and church while the fate of Galileo was altogether different. Bacon (1605) had already proposed an integrated policy for science, exploration, invention and technology at the beginning of the 17th century. There was an exceptionally fortunate *congruence* of science, culture and technology in Britain which made it possible to use science, including Newtonian mechanics, on a significant scale in the invention and design of a wide variety of new instruments, machines, engines, canals, bridges, water wheels and so forth. For example, the British industrial revolution depended on water power (*not* on steam power) for over half a century. It was Joseph Smeaton in his papers and drawings presented to the Royal Society in the 1770s whose experimental work made possible a scientific and technological breakthrough in the design of water wheels more than doubling the productivity of water power. The use of iron rather than wood, first of all for the gears and later

Table 6.5   Labour productivity in cotton: operative hours to process 100 lbs of cotton

	OHP
Indian Hand Spinners (18th century)	50000
Crompton's Mule (1780)	2000
100-Spindle Mule (c. 1790)	1000
Power-assisted Mules (c. 1795)	300
Roberts' automatic Mule (c. 1825)	135
Most efficient machines today (1990)	40

Source: Jenkins (1994), p. xix.

for the entire water wheel, was made possible through Smeaton's work as a consulting *engineer* for the Carron Iron Works, by then already the largest iron foundry in Europe.

This is only one example, although a very important one, of the positive interplay between science, technology, culture and entrepreneurship which characterised the British national system of innovation. The *congruence* of these four sub-systems of society extended also to the political sub-system, which promoted all of these. According to many accounts (e.g. Needham, 1954) it was the failure of the Chinese Empire to sustain congruence between these sub-systems which led to the failure of China to sustain its world technological leadership. The conflict between church, state and science (e.g. Galileo) hindered a more fruitful development of both science and technology in the Italian city-states and elsewhere in Europe. The different role of science in Britain and Italy has been especially well documented by Jacob (1988).

This was not the only factor which weakened the city-state innovation systems. Even more decisive were the scale economies made possible by factory production, capital accumulation and specialised division of labour. It was an Italian economist, Antonio Serra who first recognised the extraordinary importance of increasing returns to scale but he died in prison whereas Adam Smith was honoured by the British Prime Minister ('We are all your pupils now'). Enterprises and workshops were still very small in 18th century Britain but the shift from cottage industry to factory production and the constant improvements in machinery were still enough to confer a huge advantage on British manufacturing firms. Nowhere was this more obvious than in the cotton industry (Table 6.5) where the combination of technical inventions, investment in machinery, factory organisation, and entrepreneurship in ever-wider markets (facilitated still by naval power) opened an enormous productivity gap between Britain and all other producers. Some enterprises in the two leading industries, cotton and iron, already deployed hundreds of people by 1800.

Investment in *industry* certainly owed a great deal to profits from *trade* but this could not have taken place without a change in the culture and attitudes of the landlord and middle classes as well as changes in the capital markets. The investment in the transport infrastructure by the British landlord class was unique in Europe and caused Marx to remark that Britain had a bourgeois aristocracy. The bourgeoisie and the landlords in Britain behaved differently following the victory of Parliament over the monarchy and the aristocracy in the English Civil War in the mid-17th century. This victory made irreversible political and social changes despite the restoration of the monarchy in 1660. The investment in trade, transport and industry became even more important than the ownership of land. The local political initiative of landlords in promoting a wave of investment in canals in the late 18th century was exceptionally important in the early take-off of several key industrial districts whose access to national and international markets had hitherto been hindered by poor communications and transport.

Schumpeter always maintained that the spread of innovations was necessarily uneven both with respect to timing and to space and this was certainly the case with the spread of those innovations which comprised the British industrial revolution. They were not evenly spread over all parts of the country, they affected only a few industries at first and they diffused relatively slowly to other European countries. The main centres of innovation, of urbanisation and of the rapid growth of new industries were not in the London region but in the North of England, especially in Lancashire and Yorkshire, in the Midlands and in Scotland. Originally, the reasons for the success of the new 'sub-national' industrial regions or districts had little or nothing to do with economic policy at a regional level. The main advantage of the North was probably the more rapidly flowing rivers of the Pennine Hills which provided the consistency and strength of flow for Smeaton's water wheels. The iron industry was obviously also influenced by the location of wood for charcoal and later, coal and iron ore deposits but much iron ore was still imported in the 18th century.

However, although geological factors such as rivers for navigation or water power and deposits of minerals or the lack of them, played an important role in determining the early growth of various industries, these *natural* advantages were soon overtaken by *created* advantages such as the transport infrastructure, the location of ports and access to skills and to markets. Lancashire enjoyed the advantage of the port of Liverpool which was the centre of the North Atlantic trade with North America. Many economists, and especially Marshall, pointed to the external economies which resulted from many firms in the same industry located in the same industrial district where 'the secrets of industry are in the air' (Foray, 1991). To this day, these external economies of agglomeration have continued to be extremely important in industries as diverse as semi-conductors, toys, and machine tools. They are an essential part of the argument of Piore and Sabel favouring small firm networks as against large mass production firms. They are also one of the main reasons for some economists to propose that sub-national regional innovation systems have now become more important than national systems themselves.

There is much in the experience of the British industrial revolution which appears at first sight to favour this view. Above all, the accumulated specialised skills in Lancashire were one of the major reasons for the extraordinary success of the Lancashire cotton industry, undoubtedly the leading sector of the British industrial revolution, accounting for 40% of all British exports in 1850 and still for over a quarter of a much larger total in 1900.

In their explanation of the reasons for British dominance in cotton persisting throughout the 19th century, Mass and Lazonick (1990) attribute this 'sustained competitive advantage' to a cumulative process in which the development and utilisation of several key productive factors reinforced each other. These affected labour costs, marketing costs and administrative costs. In all of these areas, industry scale economies (Marshall's external economies of scale) were important. In the case of labour:

> During the nineteenth century the development and utilisation of labour resources provided the British cotton industry with its unique sources of competitive advantage. The major machine technologies . . . required complementary applications of experienced human labour to keep them in motion. Experience gave workers not only specific cognitive skills (of which a process such as mule spinning was much more demanding . . .) but also (and more important over the long run) the general capability to work long hours at a steady pace without damaging the quality of the product, the materials or the machines (Mass and Lazonick, 1990, p. 4).

Mass and Lazonick lay particular stress on the habituation to factory work and cumulative skills of the labour force but they also stress that the trade union organisation at that time and in that sector (surprisingly for some stereotyped ideas of British industrial relations of later periods and other industries), were particularly congruent with incentives to sustain and increase productivity. Great responsibility was given to the more skilled workers (who often had previous experience in domestic craft work) for recruitment, training and supervision of the less skilled.

> Besides the general habituation to factory work that came from growing up in
> factory communities and entering the mills at a young age, cotton workers devel-
> oped specialised skills in spinning particular types of yarn and weaving particu-
> lar types of cloth (Mass and Lazonick, 1990, p. 5).

In common with other historians they point to the economies of agglomeration in relation to pools of specialised skilled labour in various Lancashire
towns: Bolton (fine yarns), Oldham (coarse yarns), Blackburn and Burnley
(coarse cloth), etc. Similar arguments apply to the availability of skilled
mechanics adept at maintaining (and improving) the local machinery. The
gains from increasing productivity were generally shared with the skilled
workers, whose union power ensured this.

> By the 1870s cotton industries around the world could readily purchase British
> plant and equipment and even British engineering expertise. But no other cotton
> industry in the world could readily acquire Britain's highly productive labour
> force; no other industry in the world had gone through the century-long devel-
> opmental process that had produced the experienced, specialised and coopera-
> tive labour force that Britain possessed (Mass and Lazonick, 1990, p. 8).

Similar arguments apply to the machine-building industry and to mill and
machine design. Whereas the early mill-wrights came from the earlier tradition of corn-mills, wind-mills, etc., with the increased specialisation and
sophistication of machinery, special and cumulative skills became increasingly important here too. All of this led to high levels of machine utilisation as well as lower initial costs of machinery.

Again in relation to material costs, the highly concentrated Liverpool
cotton exchange provided Lancashire with an exceptional advantage.
Foreign buyers found it cheaper to buy in Liverpool than anywhere else in
much the same way that the Amsterdam flower market re-exports to the
entire world today. The Manchester ship canal and the railway from
Liverpool from 1830 onwards meant that transport costs for Lancashire
were extremely low. Lancashire spinners could avoid the heavy warehousing costs of more distant competitors. It was not quite 'just-in-time' but was
well in that direction. The Liverpool market gave Lancashire enormous
flexibility in grades and types of cotton and spinners took advantage of
price changes on a weekly basis. Furthermore, Lancashire had a unique
capability to work with inferior grades of cotton for any market in the
world and even to cope with the partial switch to Indian cotton at the time
of the American Civil War.

The world-wide marketing structure was yet another cumulative advantage of the Lancashire industry, which like all the other factors mentioned
provided external economies for the firms in the industry. The structure
of the Lancashire industry itself with the very well-informed merchants,

converters and finishers meant that it had the capability to deliver whatever product the customer demanded to any part of the world rapidly. Again, inventory, transport and communication costs could be kept low through this industry-wide advantage.

Similar economies of agglomeration applied to other industries such as pottery (Staffordshire), cutlery (Sheffield), hosiery (Nottinghamshire) or wool (Yorkshire). There is no doubt that these sub-national systems of innovation or industrial districts, as Marshall called them, made major contributions to the success of the industrial revolution in Britain. However, it by no means follows that the national system was unimportant or that it was simply the sum of the sub-national systems. Each of the industrial districts could flourish not only because of the specialised *local* advantages and institutions (pools of skilled labour, exchange of experience, trade associations, etc.) but also because of *national* advantages conferred by British political, cultural, economic and technological institutions. Easy access to a large and rapidly growing domestic market as well as to foreign markets, access to the capital market and a legal system which protected property and its accumulation, and access to a national pool of engineering and scientific knowledge. In fact, the national and sub-national systems complemented each other.

It is hard to believe that the British industrial revolution would have been more successful if Britain had been divided into 20 or 30 separate states, cities and principalities as Germany and Italy then were. In fact, Friedrich List and most of those concerned to catch-up with Britain in the 19th century advocated a confederation of German states preceded by a Customs Union (*Zollverein*) and bound together by a national railway network and other national institutions because they perceived the many advantages of a unitary nation-state.

The *national* advantages of Britain which complemented the specialised sub-national industrial districts were admirably summed up by Supple (1963):

> Britain's economic, social and political experience before the late 18th century explains with relatively little difficulty why she should have been an industrial pioneer. For better than any of her contemporaries Great Britain exemplified a combination of potentially growth-inducing characteristics. The development of enterprise, her access to rich sources of supply and large overseas markets within the framework of a dominant trading system, the accumulation of capital, the core of industrial techniques, her geographical position and the relative ease of transportation in an island economy with abundant rivers, a scientific and pragmatic heritage, a stable political and relatively flexible social system, an ideology favourable to business and innovation – all bore witness to the historical trends of two hundred years and more, and provided much easier access to economic change in Britain than in any other European country (Supple, 1963, p. 14).

4. THE UNITED STATES NATIONAL SYSTEM OF INNOVATION

The economies of scale achieved for British firms and the British industrial districts by the removal of internal trade barriers and by British trading and naval superiority were even more important in the rise of the United States economy. During the second half of the 19th century and the first half of the 20th century it was the United States economy which grew much more rapidly than any other (Table 6.6).

Not surprisingly, the country whose 'national system of innovation' most closely resembled the British system in the 18th century were the former British colonies of USA. However, in the first half of the 19th century, despite a rich endowment of natural resources and many favourable institutions, growth was still retarded by the lack of an appropriate transport infrastructure to take advantage of the natural endowment and size of the country and its market. It was the advent of railways and the new technologies of the late 19th century which enabled American entrepreneurs to forge far ahead of the rest of the world. At first, the United States imported much of this technology from Europe. Many of the key inventions in cotton spinning and weaving were smuggled out of Britain and across the Atlantic by British craftsmen as it was then illegal to export this technology. Arkwright's water frame was an example of a machine that was carefully memorised and then re-built in America. But from the very beginning American inventors modified and reshaped these technologies to suit American circumstances. By the end of the century American engineers and scientists were themselves developing new processes and products in most industries, which were more productive than those in Britain.

As we have seen, among those institutions most favourable to economic growth in Britain were the scientific spirit pervading the national culture and the support for technical invention. These features were readily transferred to the United States and respect for science and technology has been an

Table 6.6   Relative productivity levels (US GDP per hour = 100)

	1870	1913	1950
UK	104	78	57
France	56	48	40
Germany	50	50	30
Fifteen countries	51	33	36

Source: Abramovitz and David (1994).

enduring feature of American civilisation from Benjamin Franklin onwards. As de Tocqueville observed in his classic on *Democracy in America* (1836): 'In America the purely practical part of science is admirably understood and careful attention is paid to the theoretical position which is immediately requisite to application. On this head the Americans always display a free, original and inventive power of mind' (p. 315).

The early immigrants were obliged as a matter of life and death, to learn by doing about agricultural techniques in the American Continent and agricultural research emerged early as an outstanding feature with strong public support. Whereas in Europe, with the partial exception of Britain, feudal institutions often retarded both agricultural and industrial development, the United States never had any feudal institutions either in agriculture or any other part of the economy. Moreover, the relative abundance of land, the westward-moving frontier, the destruction of the native civilisations or their confinement to a relatively small part of the territory, all favoured a purely capitalist form of economic development with a relatively egalitarian distribution of income and wealth amongst the white immigrants in the early period.

The big exception to these generalisations was of course the slave economy of the South. It is difficult to assess the degree to which the economic growth of the South in particular and of the Union in general was retarded by the prevalence of this slave economy but it was in the period which followed the victory of the North in the Civil War that the United States achieved rates of growth well above any previously achieved by Britain. This was a case of the sub-national system of the South *retarding* national economic growth until the victory of the Union and the major institutional changes which ensued, especially the abolition of slavery. Even after its abolition, slavery left an enduring legacy of social and economic problems, some of which persist to this day but the maintenance of the Union meant that the predominantly capitalist path of development in the North and West prevailed in the whole country. In these circumstances an entrepreneurial culture could flourish as nowhere else.

Historians such as Abramovitz and David (1994), who have examined American economic history after the Civil War point to several characteristics of the United States economy which were in combination exceptionally favourable to a high rate of economic growth. These were (i) resource abundance in both land, minerals and forests; (ii) an exceptionally large and homogeneous domestic market facilitating production, marketing and financial economies of scale, especially in the extractive, processing and manufacturing industries.

Abramovitz and David argue that the higher relative price of labour in North America interacted with these advantages to induce substitution of

Table 6.7   *Comparative levels of capital/labour ratios 1870–1950*
             (USA = 100)

	Germany	Italy	UK	Average of 13 European countries	Japan
1870	73	–	117	–	–
1880	73	26	106	68	12
1913	60	24	59	48	10
1938	42	32	43	39	13
1950	46	31	46	39	13

Source: Abramovitz and David (1994), p. 8.

capital and natural resource inputs for skilled labour. This stimulated already in the first half of the 19th century the development of a specific American labour-saving, capital-intensive technological trajectory of mechanisation and standardised production, which at the lower end of the quality range had enabled US manufacturing to surpass British productivity levels already by 1850. As the 19th century advanced, 'the engineering techniques of large-scale production and high throughput rates became more fully explored and more widely diffused. American managers became experienced in the organisation, finance and operation of large enterprises geared to creating and exploiting mass markets' (Abramovitz and David, 1994, p. 10).

The extent to which this specific American trajectory of tangible capital-using technology diverged from that of Europe (and Japan) can be clearly seen from Table 6.7. Until the 1880s the UK still had an overall capital/labour ratio higher than that of the United States but by 1938, like all other countries, the ratio had fallen to less than half that of the United States. The large cost reductions and productivity gains associated with this North American technological trajectory could be illustrated from numerous industrial sectors. The extraordinary productivity gains in mining and mineral processing are emphasised in particular by Abramovitz and David, whilst the productivity gains in agriculture are very frequently cited by other historians. The examples of *steel* and *oil* are particularly noteworthy because of the key role of these commodities in all kinds of tangible capital-using investment projects, in capital goods themselves, in transport and in energy production and distribution. Cotton, iron, canals and water-power were the leading sectors in the early British industrial revolution; oil, steel and electricity were the leading sectors in the huge American spurt of growth from 1880 to 1913.

Viotti (1997) points out that these differences and the case of the chemical industry in Germany mean that catching up in the late 19th century and early 20th century was rather different from what it has become in the late 20th century. The United States and Germany, he suggests, caught up by *radical* innovations in new industries, not by incremental innovations in cotton spinning and weaving. Today, the late-comer countries may not have the option of radical innovations in new industries and have no alternative but to pursue the path of imitation and *learning*. However, he makes a distinction between *active* learning systems and *passive* learning systems, taking the examples of South Korea and Brazil to illustrate his point. We shall pursue this example in Section 5.

5.   LATE-COMER CATCH-UP IN THE 20TH CENTURY

Very large economies of scale were characteristic of the forging ahead process in the United States, especially in steel, chemicals, oil, minerals and electricity. Even after the Second World War, when the OECD (previously OEEC and ERP) organised many European missions to study the productivity gaps between European and American firms, they frequently stressed scale of plant and size of domestic market as two of the biggest comparative advantages of US firms. This kind of thinking lay behind much of the political impulse to establish first the European Coal and Steel Community and later the European Common Market (Customs Union) and the European Economic Community. Just as the German nationalists, following Friedrich List, believed that a German Customs Union would greatly facilitate catch-up with Britain, so the European federalists believed that a European Common Market would accelerate European catch-up with the United States. This philosophy still influences the debate on EMU today.

Catch-up by Western Europe did indeed take place between 1950 and 1975 although it certainly cannot be attributed uniquely to scale economies and market enlargement. As with the first British industrial revolution, a general capability for institutional and technical change was essential and not merely scale economies. European research and development activities, technology transfer, education and training, and management techniques were all greatly improved. Investment by the United States firms in Europe and by European firms in the USA also facilitated the transfer of technology and management techniques. All these things were necessary even to achieve the scale economies themselves.

Not surprisingly, however, economists who were interested in catch-up by 'late-comer' countries were especially impressed by the scale economies of North American and European firms and when they came to study catch-up phenomena, they stressed this point in particular. Gerschenkron (1962, 1963) studied the catch-up by 19th century German and later Russian firms in the steel industry and argued that the new (late-comer) firms could acquire and use the latest technology, at much lower costs than those in the pioneering countries, by transfer agreements, inward investment and the recruitment of skilled people. Even more important in his view was the fact that the pioneering firms and countries had already established a growing world market so that the catch-up firms did not have to face all the uncertainties, costs and difficulties of opening up entirely new markets. Gerschenkron's theory of *late-comer* advantages stressed that the pioneers could not possibly *start* with large plants, whereas the late-comers could move very rapidly to large-scale production, while their mature competitors might be burdened with smaller plants embodying now obsolete technology.

Jang-Sup Shin (1995) in his study of the *Korean* steel industry endorsed this Gerschenkronian explanation, pointing out that Posco, the largest Korean steel firm was able to leapfrog European and American firms with respect to plant size and technology and thus enter the world market as a low-cost producer. He extended this analysis to the case of the semi-conductor industry arguing that here too the plant-scale advantages of the Korean producers of memory chips enabled them to leapfrog the European semi-conductor industry and to compete with the most successful Japanese and American firms. However, he accepted that the Gerschenkron late-comer scale economy advantages had to be complemented by a 'national system of innovation' explanation of successful catch-up since neither in the case of steel, nor in the case of semi-conductors could catch-up have taken place without many institutional changes, especially in education, training and R&D.

Bell and Pavitt (1993) pointed to another problem with Gerschenkronian catch-up theory: a country which simply instals large plants with foreign technology and foreign assistance will not experience the build-up in technological capability over several decades, which has been characteristic of the leading countries. Consequently, below capacity working and low output capital ratios have often persisted in developing countries. *Active* learning policies of the type prescribed by Bell and Pavitt, by Viotti and by Alice Amsden, will be essential to overcome this disadvantage of late-comers.

Perez and Soete (1988) provided a more general theory of the science and technology infrastructure needed for effective catch-up. They showed that even the costs of *imitation* could be rather high in the absence of an infrastructure which is taken for granted in mature industrialised countries. Even more important, they showed that these costs would vary systematically at different stages of evolution of a product or a technology. Thus, while Gerschenkron could be regarded as the leading theorist of late-comer advantages, Perez and Soete reflected the experience in numerous developing countries of late-comer *disadvantages* and difficulties in catching up the leaders in technology. However, they did also point to 'windows of opportunity' in the acquisition and assimilation of technologies, provided the catch-up countries followed appropriate social, industrial and technology policies.

Gerschenkron himself argues that countries could only enjoy late-comer advantages if they could also make innovations in their *financial* system so that the huge scale of investment needed for very large plants could be accommodated. However, there is another important point about late-comer advantages which Gerschenkron did not sufficiently explore: the plant scale economies of a particular historical period were not necessarily characteristic of *all* industries or of other periods. As Perez and Soete showed, scale economies are industry-specific and technology-specific. In a number of industries, such as aircraft or drugs, scale economies in *design* and *development* costs were much more important than *plant*-scale economies in *production*. In still other industries, scale economies in *marketing* may be decisive. In the steel industry itself as well as in semiconductors, plant scale economies have changed with technology.

Nevertheless, Gerschenkron's theory of late-comer advantages was an important complement to infant industry arguments. The much higher growth rates in some catch-up countries are obviously attributable in part to the fact that costs of technology acquisition and implementation are lower and the risks and uncertainties are less in catch-up situations. Imitation is usually easier and less costly than innovation. A very big gap in technology does provide a *potential* for fast catch-up.

Finally, as traditional international trade theory has always stressed, late-comer countries will usually enjoy labour cost advantages and these may be very large now because of the wide disparities in world-wide *per capita* incomes. These labour-cost advantages may also be reinforced by lower costs of particular materials and of energy, as well as climatic advantages. All of these things as well as the narrow and the broad national innovation systems affect the potential for catch-up and its realisation.

It also seems to be the case that geographical and cultural proximity to nations which have led either in forging ahead or in catching up has a considerable effect on rate of catch-up. It would be difficult otherwise to explain the clear-cut *inter-continental* differences which are apparent. Britain was first caught up and overtaken by neighbouring European countries and by countries partly populated by British and other European immigrants (the United States, Canada, Australia, etc.). The most successful catch-up countries in the late 20th century have been those which are geographically (and in some respects culturally) close to the leading catch-up country of the 20th century – Japan.

Thus, it is not altogether surprising that East Asian countries and some South-East Asian countries grew much faster than Latin American countries in the 1980s and 1990s, despite the fact that the Asian countries started from a much lower level of industrialisation and productivity than most Latin American countries (Table 6.8). This would appear at first sight to support a simple convergence theorem – the later the faster. But before jumping to any such conclusion it is essential to recognise that not all late-comer countries were catching up; some were falling further behind and some were standing still. The countries and sub-continents making the fastest progress have actually varied enormously both in 19th and 20th centuries. Uneven development is a much more accurate characterisation of growth than convergence. In a well-known paper, De Long (1988) showed that Baumol's (1986) attempt to establish the convergence theorem using Maddison's data was fundamentally flawed:

> ... when properly interpreted Baumol's finding is less informative than one might think. For Baumol's regression uses an *ex post* sample of countries that are now rich and have successfully developed. By Maddison's choice, those nations that have not converged are excluded from his sample because of their resulting persistent relative poverty. *Convergence is thus all but guaranteed in Baumol's regression*, which tells us little about the strength of the forces making for convergence among nations that in 1870 belonged to what Baumol calls the 'convergence club.' . . . Because [Maddison] focuses on nations which (a) have a rich data base for the construction of historical national accounts and (b) have

Table 6.8   Starting levels for industry, Latin America and Asia 1955

	Ratio of manufacturing to agricultural net product	US$ net value of manufacturing per capita
Argentina	1.32	145
Brazil	0.72	50
Mexico	1.00	60
Venezuela	1.43	95
Colombia	0.42	45
South Korea	0.20	8
Thailand	0.28	10
India	0.30	7
Indonesia	0.20	10

Source: Maizels (1963).

successfully developed, the nations in Maddison's sixteen are among the richest nations in the world today (De Long, 1988, pp. 1138–9, emphasis added).

De Long showed that for another sample of countries, drawn *ex ante*, there was no correlation between starting level of productivity and subsequent growth performance.

Following up De Long's critique of convergence theory, Chabot (1995) showed that for the period 1820–1870 the capacity for income growth varied *directly* not *inversely* with countries' 1820 level of GDP per capita:

> The result is directly antithetical to what convergence theory predicts. The case is demonstrated remarkably well by two countries, the United States and the UK. Both were amongst the group of three to four most promising nations in 1820 and both experienced phenomenal subsequent growth rates. Clearly something more than the logic of convergence and catch-up was at work (p. 60).

Sections 3 and 4 of this paper have attempted to show that the 'something more' was specific national innovation systems.

Chabot further showed that for the period 1870– 1950, *forging ahead* by the United States in labour productivity took place in relation to all other OECD countries except the Nordic countries (Table 6.9). Only for the period 1950–1992 did he find some limited support for convergence and he

Table 6.9   *Falling behind-rates of divergence or convergence towards the US labour productivity level, 1870–1950*

Country	Rate
Australia	−0.95
Austria	−0.81
Belgium	−0.84
Canada	0.10
Denmark	−0.46
Finland	−0.20
France	−0.37
Germany	−0.88
Italy	−0.37
Japan	−0.30
The Netherlands	−0.87
Norway	−0.15
Sweden	0.04
Switzerland	−0.14
UK	−0.77

Source: Maddison (1995), as quoted in Chabot (1995).

concluded 'in the whole of modern economic history, there is only one period which offers any substantive support for international convergence, and even that is subject to non-trivial qualification' (p. 62). Although Gerschenkron was undoubtedly right to detect some major advantages for late-comer countries and to show that *in some circumstances* late-comers, starting from a very low level of productivity could enjoy growth rates much higher than the established leading countries, it certainly does not follow that late-comers will *always* tend to converge with the leaders. Whether they do so or not depends, as was suggested at the outset, on social capability for technical and institutional change, i.e. on the national systems of innovation and on the nature of the new waves of technology pervading the system. It also depends on a favourable conjuncture of international relationships.

Whilst it is true that most Asian countries were 'later' late-comers than most Latin American countries in their industrialisation, their faster growth in the 1980s and 1990s cannot be explained by this alone. Nor indeed can it be explained as Krugman (1994) attempted to do, primarily by fast growth of capital and labour inputs, with technical change playing very little part. Neither is the World Bank Report (1993) on the *East Asian Miracle* entirely convincing in its explanation of the 'miracle'. Both Krugman and the World Bank Report greatly underestimate the role of technical change and in particular they fail to recognise the degree to which the 'Tigers' since the 1970s concentrated their investment, their R&D, their infrastructural development, their training and their technology input on the electronic and telecommunication industries. 'Catch-up' is not a spontaneous process associated with late-coming, nor the inevitable outcome of market forces in a liberal economy. By a combination of good fortune and of good judgement, as well as proximity to Japan, the Tigers (and later some other Asian countries) increased their commitment to the manufacture and export of electronic products at a time when they were the most rapidly growing part of world exports.

Clearly, the huge achievements of the Tigers in export performance in the 1980s and 1990s were greatly facilitated by the commodity composition of their exports and imports, both of which were heavily related to the fastest growing sectors of the world economy and of world trade (Table 6.10). Singapore is the most extreme example of this with electronic and telecommunication products accounting for over a third of total industrial production and nearly two-thirds of exports by the mid-1990s. Hong Kong, however, transferred much of its electronics manufacturing to China in the 1980s and 1990s. Elsewhere in Asia networks of interdependent suppliers of electronic components, sub-systems and final products were the typical feature of rapidly growing manufacturing industries. Both imports and exports of these products grew extremely rapidly. Not only did the World

Table 6.10   *Exports of ICT equipment* to major OECD countries as a share of total manufacturing exports to those countries from each of the following countries*

	1970	1980	1992
Japan	21	17	29
Germany	7	5	6
USA	14	15	22
France	6	5	6
The Netherlands	6	7	8
UK	6	7	13
Taiwan	17	16	28
South Korea	7	13	26
Singapore	20	36	65

Note: * Computers, office machines, telecommunication equipment and other electronic equipment.

Source: OECD trade data base.

Bank Report neglect the pattern of structural change in the East Asian economies, it also neglected the changing pattern of research and development activities and of technology transfer.

The World Bank Report *did* recognise the importance of *education*. However, it differed from the earlier work of institutional economists such as Amsden (1989) and Wade (1990) in neglecting the role of government policy in many other areas, such as the protection of certain industries, the promotion of exports, the subsidies to specific firms and the promotion of R&D activities. In general, it ignored *industrial* policy and had little to say about training or technology transfer. In all these respects, the policies of South Korea, Taiwan and Singapore have resembled those prescribed long ago by Friedrich List. In pointing this out, Freeman (1993) made some comparisons and contrasts between Brazil and South Korea.

This comparison has been made much more thoroughly since then by several Brazilian scholars (Villaschi, 1993; Albuquerque, 1997b; Viotti, 1997). Albuquerque distinguishes several different categories of 'national innovation systems', while Viotti makes an interesting distinction between 'Active' and 'Passive' learning systems building on the earlier work of Villaschi (1993) and Bell and Cassiolato (1993) on 'learning to produce and learning to innovate'. All of these accounts emphasise the role of *active policies* at the national and firm level in the import, *improvement* and adaptation of technology as characteristic of successful catch-up.

Viotti (1997) presents impressive evidence of the contrasts between Brazil and South Korea in the fields of education, and of research and development (Table 6.11). In presenting this evidence, he points out that the number of tertiary students per 100,000 inhabitants in Brazil (1079) is approximately just a fourth of that of South Korea (4253) and the concentration on *engineering* is much greater in the Korean tertiary education system compared with both science and humanities. Amsden (1989) in her classic work on Korean catch-up, gave some vivid examples of the role of training in the steel and cement industries in the early period of catch-up. This has become even more important in the electronic industry. For example, Samsung not only trains thousands of its own employees at every level but also regularly provides intensive training for its sub-contractors. Such intensive training efforts are essential for an *active* policy of continuous improvement of technology even more than for simple imitation. Whereas *static* economies of scale can be achieved simply by building a larger plant, the far greater *dynamic* economies of scale depend on such active learning policies and increasingly on engineering activities and in-house R&D at plant level, as shown so clearly by Bell and Cassiolato (1993) and by Bell and Pavitt (1993). The rapid change of product design and the associated change of components characteristic of the electronic industry have further increased the importance of these active learning and training policies.

Viotti has further shown that Korean industry has relied far less on foreign investment than Brazil and has relied more on imports of capital goods and on increasingly active efforts to improve upon imported technology through the *in-house* R&D efforts of Korean firms themselves. Hobday (1995) has pointed to the variety of strategies in the East Asian countries, all designed in different ways steadily to upgrade local technological capability. The contrast between the rapid rise in the performance of in-house R&D in *firms* in both South Korea and Taiwan, and its low level, stagnation or non-existence in firms in most developing countries is especially notable. Table 6.11 illustrates the contrast with Brazil.

The rise of in-house R&D in the 1970s led to an extraordinary increase in numbers of patents (Table 6.12) and this is perhaps the most striking confirmation of the *active* learning system in South Korea and Taiwan. Between 1977–1982 and 1990–1996, the number of patents taken out in the USA by Brazil, Argentina, Mexico and Venezuela nearly doubled from 570 to 1106, but in the same period the numbers taken out by the four 'Tigers' increased nearly 30 times over, from 671 to 18,763.

In the case of South Korea nearly half of the patents taken out between 1969 and 1992 were in six technical fields in the electronics area (semiconductors, computers, imaging and sound, instruments, electrical devices

Table 6.11 Indicators of national efforts in S&T–Brazil, South Korea, Japan and the United States[a]

	Brazil	South Korea	Japan	USA
Scientists and engineers engaged in R&D (per million population)	235[b] (1993)	1990 (1992)	5677 (1992)	3873 (1988)
Expenditure for R&D as percentage of GNP	0.4[c] (1994)	2.1 (1992)	3.0 (1991)	2.9 (1988)
Expenditure in R&D by source of funds (%)	1994[c]	1992	1992	1992
Government	81.9	17.2	19.4[f]	43.3[f]
Productive enterprise	18.1	82.4	71.0[f]	51.6[f]
Other	–	0.4	9.6[f]	5.1[f]
Total patents granted in 1991	2479[d]	3741[e]	36100[f]	96514[f]
Patents granted to residents (%)	14[d]	69[e]	84[f]	53[f]
Number of tertiary students per 100,000 inhabitants (1992)	1079	4.253	2340	5652

Notes:
[a] Numbers between parenthesis correspond to the year of the data.
[b] Computed from MCT (1995).
[c] CNPq (1995, p. 23).
[d] MCT (1996, p. 37).
[e] Lall (1992a, p. 197), the statistics of patents for South Korea are for the year 1986.
[f] STA/NISTEP (1995).

Source: Viotti (1997).

*Table 6.12   Emerging sources of technology in terms of ownership of US
patents*

Year	Patents granted during					
	1977–1992	Share	1983–1989	Share	1990–1996	Share
Taiwan	382	0.10	2292	0.41	11040	1.43
South Korea	70	0.02	580	0.10	5970	0.77
Israel	641	0.16	1507	0.27	2685	0.35
Hong Kong	272	0.07	633	0.11	1416	0.18
South Africa	491	0.12	699	0.12	787	0.10
Mexico	245	0.06	289	0.05	314	0.04
Brazil	144	0.04	212	0.04	413	0.05
PR China	7	0.00	142	0.03	353	0.05
Argentina	130	0.03	135	0.02	187	0.02
Singapore	17	0.00	65	0.01	337	0.04
Venezuela	51	0.01	122	0.02	192	0.02
India	56	0.01	96	0.02	204	0.03
East and Central Europe	3444	0.87	2417	0.43	1317	0.17
Sub-total	5950	1.51	9189	1.62	25215	3.26
Others	731	0.19	902	0.16	1494	0.19
Total	393629	100.00	565739	100.00	772927	100.00

Source: Kumar (1997) based on data presented in US Patents and Trademarks Office
(1997) TAF special report: all patents, all types – January 1977–December 1996,
Washington, DC.

and photocopying). In the case of Taiwan the increase in total numbers of patents was even more remarkable but they were spread over a wider technical area, including especially metal products and machinery as well as electrical and electronic devices (Choung, 1995). Firms in both South Korea and Taiwan were so successful in their catch-up that they began to export technology themselves and to invest overseas in older industrial countries like Britain as well as in the less developed countries of South-East Asia.

Although very useful for international comparative purposes, *United States* patent statistics are of course not the only ones which are significant. Since the establishment of the European patent, the European Patent Office (EPO) statistics are increasingly valuable. Even more interesting for catch-up countries are the measures of *domestic* patenting in each individual country. In a pioneering paper, Albuquerque (1997a) analyses these statistics and more interestingly from the standpoint of this paper shows that the number of *Brazilian* domestic patents have shown no clearly increasing trend in the last 15 years after reaching a peak in 1981–1982.

The extraordinary growth of East Asian patenting in the USA is not of course only an indication of active technology improvement. It is also influenced by the commercial and export strategies of firms. Hobday (1995) has particularly stressed the key role of learning by exporting in East Asian catch-up. The success of East Asian firms in exports complements their success in obtaining *United States* patents. Moreover, insofar as they continue to make progress towards the world technological frontier, they have encountered increasingly severe competition from the established technological leaders and from the pressures of these leaders to liberalise all aspects of their economic, financial and trading systems.

The dominance of the United States firms in the world software industries and in all the supporting services for the Internet and in world financial services presents some especially acute problems for those catch-up countries which are making good progress in closing the gap in manufacturing.

The liberalisation of capital movements which has already taken place exposes all countries to the instability and shocks which occur in any part of the system. Events in the late 1990s have shown that these shocks can be propagated throughout the system and that however good the narrow innovation system it is always still part of a broader global economic and political system. Trends in the political, cultural and economic sub-systems are influenced very strongly by institutions which are only tenuously related to science and technology. These points are further discussed in Section 7 of this paper.

6. CONCLUSIONS

Section 3 of this paper suggested that it was from the time of the British industrial revolution in the 18th century that full *national* systems of innovation emerged. Bairoch's (1993) estimates of the widening gap between developing countries and industrialised countries show this gap growing very rapidly from this time onwards and Sections 3 and 4 of the paper attempted to show that this huge gap between the 'forging ahead' countries and the rest could best be explained in terms of such concepts as the 'national systems of innovation'. Section 5 further showed that this concept is also necessary to explain varying rates of late-comer catch-up and the failure of late-comer catch-up in some circumstances.

Whilst economic historians have had few difficulties in accepting the crucial importance of technical and institutional change in the theory of economic growth, the growth modellers have found this a continuing problem. Some early growth models put the main emphasis on accumulation of (tangible) capital through investment and the growth of the labour force and left all other influences to be subsumed in a 'residual factor'. Although the so-called 'New Growth Theory' broke away from this tradition and moved 'intangible investment' in education, research and development to the centre of the stage, the old approach lingers on, as can be seen for example in Krugman's (1994) attempt to debunk the 'East Asia Miracle' and to explain East Asian growth mainly in terms of capital and labour accumulation.

The treatment of all the complexities of technical and institutional change in early growth models came in for heavy criticism at the time both from historians and from many economists, especially as most of the models showed that the 'Third Factor' apparently accounted for most of the growth. Balogh (1963) dubbed the 'Third Factor' the 'Coefficient of Ignorance' while Supple (1963) concluded that

> it must surely be clear that any discussion of the relationship between capital formation and economic growth necessarily entails the appraisal of a host of other issues. And these in their turn lead to the conclusion that the accumulation of capital is in itself by no means the central aspect of the process of economic growth (p. 22).

In response to this criticism various attempts were made to disaggregate the residual factor in the aggregate production function, notably by Denison (1962, 1967), who used what Dosi (1988) described as an 'entire Kama-Sutra of variables' in his efforts to make systematic comparisons of growth rates. Yet none of these efforts could survive the trenchant criticism of Nelson (1981) and others who pointed to the *complementarity* of all these variables. The contribution of capital accumulation to growth depends not only on its quantity but on its *quality*, on the direction of investment, on the skills of entrepreneurs and the labour force in the exploitation of new investment, on the presence (or absence) of social overhead capital and so forth.

A brave and highly original contribution to the growth modelling debate came from Adelman (1963). She recognised early on that the assumption of constant returns to scale in many models raised big problems and in the so-called 'New Growth Theory' this assumption has been dropped in favour of Young's (1928) increasing returns to scale (Romer, 1986; Grossman and Helpman, 1991).

These models usually also follow her in attempting to assign a specific role to technical change (or as she termed it 'the stock of knowledge from applied science and technology'). In her model Irma Adelman also separated

'Natural Resources' from other forms of capital in much the same way as the classical economists separated land. This distinction is likely to become increasingly important with the growing recognition of the importance of ecological factors and resource conservation in economic growth. She also separated technical change from other forms of institutional change. Thus, she specified the production function as

$$Y_t = f(K_t N_t L_t S_t U_t) \qquad (6.1)$$

where K_t denotes the amount of the services of the capital stock at time t; N_t stands for the rate of use of natural resources; L_t represents the employment of the labour force; S_t represents 'society's fund of applied knowledge'; U_t represents the 'social-cultural milieu within which the economy operates' (Adelman, 1963, p. 9).

Adelman was also unusual in her frank recognition of the immense difficulties in the production function approach and of the interdependence of her variables. For example,

> . . . both the quality and the composition of the labour force vary through time and are not independent of the rates of change of the other variables in the system. Specifically, changes in the skills and health of the labour force are directly dependent upon changes in society's applied fund of technical knowledge (S_t).

Like other modellers, she suggests that the conceptual problems 'which arise from the heterogeneity and incommensurability of the production factors may be reduced somewhat if we think of each input as a multi-component vector rather than as a single number'.

However, this is still not the greatest difficulty with the production function approach. Again, as Irma Adelman so clearly points out:

> Even more difficult than the measurement problems raised by these production factors are those posed by an attempt to quantify our last two variables. S_t and U_t represent heuristic devices introduced primarily for conceptual purposes . . . At some time in the future a method may be evolved for the ordinal evaluation of S_t and U_t but such a method does not now exist and accordingly neither variable can be used as an analytical tool (pp. 11–12).

This situation has scarcely changed since 1963 despite some advances in the measurement of R&D and of education and despite the somewhat greater realism about technical and institutional change in the more recent 'new' growth models (Verspagen, 1992).

All of this does not mean that the modelling attempts and developments in growth theory of the past half century have been a complete waste of effort. Adelman's argument for the heuristic value of growth modelling still stands and her own attempt to use her production function to illustrate the differences and similarities in the growth theories respectively of Adam Smith, Ricardo, Marx, Schumpeter, Harrod, Kaldor and the neo-Keynesians is an excellent example of these heuristic advantages. But when all is said and done the main conclusion of the whole debate has been to vindicate the contention of many economic historians and neo-Schumpeterian economists that technical change and institutional change are the key variables to study in the explanation of economic growth.

In his fairly sympathetic treatment of neo-classical growth theory Gomulka (1990) concluded that

> The cumulative effect of the theoretical and empirical work has been to highlight more sharply and widely than ever before how really central is the role, in long-term economic growth, of the activities producing qualitative change in the economy. Technological changes have assumed the primary role by virtue of their being typically the original impulses which tend to initiate other qualitative changes. By the same token, the work has also helped to delineate the very limited usefulness of the (standard) growth theory based on the assumption that these qualitative changes are cost free and exogenously given (p. 19).

Sections 1–5 have attempted to justify the view that technical change and the institutions which promoted it played a central role both in the forging ahead process and in the catching up process. This is by no means to deny, however, the role of other influences – economic, political and cultural – which constitute the 'broad' national system of innovation. Although the work on national systems has made a promising start on the very complex task of 'putting history back into economics' it has certainly not done enough to satisfy the critics, many of whom are uneasy about neo-classical growth models, but also lack confidence in alternative 'evolutionary' explanations of economic growth.

Some of the most promising lines of future research on national systems would appear to be in the study of catch-up failure and *falling behind* in economic growth. In cases such as Britain and Argentina, both of which slowed down and fell behind in the 20th century, many of the explanations offered point to the lack of congruence between various sub-systems of society, social institutions which have been favourable to economic growth in one period of technological development may not be so favourable when there are fundamental changes in technology.

Hughes (1982) has shown that Berlin and Chicago forged ahead of London in the applications of electric power in part because of the multiplicity of standards in Britain and mis-management of the new infrastructure. These kinds of points indicate that various 'out of synch' phenomena had emerged towards the close of the 19th century in Britain – between technology and culture, technology and politics, technology and the economy and even between technology and science. In the mid-19th century, very few people foresaw this relative British decline. Even Friedrich List, the outstanding exponent of catch-up theory on the Continent of Europe, died believing that Germany could never overtake Britain. Much later on, in the 1960s, the 'Dependency' theorists were so impressed by the advantages of the United States and Western Europe that they thought it impossible for countries in Asia, Latin America or Africa ever to catch up.

The advantages of fore-runners may indeed appear overwhelming at first to late-comers. Not only do they apparently command an unassailable lead in technology, but they also enjoy many static and dynamic economies of scale and privileged prestigious positions in world markets. It is for this reason that successful catch-up is often referred to as a 'miracle' (The German and Japanese 'miracles' of the 1950s, 1960s and 1970s; the Korean and Taiwanese 'miracles' of the 1980s and 1990s). But if any process is to be regarded as a 'miracle' it should be 'forging ahead' rather than catching up.

At the present time (late 1990s) the United States appears to have enormous advantages compared with its principal competitors. The successful catch-up of Japan and other East Asian countries was based on their intensive active learning in *hardware* design, development and manufacturing. Now, however, it is increasingly *software* design, development, production and marketing which is the key to commercial success. Here the United States has some considerable fore-runner advantages. It has by far the strongest software industry in the world with major advantages in scale economies in business applications. This has led in turn to English language domination in software generally and especially on the Internet – a global infrastructure, dominated by US service providers and content providers. Finally, the United States firms also lead in many other service industries and the victory of the USA in the Cold War has established the US as the only 'super-power' in a military sense. This power can be used to protect the interests of US firms world-wide including their intellectual property.

It is impossible to predict however how long these advantages can be retained despite the tightening of intellectual property restrictions. Very many countries have rapidly growing young software firms including Eastern Europe, as well as Eastern Asia, Latin America and countries with strong English language capability, such as India. Moreover, political and social events may predominate over more narrow technological and economic factors.

Social scientists face a more complex problem than biologists because the 'selection environment' confronting innovators is not simply the natural environment but also several different sub-systems of human societies – scientific, technological, economic, political and cultural. Each of these has its own unique characteristics and successful diffusion depends on the establishment of some degree of congruence between them.

The growing environmental problems facing the whole world may also impose a rather different pattern of economic and political development than that which has prevailed in the 20th century. The development of environmentally friendly technologies and their universal diffusion may impose a more cooperative civilisation and an entirely new pattern of institutional change and of knowledge accumulation. The great variety of new possibilities in science, technology, economics, politics and culture means that despite the present-day predominance of the United States, permanent convergence based on US hegemony is a rather unlikely scenario. Viotti may be underestimating the feasibility of new clusters of radical innovations in catch-up countries.

The natural environment confronts all living creatures but the accumulation of scientific knowledge and of technological knowledge and artefacts are uniquely human processes even though they may have originated, as with other animals, in the search for food and shelter and the communication associated with this search. There are birds and mammals which also make use of 'tools' in the sense of twigs, branches or stones, but the systematic *design* and *improvement* of tools and other artefacts are uniquely purposeful human activities, with their own partly autonomous selection environment. Economists often use a biological analogy to analyse the competitive behaviour of firms in a capitalist economy and the survival of the supposedly 'fittest' firms. This is a case of the borrowing back of an analogy which Darwinian theory originally took over from economics. But again the selection environment which confronts firms in their competitive struggle is actually very different from the natural environment confronting animals and plants and this economic environment is itself rapidly changing in ways which are unique. Finally, the political system and the cultural milieu are again uniquely human and powerfully influence the evolution of the economy, as they also reciprocally influence the evolution of science and technology. Evolutionary theories which deal *only* with the survival of *firms* (Alchian, 1951) or *only* with the survival of artefacts or of nations are inadequate for the study of economic growth (Freeman, 1994).

We have no alternative but to confront the unique features of human history, even though we may quite legitimately search for patterns of recurrence and for explanations of recurrence and of non-recurrence. One of the most obvious unique features is the rate of knowledge accumulation in human societies and the varying modes of disseminating this knowledge between individuals and groups. These features are ubiquitous and justify continuous attention by historians of economic growth, searching both for regular patterns as well as for the emergence of new features.

7.   SPECULATIONS

In this search, economists and other social scientists will need to pay attention to changing systems of innovation at all levels – the global level, the continental and sub-continental levels, the national level and the sub-national level. This paper has concentrated on developments at the *national* level in the belief that the major phenomena of forging ahead, catch-up and falling behind in the 19th and 20th centuries can most plausibly be explained in terms of national systems, albeit in an international context and recognising uneven development at the sub-national level.

All of this may change in the 21st century. In particular, the capacity to use information and communication technology will probably be a decisive factor in world competition and this in turn will lead to the dominance of firms and networks with capability in *service* activities. The models which economists have used have largely been based on *manufacturing* activities, although of course agriculture and services have always been important. Now manufacturing may increasingly be located outside Europe, Japan and the United States. Major manufacturing firms such as General Electric or Ericsson have for some time had a deliberate strategy of increasing the share of *service* activities within their total turnover. Manufacturing employment has already declined substantially in firms such as these and accounts now for much less than half the total, even though they are still often thought of as mainly manufacturing organisations. Financial, marketing, software, design and R&D services may often predominate now in the portfolio of large MNCs.

This does not mean that manufacturing will cease to be important. It will always be important, just as agriculture will always be important even though it occupies a small proportion of the labour force. It may more often be sub-contracted and competitive power will increasingly depend on the capability to manage international networks in production and marketing, with the core activities of research, design and development of software and hardware, based mainly in the national 'home' base as long as their base can provide the necessary supporting scientific, technological, educational, financial and communication infrastructure.

Power in these networks will depend on a variety of information services and knowledge-based activities but not only on these. These networks are embedded in social systems where increasing inequality is now the rule and to some degree exacerbated by these developments. Both environmental and social problems are likely to become more acute in these circumstances.

Political and cultural changes may then take precedence in the complex interactions between the various sub-systems of society at all levels of the global system. Breadth, enlightenment and social solidarity are essential in the end for any innovation system. Otherwise, as Gomulka has suggested, people may reject the constant turmoil and uncertainty of contemporary competitive innovation systems and insist on the primacy of quality-of-life objectives.

NOTE

*   This paper was originally written for a research project on local systems of innovation in the Mercosur countries carried out by a network of academic institutions in Brazil, Argentina and Uruguay under the coordination of José E. Cassiolato and Helena M.M. Lastres of the Federal University of Rio de Janeiro, Brazil and sponsored by the Organisation of American States and the Brazilian National Council for Scientific and Technological Development. A longer version was published in the book *Globalização e Inovação Localizada: Experiências de Sistemas Locais no Mercosul*, Brasília, IBICT, a collection of papers of the first part of the project (Cassiolato and Lastres, 1999). An extended discussion of some of the themes in Sections 2 and 3 can now be found in Freeman and Louçã (2001).

REFERENCES

Abramovitz, M.A. (1986). 'Catching up, forging ahead and falling behind'. *Journal of Economic History* 46, 385–406.

Abramovitz, M.A. and David, P.A. (1994). 'Convergence and Deferred Catch-up: Productivity Leadership and the Waning of American Exceptionalism'. CEPR Publication No 401. Stanford University, Stanford, CA.

Adelman, I. (1963). *Theories of Economic Growth and Development.* Stanford University Press, Stanford, CA.

Albuquerque, E. (1997a). 'Domestic Patents and Developing Countries', SPRU (Brighton) and UERJ (Rio de Janeiro), Mimeo.

Albuquerque, E. (1997b). 'National Systems of Innovation and Non-OECD Countries: Notes About A Tentative Taxonomy', SPRU (Brighton) and UERJ (Rio de Janeiro), Mimeo.

Alchian, A. (1951). 'Uncertainty, evolution and economic theory'. *Journal of Political Economy* 58, 211–222.

Amsden, A. (1989). *Asia's Next Giant: South Korea and Late Industrialisation.* Oxford University Press, Oxford and New York.

Bacon, F. (1605). *The Advancement of Learning*, London.

Bairoch, P. (1993). *Economics and World History: Myths and Paradoxes.* Chicago University Press, Chicago, IL.

Bairoch, P. and Levy-Leboyer (1981). *Disparities in Economic Development Since the Industrial Revolution.* St. Martin's Press, New York.

Balogh, T. (1963). 'Comments on the paper by Tinbergen and Bos'. In: OECD, *The Residual Factor in Economic Growth.* OECD, Paris, pp. 180–187.

Baumol, W.J. (1986). 'Productivity growth, convergence and welfare: what the long run data show'. *American Economic Review* 76, 1072–1085.

Bell, M. and Cassiolato, J. (1993). 'The Access of Developing Countries and to New Technology'. Mimeo, FECAMP/UNICAMP, Campinas.

Bell, M. and Pavitt, K.L.R. (1993). 'Technological accumulation and industrial growth: contrasts between developed and developing countries'. *Industrial and Corporate Change* 2, 157–210.

Cassiolato, J. and Lastres, H. (1999) (eds.), *Globalização e Inovação Localizada: Experiências de Sistemas Locais no Mercosul*, Ibict, Brasília.

Chabot, C.N. (1995). 'Long-run productivity growth, technological change and the international economy'. M.Sc. Dissertation. SPRU, University of Sussex.

Choung, Jae-Yong (1995). 'Technological Capabilities of Korea and Taiwan: An Analysis Using Patent Statistics'. STEEP Discussion Paper, No. 26. SPRU, University of Sussex.

DeBresson, C. (1989). 'Breeding innovation clusters: a source of dynamic development'. *World Development* 17, 1–6.

DeBresson, C. and Amesse, F. (1991). 'Networks of innovators: a review and introduction to the issue'. *Research Policy* 205, 363–379.

De Long, B. (1988). 'Productivity growth, convergence and welfare: comment'. *American Economic Review* 78 (5), 1138–1154.

Denison, E.F. (1962). *The Sources of Economic Growth in the United States*. Committee for Economic Development, New York.

Denison, E.F. (1967). *Why Growth Rates Differ: Post-War Experience in Nine Western Countries*. Brookings Institution, Washington, DC.

De Tocqueville, A. (1836). *Democracy in America*. Oxford University Press, Oxford.

Dosi, G. (1988). 'Sources, procedures and microeconomic effects of innovation'. *Journal of Economic Literature* 36, 1126–1171.

Edqvist, C. (1997a). 'Institutions and organisations in the system of innovation: the state of the art'. TEMA-T, Working Paper ISSN 1101-1289. University of Linköping.

Edqvist, C. (1997b). 'Systems of innovation approaches – their emergence and characteristics', Chapter 10. In: Edqvist, C. (ed.), *Systems of Innovation, Technologies, Institutions and Organisations*. Pinter, London.

Foray, D. (1991). 'The secrets of industry are in the air: industrial cooperation and the organisational dynamics of the innovative firm'. *Research Policy* 20, 393–405.

Freeman, C. (1993). 'Technological revolutions and catching-up: ICT and the NICs'. In: Fagerberg, J., Verspagen, B. and von Tunzelmann, N. (eds.), *The Dynamics of Technology, Trade and Growth*. Edward Elgar, Aldershot, UK and Brookfield, US, pp. 198–221.

Freeman, C. (1994). 'The economics of technical change: a critical survey article'. *Cambridge Journal of Economics* 18 (5), 463–514.

Freeman, C. (1995). 'History, Co-Evolution and Economic Growth'. Working Paper-95-76. IIASA, Austria.

Freeman, C. and Louçã, F. (2001). *As Time Goes By: From the Industrial Revolutions to the Information Revolution*. Oxford University Press, Oxford.

Gerschenkron, A. (1962). *Economic Backwardness in Historical Perspective*. Harvard University Press, Cambridge, MA.

Gerschenkron, A. (1963). 'The early phases of industrialisation in Russia'. In: Rostow, W.W. (ed.), *The Economics of Take-Off into Sustained Growth*. Macmillan, London.

Gomulka, S. (1990). *The Theory of Technological Change and Economic Growth.* Routledge, London.

Grossman, G.M. and Helpman, E. (1991). *Innovation and Growth in the Global Economy.* MIT Press, Cambridge, MA.

Hobday, M. (1995). *Innovation in East Asia: the Challenge to Japan.* Edward Elgar, Aldershot, UK and Brookfield, US.

Hu, Y.S. (1992). 'Global or transnational corporations are national firms with international operations'. *Californian Management Review* 34, 107–126.

Hughes, T.P. (1982). *Networks of Power Electrification in Western Society, 1800–1930.* Johns Hopkins University Press, Baltimore, MD.

Humbert, M. (ed.) (1993). *The Impact of Globalisation on Europe's Firms and Industries.* Pinter, London.

Jacob, M. (1988). *The Cultural Meaning of the Scientific Revolution.* McGraw-Hill, New York.

Jang-Sup Shin (1995). 'Catching up, technology transfer and institutions: a Gerschenkronian study of late industrialisation from the experience of Germany, Japan and South Korea with special reference to the iron and steel industry and the semi-conductor industry'. Ph.D. Dissertation. Cambridge University, Darwin College.

Jenkins, D.T. (ed.) (1994). 'The Textile Industries, Vol. 9'. In: Church, R.A. and Wrigley, E.A. (eds.), *The Industrial Revolution in Britain.* Blackwell, Oxford.

Krugman, P. (1994). 'The myth of Asia's Miracle'. *Foreign Affairs* 71, 62–78.

Kumar, N. (1997). 'Technology Generation and Technology Transfer in the World Economy: Recent Trends and Implications for Developing Countries, 9702'. INTECH, UNU, Maastricht.

Landes, D.S. (1970). *The Unbound Prometheus: Technological and Industrial Development in Western Europe from 1750 to the Present.* Cambridge University Press, Cambridge.

List, F. (1841). *The National System of Political Economy*, English Edition. Longman, London, 1904.

Lundvall, B.-Å. (ed.) (1992). *National Systems of Innovation: Towards A Theory of Innovation and Interactive Learning.* Pinter, London.

Maddison, A. (1995). *Monitoring the World Economy, 1820–1992.* Development Centre, OECD, Paris.

Maizels, A. (1963). *Industrial Growth and World Trade.* Cambridge University Press and NIESR, Cambridge.

Mass, W. and Lazonick, W. (1990). 'The British cotton industry and international competitive advantage: the state of the debates'. Working Paper 90-06. Department of Economics, Columbia University, New York.

Mjøset, L. (1992). *The Irish Economy in a Comparative Institutional Perspective.* National Economic and Social Council, Dublin.

Needham, J. (1954). *Science and Civilisation in China.* Cambridge University Press, Cambridge.

Nelson, R.R. (1981). 'Research on productivity growth and productivity differentials: dead ends and new departures'. *Journal of Economic Literature* 19, 1029–1064.

Nelson, R.R. (ed.) (1993). *National Innovation Systems: A Comparative Analysis.* Oxford University Press, Oxford.

Ohmae, K. (1990). *The Borderless World.* Harper, New York.

Patel, P. (1995). 'Localised production of technology for global markets'. *Cambridge Journal of Economics* 19, 141–153.

Perez, C. and Soete, L. (1988). 'Catching up in technology: entry barriers and windows of opportunity'. In: Dosi, G. et al. (eds.), *Technical Change and Economic Theory*. Pinter, London, pp. 458–479.

Porter, M. (1990). *The Competitive Advantage of Nations*. Free Press, Macmillan, New York.

Reinert, E. (1997). 'The role of the state in economic growth'. Working Paper, 1997-5. S.U.M. University of Oslo.

Romer, P. (1986). 'Increasing returns and long-run growth'. *Journal of Political Economy* 94, 1002–1037.

Supple, B. (ed.) (1963). *The Experience of Economic Growth*. Random Publishing House, New York.

Verspagen, B. (1992). *Uneven Growth between Interdependent Economies: An Evolutionary View on Technology Gaps, Trade and Growth*. University of Limburg, Maastricht.

Villaschi, A.F. (1993). 'The Brazilian National System of Innovation: Opportunities and Constraints for Transforming Technological Dependency'. D.Phil. Thesis. University of London, London.

Viotti, E.B. (1997). 'Passive and Active National Learning Systems'. Ph.D. Dissertation. New School for Social Research.

Wade, R. (1990). *Governing the Market*. Princeton University Press, Princeton, NJ.

World Bank (1991). *World Development Report, 1991*. Oxford University Press, New York.

World Bank (1993). *East Asian Miracle*. World Bank, Washington, DC.

Young, A.A. (1928). 'Increasing returns and economic progress'. *Economic Journal* 38, 527–542.

7. Rise of East Asian economies and the computerisation of the world economy*

The interdependence of technical and economic influences in the diffusion of computer technology became especially clear in the 1970s and 1980s. Although engineers and scientists such as Diebold (1952) and Wiener (1949) had clearly forecast universal computerisation, it was only with the development of micro-electronics (LSI and VLSI), and above all with the advent of the micro-processor in the 1970s, that the applications of the computer in every factory and office which had been foreseen by the visionaries in the 1940s became an everyday reality. The new developments in telecommunication and computer technology meant that vast quantities of data could not only be recorded, processed and stored in fractions of a second but they could also be transmitted world-wide extremely cheaply.

Although there is some reluctance to use the expression 'revolution', most people now agree that the development of Information and Communication Technology has led to a technological transformation, variously described as the 'Information Revolution', the 'Microelectronic Revolution' or the 'Computer Revolution'. But this can mean very different things to different people (Table 7.1).

The first approach, pioneered by sociologists such as Daniel Bell (1973) and economists such as Fritz Machlup (1962) puts the emphasis on *information* activities wheresoever they are performed. Machlup's pioneering book was entitled *The Production and Distribution of Knowledge*, whilst Bell introduced the notion of the 'post-industrial society'. Sociologists and economists taking this route tend to stress the gradual growth of information-related *occupations* and of 'white collar' work compared with 'blue collar' as a long-term trend characteristic of the 20th century, and leading to what is often described as the 'Information Society'. This approach is not necessarily concerned with electronic or computer technology at all, although Machlup does have a section on electronic computing.

The second approach regards the IT 'industries' as major new branches of the economy capable of imparting an upward impetus to employment in their own right. Thus, for example, it is pointed out that as a result of its

Table 7.1   Various ways of looking at ICT

Approach to Information Technology	'Information Society'	'IT' Sector	Automation	ICT Paradigm
Main focus of approach	Knowledge occupations	Micro-electronics Computers Telecom- munications	Process innovations	Pervasive technology
Representative work or analysis	Machlup Bell Porat	Macintosh IT industry Classification systems and lobbies	Wiener Jenkins and Sherman	Diebold Imai Perez Petit
Major economic consequences	Informatisation postindustrial society	Rise of electronics industry	Unemp- loyment and deskilling as main problems	New industries, new services *and* trans- formation of old
Approach to software	Software as just another occupation	Emphasis on software *industry* and hardware suppliers	Software neglected	Emphasis on software *users*, interfaces and standards
Implications for technology policy	No special implications for technology policy	Support for electronic industry R&D	Slow down technical change	Genetic technology programmes linked to diffusion networks

extraordinary growth in the 1960s and 1970s, the electronics industry in Japan or the United States now employs more people than the automobile industry, once regarded as a typical 'engine of growth' of employment and economic activity more generally. The 'IT sector' in this approach comprises both manufacturing and service industries, whose growth may be analysed in the same way as that of vehicles, electrical machinery or garages and motor repair services, once the necessary reclassification of industrial output and employment statistics has been satisfactorily performed.

The third approach regards the debate about new technology as essentially a continuation of the 'automation' debate of the 1950s and uses expressions such as 'factory automation' or 'office automation' as though they were virtually synonymous with information technology. Those who take this view regard all the important questions as having been resolved long ago by economists such as Einzig (1957). The emphasis in this approach is almost entirely on *process* innovation.

The fourth approach, which is that of this paper, defines 'information and communication technology' both as a new range of products and services *and* as a technology, which is capable of revolutionising the processes of production and delivery of all *other* industries and services. This approach puts the emphasis on the new *technology* and not just on the *information*. The *scope* for such a new technology itself is new, having emerged in the last couple of decades as a result of the convergence of a number of inter-related advances in the field of micro-electronics, fibre optics, software engineering, communications, laser and computer technology. An approach to information activities which ignores the specific features of the new technologies is in danger of over-looking many of the economic and social aspects of these technologies including their employment and skill effects. Moreover, the third approach (automation) has an implicit bias towards job displacement, and the second (IT industries) towards job creation, but each is needed to complement the other. The fourth approach combines features of all the others and attempts to overcome their one-sidedness.

The pervasiveness of ICT is now more or less universally accepted and despite the classification problems many features of this pervasiveness can be measured. Measures of R&D show that in most leading industrial countries electronic and telecommunication R&D account for between 20 and 30 per cent of total manufacturing and services R&D. But these measures exclude most software applications development. Canada was the first country to attempt systematic measurement of this software R&D performed outside R&D Labs. It amounted to 23 per cent of total industrial R&D in Canada in 1988. This means that in the leading industrial countries electronics plus software development probably accounts for about half of all new R&D in industry. In Korea and Japan it probably accounts for over half. Electronics alone is over 40 per cent in Korea. This is an extraordinarily high concentration of R&D activities and fully justifies the description of ICT as a technological revolution. Figures of investment tell a similar story but a satisfactory series of comparable ICT investment statistics does not yet exist.

These examples show that the statistics are still very unsatisfactory. However, slowly improvements are being made and one of the areas where advances have come is in international trade statistics. These show (Table 7.2) that ICT goods, classified by GATT as 'office machinery' and 'telecommunication equipment' are by far the fastest growing category in

Table 7.2   Rates of growth of exports in 1980–1989

ALL PRIMARY COMMODITIES	2
of which	
Food	3
Raw Materials	4
Ores, Minerals	4
Fuels	−5
ALL MANUFACTURES	8
of which	
Iron and Steel	4
Textiles	6
Chemicals	7
Clothing	10
Machinery and Transport	8
of which	
ICT Goods	13

Source: GATT (1990).

international trade. They account already for a quarter of all exports of manufactures from Japan and more than a quarter for several other East Asian countries.

ICT not only affects every industry and service but also every *function* within each industry i.e. R&D, Design, Production, Marketing, Transport and general administration. It is *systemation* rather than automation, integrating the various previously separate Departments and functions (Table 7.3). In *Design and Development* every industry now depends on computers. This is not just a question of CAD, although this is of great and growing importance, especially in complex products, such as aircraft, large buildings, ships and chemical plants, as well as the products of the electronics industry itself. It is also a question of the accuracy, speed and volume of all kinds of calculations and access to data banks at all stages of the research and development process. The development of a new drug depends increasingly on super-computers and even simple operations such as scanning of scientific abstracts are now heavily computerised. Moreover, the CAD systems of component and assembly firms are increasingly linked together and both are linked to data banks on the properties of new and old materials. Roy Rothwell (1991) has described this process as the 'electronification of design' and cites the Boeing 777 with its network of inter-linked computers as a leading example of the transformation of the R&D process. The new developments in telecommunications also mean that research laboratories, design offices, and manufacturing plants in different locations can

Table 7.3   Change of techno economic paradigm

'Fordist' Old	ICT New
Energy-intensive	Information Intensive
Design and engineering in 'drawing' offices	Computer-aided designs
Sequential design and production	Concurrent engineering
Standardised	Customised
Rather stable product mix	Rapid changes in product mix
Dedicated plant and equipment	Flexible production systems
Automation	Systemation
Single firm	Networks
Hierarchical structures	Flat horizontal structures
Departmental	Integrated
Product with service	Service with products
Centralisation	Distributed intelligence
Specialized skills	Multi-skilling
Government control and sometimes ownership	Government information, coordination and regulation
'Planning'	'Vision'

Source: Adapted from Perez (1990).

exchange data, designs and calculations, divide and coordinate tasks and tests in a matter of seconds. But as Rothwell is careful to point out the organisational and managerial capability to use such systems efficiently varies a great deal by firm, by industry and by country.

The emphasis on shorter lead-times and speeding up design and development is probably strongest in the electronic industry itself because of the extremely rapid succession of new generations of integrated circuits and related products. It is important too in other industries which use electronic 'black boxes' such as machinery and instruments and in industries such as clothing and automobiles when fashion and speed to market for new models can play a big role. It was always important in military design and development and to a lesser extent in the construction industry. Whilst shortening of lead times is certainly not an entirely new feature of R&D management (see for example, Freeman, 1962 for an example in mining machinery), it has received far greater attention with the diffusion of the ICT techno-economic paradigm. It is closely associated with wider product range, more flexible production systems and customisation and has been facilitated by a whole number of techniques in addition to CAD, such as fast prototyping and total quality control at all stages of development.

Speed to market and integration of design and *production* have also been greatly facilitated by computerisation. Many observers have commented on Japanese techniques of integrating R&D, production and marketing. Baba (1985) spoke of using 'the factory as laboratory' Takeuchi and Nonaka (1986) spoke of 'playing rugby' instead of 'running relay races'. The MIT world vehicle project showed in some detail how design and production engineering were integrated to generate shorter lead times in the automobiles industry (Graves, 1991). It must be emphasised that not all of these management techniques depended on computerisation or other technical innovations. 'Lean production systems' preceded computerisation as did other management innovations associated with the 'Toyota-Ohno' system.

Much more directly related to widespread computerisation are of course flexible production systems. It is because of this 'new style of manufacturing' that diffusion research can no longer concentrate, as in the 1960s, exclusively on discrete products but must take account of system changes as well. For this reason, there is now a proliferation of studies on the diffusion of 'computer-integrated manufacturing', 'flexible manufacturing systems', 'computer-aided manufacturing', 'computer-aided design' and so forth (see, for example, Arcangeli et al., 1991; Ayres, 1991).

These studies of diffusion, whether they are of individual products or of networks and systems point unanimously to the conclusion that there are few 'standard' solutions in the machine-building and other metal-working industries. Configurations of robots, machine-tools, guided vehicles and other equipment vary enormously and so too does the programming and organisation of the production process. All are path dependent and related to the locally available skills, training systems, managers, industrial relations systems and so forth. Fleck's (1983, 1988, 1993) work on robotics in particular has shown that the adaptation of robot design to local situations and needs has been one of the strong points of the relatively successful diffusion in Japan. He coined the expressions 'Innofusion' and 'diffusation' to characterise the dependence of diffusion on site-specific incremental innovations (Fleck, 1988).

In *flow production* industries, such as chemicals, oil refining, food and drink, computerisation mainly takes the form of process control instrumentation linked to computers. Many possibilities exist for economies in materials and energy consumption as well as in quality control and improvement. But again the efficient introduction of computers and related instruments and equipment depends very much on local skills, local resources, local special features of plant design and so forth.

The integration of functions within the firm is no less relevant to *marketing* than to production and design. Speed of response to market changes and reduction of stocks at various points in the distribution chain are typical of the competitive advantages achieved by firms like IKEA and Benetton, which have computerised warehousing and distribution systems, linked to retail outlets downstream and suppliers upstream. The involvement of future *users* of new products and services is nowhere more important than in the introduction of computerised systems and new software as a whole number of PICT projects have amply confirmed (Coombs et al., 1991; Low and Woolgar, 1991; Fleck, 1993; Quintas, 1994).

All of these conclusions apply *a fortliori* to service industries as well as to service functions within manufacturing industries. A particularly important feature of the ICT revolution is the scale of technical and organisational change in service activities, especially those like financial services which are mainly concerned with the storage, analysis, processing and transmission of vast quantities of information. The scale of investment in these industries is now greater than that in most manufacturing industries and (usually for the first time) R&D activities are beginning to be significant, mainly in the development of new software and associated services. Service industry R&D in the United States has increased from less than 2 per cent in the 1960s to nearly 10 per cent of total business R&D in 1990 and it is now 9 per cent in the EC. These figures almost certainly underestimate service R&D because of the problem of software R&D, already referred to. These changes within service industries have led Barras (1986, 1990) to re-define the relationship between hardware suppliers and service industries as the latter increasingly make their own innovations and cease to be so dependent on hardware suppliers, as they were with earlier waves of technical change.

The scale of R&D in the new applications of ICT, the extraordinary growth of the software industry and related business services, the scale of investment in computerised equipment and in the telecommunication infrastructure, the rapid growth of the industries supplying ICT products and services and the use of computers within every function in every industry have led some observers, such as Peter Drucker to characterise the ICT Revolution as a change in the economy comparable to the Industrial Revolution itself and going beyond all previous waves of technical change.

Certainly, it can be argued that the extent and scale of the technical and organisational changes appear to go beyond those associated with electrification a century ago or with diffusion of the energy-intensive Fordist mass production system half a century ago. And yet the growth of the world economy has slowed down drastically compared with what now appears as the 'Golden Age' of economic growth in the 1950s and 1960s.

The complexity of the transition from the Fordist techno-economic paradigm to the ICT paradigm may well explain part of the slow-down in

Table 7.4   Labour productivity in OECD countries business sector 1960–1990 (percentage change)

	1950–1973	1973–1979	1979–1990
Belgium	5.2	2.8	2.4
Canada	2.8	1.5	1.2
Denmark	4.3	2.6	2.3
France	5.4	3.0	2.7
FR Germany	4.5	3.1	1.6
Italy	6.3	3.0	2.0
Japan	8.6	2.9	3.0
Netherlands	4.8	2.8	1.5
Spain	6.0	3.3	3.0
Sweden	4.1	1.5	1.5
UK	3.6	1.6	2.1
USA	2.2	0.0	0.5

Source: OECD (1992).

productivity growth rates in almost all leading industrial countries in the 1970s and 1980s (Table 7.4).

There were, of course, other contributory causes, notably the exhaustion of the post-war 'catching-up' gains in labour productivity as Japan and many European countries overtook the United States. The productivity gaps and technology 'gaps' which had been such a prominent feature of economic analysis and policy-making in the OECD in the 1950s and 1960s had largely disappeared in the 1970s. As Europe, Japan and the USA all approached the world technological frontier, the very rapid productivity gains of the 1960s could apparently now only be achieved in the NICs or other former Third World countries. Nevertheless, there were very striking differences in productivity growth in the 1980s between the Latin American NICs and the East Asian NICs and although *all* OECD countries experienced a slow-down in productivity growth, uneven development remained a feature of the world economy (Dosi and Freeman, 1992) aggravated by the collapse of the socialist economies of Eastern Europe, contrasted with the high growth performance of Communist China. This section of the paper will endeavour to relate some of these differences to relative success and failure in the diffusion of the new ICT paradigm.

Carlota Perez (1983, 1990) argued that slow-down would result from 'mis-match' between the old institutional framework and the new technology. This can certainly be observed in many cases, but as both she and Johnson (1992) have stressed, institutions are not only sources of inertia ('institutional drag') but also facilitators of change. Whilst some industries and countries may be 'locked in' to old ways of doing things, others may initiate reforms which enable them to produce and to use ICT products and services very widely and efficiently.

Although PICT research is highly relevant to the debate on the so-called 'Solow Paradox' (computers everywhere but where are the productivity gains?), the programme has not yet made a commensurate contribution to this debate. It has been argued already that ICT is such a pervasive technology that it has changed methods of design, development, production, administration, distribution and management in virtually every sector of the economy. Since the technology embodies a large cluster of radical innovations as well as numerous incremental innovations, this means that many institutional changes are associated with its diffusion (as briefly summarised in Table 7.3).

The capability to initiate such institutional changes is very uneven in different parts of the world economy and so too is their efficient implementation. In part this is a matter of the scale and nature of the institutional heritage from the past (path dependence). An obvious example is the educational and training system. As Diebold insisted already in 1952, computerisation of production systems is possible only when accompanied by a vast transformation of the skill profile of the work force. As against those who stressed unemployment and de-skilling as the probable consequence of computerisation, he stressed on the contrary the need for creative skills in the re-design of the entire capital stock and in the maintenance of this new capital and argued that this would require the breaking down of departmental and disciplinary barriers within organisations and completely new forms of organisation which facilitated horizontal communication and original initiatives at all levels of the work force.

On the whole, experience has vindicated his standpoint. Computerisation does indeed demand a huge number of new skilled people as well as the retraining and re-skilling of most others. Every computer requires software so that there has been a persistent shortage of software engineers and programmers in almost every industrial country for decades. Only in the most recent recession of the 1990s are there some indications that this shortage has abated at least for the less skilled software occupations. Despite numerous innovations in software design and engineering there has been a permanent software crisis and shortage of high quality software designers. There are innumerable examples of system failures because of software problems (Brady, 1986; Brady and Quintas, 1991; Quintas, 1994). Spectacular failures have occurred not only with computer integrated manufacturing systems (CIM) but also in banks, in weapon systems, in government departments, in telecommunication networks and in distribution.

This means that those countries which had an educational and training system capable of a rapid and effective response to these huge demands for new skills had a big comparative advantage in the efficient implementation of ICT. Countries which had considerable inertia and rigidity in these systems, on the other hand were placed at a disadvantage and experienced relative stagnation in their production systems and competitive strength. Much depended too on management style, on industrial relations and structure of the software industry.

One solution to the software problem is of course to use standard packaged software for standard functions in areas such as accountancy, payroll, stock control and so forth. The US software industry has excelled in the development and marketing of these standard packages world-wide, aided by the early US lead, the English language predominance in the computer industry and, until recently, some proprietary standards.

However, many software applications involve unique features so that an organisation which relied entirely on standard packages would be relatively limited in its capacity to initiate changes in its design, production and marketing systems. It would also be limited in its response to external changes in hardware and software systems. Another solution is to use consultancy services with software capability or the services of the hardware suppliers themselves. It is notable that the big hardware suppliers have been making intensive efforts to extend their service consultancy business and their software activities generally in response to the extraordinarily rapid growth of these activities, which has been for more rapid than that of the hardware industry. The market capitalisation of Microsoft early in 1993 was equal to that of Intel or IBM, and whereas IBM's mainframe hardware business is declining, its service income is growing.

There can be no doubt that consultancy services are an extremely important feature of the new techno-economic paradigm and it is significant that recent studies of diffusion have drawn attention to their enhanced role. Whereas previously the pattern of diffusion was attributed primarily to the characteristics and proximity (cultural or geographic) of the adopter population (epidemic models) or to the sales push of suppliers, now the role of third parties, whether public agencies or private consultancies, is increasingly stressed (see e.g. Midgley et al., 1992). Often they are capable of advising their clients on both technical and managerial problems and it is notable that consultants who were previously almost entirely concerned with technical and engineering problems have moved increasingly into management consultancy and systems integration. This reflects the intense interdependence of technical and organisational problems in this paradigm change. The availability and efficiency of consultancy services varies very much in different countries, despite their globalisation.

Finally, however, the efficiency and innovative capability of any firm will depend not only on its ability to use standard packages and the services of consultants but also on its own in-house capacity for R&D, design and software development. Comparisons of the Japanese and US software industries suggest that the main *structural* difference lies in the relatively greater size of the in-house software teams in Japanese firms, whereas the independent software houses and consultants are the great strength of the US industry, both in packaged and customised software (Baba et al., 1993).

Maintenance is a key issue in software activities. Some studies have suggested that a high proportion of software designers and programmers are now occupied with maintenance. However, *physical* deterioration and disrepair is not a problem with software as it is with buildings or machinery. It has even been suggested that the software industry could decline drastically once most users have installed reasonably efficient systems, since the software itself is relatively indestructible. This brings out the point that the industry depends on *permanent innovation*. Software 'maintenance' is not in fact maintenance in the old sense at all but is a new type of maintenance involving continuous adaptation both to changes in the user organisation and to changes in the external environment, including patching together new and older hardware and software systems, as well as networking relationships. As the research at all PICT centres has shown, this is an extremely creative function and probably should be described as 'innovative maintenance' or some such expression. It is true of course that electromechanical maintenance can also be creative and used for continuous incremental innovation and those firms and countries where this has already been recognised, will probably have a comparative advantage. Once again, Diebold (1952) anticipated this key role of the skilled creative maintenance function.

These two examples of education and training and of software services have served to bring out the fundamental point that national (and regional) systems vary a great deal. Economists and sociologists concerned with technical change have been increasingly preoccupied with these differences, using the expression 'national systems of innovation' (Lundvall, 1992; Nelson, 1988, 1993; Mjøset, 1992) to describe all those institutions which affect the innovative performance of a national economy.

Many improvements to *products* and to services came from interaction with the market and with related networking firms, such as sub-contractors, suppliers of materials and services (see especially Lundvall, 1985, 1988, 1992; Sako, 1992). Formal R&D was usually decisive in its contribution to *radical* innovations but it was no longer possible to ignore the many other contributions to, and influences upon the process of technical change at the level of firms and industries. Networking has always been a feature of manufacturing under capitalism but its role has been greatly enhanced by ICT with computerised networks playing a rapidly growing part. National and *regional* aspects of networking were shown to be of great and continuing importance despite the availability of global telecommunication networks.

Not only are inter-firm and market-production relationships of critical importance, but the external *linkages* within the narrower professional science-technology system are also decisive for innovative success with radical innovations. Finally, research on diffusion has revealed more and more that the *systemic* aspects of innovation are increasingly influential in determining both the rate of diffusion and the productivity gains associated with any specific diffusion process (see especially Carlsson and Jacobsson, 1993). As information and communication technology diffused through the world economy in the 1970s and 1980s, all these systemic aspects of innovation assumed greater and greater importance.

At the *international* level the innovation systems of two countries made a very powerful impression in the 1980s both on policy-makers and on researchers: the extraordinary success of first Japan and then South Korea in technological and economic catch-up. At first in the 1950s and 1960s the Japanese success was often simply attributed to copying, imitating and importing foreign technology and the statistics of the so-called 'technological balance of payments' were often cited to support this view. They showed a huge deficit in Japanese transactions for licensing and know-how imports and exports and a correspondingly large surplus for the United States. It soon became evident, however, as Japanese products and processes began to out-perform American and European products and processes in more and more industries and as Japanese *income* from technology payments rose, that this simplistic explanation was no longer sufficient. Japanese industrial R&D expenditures as a proportion of civil industrial net output surpassed those of the United States in the 1970s and total civil R&D as a fraction of GNP surpassed USA in the 1980s. The Japanese performance was now often explained more in terms of R&D-intensity, especially as Japanese R&D was highly concentrated in the fastest growing civil industries, such as electronics. Patent statistics showed that the leading Japanese electronic firms outstripped American and European firms not just in domestic patenting but in patents taken out in the United States (Patel and Pavitt, 1991; Freeman, 1987). Japanese electronic firms came to occupy the leading positions in patenting in the USA displacing the erstwhile leaders, such as IBM and GE (Figures 7.1 and 7.2).

However, although these rough measures of research and inventive activity certainly did indicate the huge increase in Japanese scientific and technical activities, they did not in themselves explain how these activities led

Systems of innovation

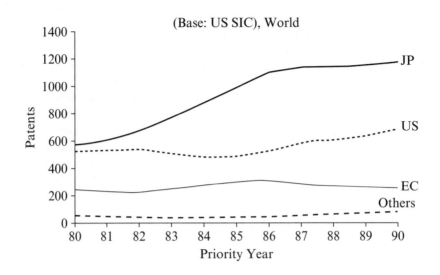

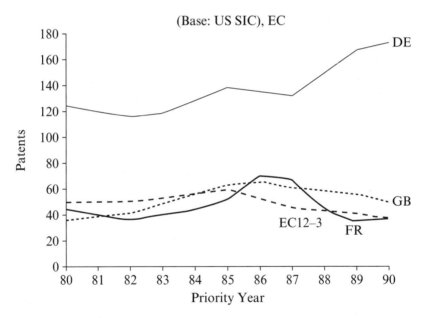

Source: Grupp and Soete (1993).

Figure 7.1 Office and data processing machines triad patents

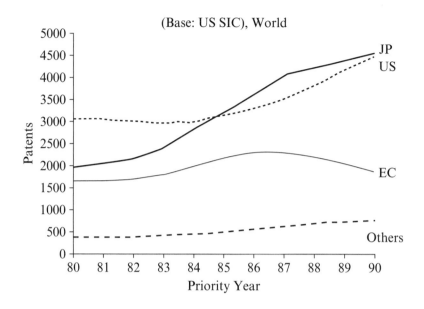

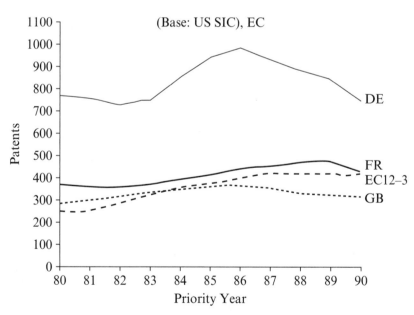

Source: Grupp and Soete (1993).

Figure 7.2 Semiconductors, telecommunications triad patents

to higher quality of new products and processes (Grupp and Hofmeyer, 1986; Womack et al., 1990); to shorter lead times (Graves, 1991; Mansfield, 1988) and to more rapid and efficient diffusion of some ICT technologies such as robotics (Fleck, 1983, 1988, 1993) and CNC. Moreover, the contrasting example of the (then) Soviet Union and other East European countries showed that simply to commit greater resources to R&D did not in itself guarantee successul innovation, diffusion and productivity gains It was obvious from much research that *qualitative* factors affecting the national and regional systems had to be taken into account as well as the purely *quantitative* indicators. The *qualitative* features of the Japanese national system of innovation, and increasingly now of other East Asian countries, are the main explanation of their relative success in diffusion of ICT.

NOTE

*   It has been a very great pleasure for me to came to know Masaaki Hirooka during the last decade. After a distinguished career as a research scientist and manager in industry, he has used his wealth of experience to make a major contribution to the research on economics of innovation. I have learnt a great deal from him and I have especially admired the papers which he gave to the 4th and 5th Conferences of the Schumpeter Society. I am therefore very happy to contribute this paper to the special issue of the *Journal of Economics and Business Administration* in his honour.

REFERENCES

Arcangeli, F., Dosi, G. and Moggi, M. (1991), 'Patterns of diffusion of electronics technologies: an international comparison', *Research Policy*, **20**, 6, 515–31.

Ayres, R.V. (1991), 'Information, computers, computer-integrated-manufacturing and productivity' in OECD (ed.) *Technology and Productivity*, Paris: OECD, 319–60.

Baba, Y. (1985), 'Japanese colour TV firms: decision-making from the 1950s to the 1990s: oligopolistic corporate strategy in the age of micro-electronics', Unpublished D.Phil. Dissertation, University of Sussex.

Baba, Y., Takai, S. and Mizutu, Y. (1993), 'The evolution of the software industry in Japan: a comprehensive analysis', RACE, University of Tokyo.

Barras, R. (1986), 'Toward a theory of innovation in services', *Research Policy*, **15**, 4, 161–73.

Barras, R. (1990), 'Interactive innovation in financial and business services: the vanguard of the service revolution', *Research Policy*, **19**, 3, 215–237.

Bell, D. (1973), *The Coming of Post-Industrial Society: A venture in social forecasting*, Harmondsworth: Penguin.

Brady, T. (1986), *New Technology and Skills in British Industry*, Skills Series 5, London: Manpower Services Commission.

Brady, T. and Quintas, P. (1991), 'Computer Software: The IT Constraint', in C. Freeman, M. Sharp and W. Walker (eds) *Technology and the Future of Europe: Global competition and the environment in the 1990s*, London: Pinter Publishers, 117–37.

Carlsson, B. and Jacobsson, S. (1993), 'Technological systems and economic performance: the diffusion of factory automation in Sweden', in D. Foray, and C. Freeman (eds) *Technology and the Wealth of Nations*, London: Pinter Publishers.

Coombs, R., Knights, D. and Willmott, H. (1991), 'Culture, control and competition: towards a framework for the study of Information Technology in organisations', *CROMTEC Working Paper No. 3*, Manchester: University of Manchester Institute of Science and Technology.

Diebold, J. (1952) *Automation: The advent of the automatic factory*, New York: Van Nostrand.

Dosi, G. and Freeman, C. (1992), 'The diversity of development patterns: on the processes of catching up, forging ahead and falling behind', paper prepared for the International Economics Association Meeting, Ravenna, 1–3 October.

Einzig, P. (1957), *The Economic Consequences of Automation,* London: Secker and Warburg.

Fleck, J. (1983), 'Robots in manufacturing organisations', in G. Winch (ed.) *Information Technology in Manufacturing Processes*, London: Rossendale, 44–56.

Fleck, J. (1988), 'Innofusion or diffusation? The nature of technological development in robotics', Edinburgh PICT, Working Paper Series, The University of Edinburgh.

Fleck, J. (1993), 'Configurations: crystallising contingency', *Journal of Human Factors in Manufacturing*, **3**, 1, 15–36.

Freeman, C. (1962), 'Research and development: a comparison between British and American industry', *National Institute Economic Review*, **20**, 21–39.

Freeman, C. (1987), *Technology Policy and Economic Performance: Lessons from Japan*, London: Frances Pinter.

GATT (1990), *International Trade 89–90*, Il, Geneva: GATT.

Graves, A. (1991), 'International competitiveness and technological development in the world automobile industry', Unpublished D.Phil. Dissertation, Science Policy Research Unit, University of Sussex.

Grupp, H. and Hofmeyer, O. (1986), 'A technometric model for the assessment of technological standards and their application to selected technology comparisons', *Technological Forecasting and Social Change*, **30**, 123–37.

Grupp, H. and Soete, L. (1993), 'Analysis of the dynamic relationship between technical and economic performances in information and telecommunication sectors', Final Report in Fulfilment of Project No. 8862 for DGXIII of the European Commission.

Johnson, B. (1992), 'Institutional learning', in B-Å Lundvall (ed.) *National Systems of Innovation*, London: Pinter Publishers.

Low, J. and Woolgar, S. (eds) (1991), 'Do users get what they want? *CRICT Discussion Paper 30*, Brunel University, March.

Lundvall, B-Å. (1985), 'Product innovation and user-producer interaction', *Industrial Development Research Series 31*, Aalborg: Aulborg University Press.

Lundvall, B-Å. (1988), 'Innovation is an interactive process: from user-producer interaction to the national system of innovation', in G. Dosi, C. Freeman, R. Nelson, G. Silverberg and L. Soete (eds) *Technical Change and Economic Theory*, London: Pinter Publishers, 349–69.

Lundvall, B-Å. (ed.) (1992), *National Systems of Innovation: Towards a theory of innovation and interactive learning*, London: Pinter Publishers.

Machlup, F. (1962), *The Production and Distribution of Knowledge in the United States*, Princeton, NJ: Princeton University Press.

Mansfield, E. (1988), 'Industrial innovation in Japan and in the United States', *Science*, 241, 1760–61.

Midgley, D.F., Morrison, P.D. and Roberts, J.H. (1992), 'The effect of network structure in industrial diffusion processes', *Research Policy*, 21, 6, 533–52.

Mjøset, L. (1992), *The Irish Economy in a Comparative Institutional Perspective*, Dublin: National Economic and Social Council.

Nelson, R. (1988), 'Institutions supporting technical change in the United States', in G. Dosi, C. Freeman, R. Nelson, G. Silverberg and L. Soete (eds) *Technical Change and Economic Theory*, London: Pinter Publishers.

Nelson, R. (1993) (ed.) *National Innovations System*, Oxford: Oxford University Press.

OECD (1992), *Economic Outlook*, Paris: OECD.

Patel, P. and Pavitt, K. (1991) 'Large firms in the production of the world's technology: an important case of "Non-Globalisation"', *Journal of International Business Studies*, 22, 1, 1–21.

Perez, C. (1983), 'Structural change and the assimilation of new technologies in the economic and social system', *Futures*, 13, 3, 441–63.

Perez, C. (1990), 'Technical change, competitive re-structuring and institutional reform in developing countries', *World Bank Strategie Planning and Review*, Discussion Paper No. 4, Washington, DC: World Bank.

Quintas, P. (1994), 'Pathes of innovation in software and systems development practice', in R. Mansell (ed.), *Emerging Patterns of Control: The management of information and communication technologies*, London: Aslib.

Rothwell, R. (1991), 'External networking and innovation in small and medium-sized manufacturing firms in Europe', *Technovation*, 11, 2, 93–112.

Sako, M. (1992), *Contracts, Prices and Trust: How the Japanese and British manage their sub-contracting relationships*, Oxford: Oxford University Press.

Takeuchi, H. and Nonaka, I. (1986), 'The new product development game', *Harvard Business Review*, 61, 1, 137–46.

Wiener, N. (1949), *The Human Use of Human Beings: A cybernetics approach*. New York: Houghton Mifflin.

Womack, J., Jones, D. and Roos, D. (1990), *The Machine that Changed the World*, New York: Rawson Associates.

PICT: 'Programme on Information and Communication Technology' A British Research Programme Supported by the Economic and Social Research Council (ESRC)

8.   A hard landing for the 'new economy'? Information technology and the United States national system of innovation*

1.   INTRODUCTION

This paper deals with a topic, which has not so far featured in the recent efflorescence of literature on national systems of innovation and might be considered as rather remote from its main direction, but is certainly of the greatest interest to all observers of the evolution of the global economy. That topic is the possibility of a 'hard landing' for the US economy and the relevance of information technology to that possibility. That such a hard landing would have major consequences for all innovation systems, whether national, regional, local or sectoral, can hardly be doubted. That this possibility is related to the recent evolution of the United States national system of innovation is more controversial, but is the central thesis of this paper.

Since the publication of two seminal books on National Systems of Innovation in the early 1990s (Lundvall, 1992, Nelson, 1993), many researchers have contributed to a rapidly growing body of knowledge in this field. Part of this work followed the tradition of the Nelson book in analysing specific national systems in individual countries or comparisons between several countries (for example, Niosi's (2000) book on the Canadian national system, or Poh-Kam Wong's (1999) comparison of Korea, Taiwan and Singapore). Another part of the literature has followed more in the direction pioneered by Lundvall and his colleagues, i.e. investigation of the concept itself and development of the theory of national systems (for example, the work of Andersen, 1999). Finally, a major new development has been a flowering of research on local regional and sectoral systems of innovation (see for example, Cassiolato et al., 2003). Of course, all of these streams of research overlap and intermingle, reflecting the general acceptance of the main thesis of the Lundvall book – that systems of innovations should be considered not purely in the *narrow* sense of R&D institutions but in the *broad* context of the embeddedness of innovation systems in the wider social and economic system (Edquist and McKelvey, 2000).

In this latter sense, work on systems of innovation is actually not different from work on political economy more generally. List's (1841) book on *The National System of Political Economy* could just as well have been entitled 'The National System of Innovation' since it deals with almost all the main features of the modern NSI literature. The reason that it is necessary today to emphasise *innovation* in studies of national economies (NSI), regional economies (RSI), sectoral systems (SSI) and the global system itself is not that innovation ever ceased to be a crucial feature of all these systems, but that mainstream economic theories and models had ceased to recognise this centrality and neglected the study of technical change and innovation, whilst paying lip-service to them. If evolutionary economics is successful in one of its main objectives – to restore innovation to its rightful place in the study of political economy – then this insistence may no longer be necessary.

The NSI literature has dealt mainly with the *positive* role of innovative performance in economic development and growth. In my opinion, it has quite correctly identified and described those characteristics of NSI, RSI and SSI, which appeared to influence successful performance and occasionally also those features, which inhibited or delayed such success. This was a valuable contribution of appreciative theory and empirical research to the understanding of economic growth, as well as to policy-making, as the qualitative changes which were investigated could not emerge from purely quantitative analysis or models. Many of these studies were historical in nature, dealing with possible explanations of prolonged periods of success of particular countries, industries or firms. A good recent example is the study by Balaguer (2000) of the sectoral system of innovation in the Taiwanese petrochemical industry, which gives a convincing explanation of the extraordinary success of this industry over several decades, despite the absence in Taiwan of any natural raw material endowment. However, such studies of long-term success, whether of NSI, RSI or SSI certainly do not preclude the possibility of cyclical downturns or even of longer periods of decline, following a prolonged period of success. All firms, industries and economies are vulnerable to the effects of crises, which may occur elsewhere in the global system and may have no direct connection with their own innovative activities. The liberalisation of capital movements, which has occurred in the last quarter of the twentieth century, and the abandonment of centralised planning in the former USSR and its allies, have rendered almost every country more vulnerable to the instability and shocks, which can be propagated throughout the system, however well local innovation systems may have been performing in a narrower sphere.

This point is sometimes contradicted by proponents of the view that more perfect markets will be more stable markets and that information technology in itself will improve the perfectibility of markets. The next section of this paper is devoted to a brief discussion of this proposition. It is followed by a third section, which argues that even though uncertainty inevitably remains a characteristic of the *individual* project or investment, a somewhat greater degree of predictability and stability accompanies the *aggregate* growth of sectoral systems, including those based on Information and Communication Technology (ICT). The possibility that ICT will impart a long-lasting upward thrust to the performance of the US economy and render it less vulnerable to cyclical phenomena (the so-called 'New Paradigm' or 'New Economy' theories) is discussed in Section 4 and Section 5. Section 4 discusses some of the special features of the United States NSI, which have distinguished it from the NSI of other countries and which might plausibly be supposed to render the US economy both more competitive and more stable. Section 5, however, whilst not underestimating the upward thrust from ICT and the capability of US firms and universities in the development and use of ICT, nevertheless argues that the long-term productivity performance of the US economy outside the ICT core industries themselves, does not yet provide convincing evidence for the beneficent economy-wide effects of ICT. American economists disagree about this question and the disputes may only be resolved by the unfolding events. However, past history does provide some suggestive evidence, which, although certainly not conclusive, does provide some support for a more sceptical view of the 'new economy'. Section 6 discusses the evidence of the 1920s boom based on mass production of the automobile, which was greeted at the time with as much enthusiasm as the ICT 'new paradigm' today, but ended in the Great Depression of the 1930s. It does not follow of course that the same thing will happen again, there are big differences, as well as some similarities between the two US booms. But the similarities provide some grounds for a sceptical view of the Internet euphoria. The international economy, briefly discussed in Section 7, gives some further grounds for taking seriously the possibility of a hard landing.

2. INFORMATION, UNCERTAINTY AND INNOVATION

It is sometimes suggested or implied that more perfect information about market prices is in itself a stabilising influence on economic behaviour. According to this view, modern communication technology, by making available accurate and comprehensive information about *prices* in world markets with extraordinary speed, helps to stabilise these markets and the activities, which they govern. Even in the case of foreign exchange markets, which are the kind of example often quoted, and where information technology is universally deployed, it seems dubious that it has any stabilising effects. In fact, from the experience of the 1990s, a strong case could be made for the opposite proposition, especially in the case of the East Asian crisis.

One of the fallacies, which underlie the simplistic view of information technology and its supposed role in providing more perfect information to all agents in various markets, is a confusion between *information* and *knowledge*. Indeed, the two terms were often used interchangeably. *Information* about *price* movements does not in itself convey *understanding* of the market's behaviour, essential though this information may be to the development of such understanding. Still less does information in itself confer the power to predict future movements or changes in the markets.

There is nothing in modern ICT, which eliminates uncertainty in relation to *investment* behaviour, the most important source of instability in capitalist economies. The remarks of Keynes (1936, p. 250) about expeditions to the South Pole remain as true today as when he first wrote them. Perhaps his famous comments actually should be revised slightly with respect to Antarctic exploration, although *not* with respect to innovative investment in the economy. Expeditions to the South Pole *have* become less risky and have almost become routine. Not so investments in a Dot.Com company. It is not possible to make accurate calculations of the future rate of return to an Internet investment project stretching into the future, however good the information in the company prospectus. There is an irreducible uncertainty about future political, economic and market developments, which affects any such calculations. So far from reducing that uncertainty, technological innovations may actually *increase* it, since they add to the dimensions of general business uncertainty, the dimension of technological uncertainty. In this respect, ICT is no different from earlier waves of technical change. Some exaggerated expectations about the future of radical new technologies are just as inevitable as the collapse of those expectations.

Information technology is only the latest one in a succession of pervasive new technologies, which have transformed the world economy and which Schumpeter designated as 'successive industrial revolutions' or Kondratiev waves (Table 8.1). Even after public demonstrations of highly successful applications of a radical new technology, this uncertainty remains and 'animal spirits' are still essential for the individual firm, even though in the *aggregate*, the future of the technology is bright.

There could scarcely be a more striking confirmation of this proposition than the volatility of the stock markets in relation to the firms embarking on Internet-related investment. Some firms have become an overnight

Table 8.1 Condensed summary of the Kondratiev waves

Constellation of technical and organisational innovations	Examples of highly visible, technically successful and profitable innovations	'Carrier' branch and other leading branches of the economy	Core input and other key inputs	Transport and communication infrastructure	Managerial and organisational changes	Approximate timing of the 'upswing' (boom) / 'downswing' (crisis of adjustment)
Water-powered mechanisation of industry	Arkwright's Cromford Mill (1771) Henry Cort's 'Puddling' process (1784)	Cotton spinning, iron products, water wheels, bleach	Iron, raw cotton, coal	Canals, turnpike roads, sailing ships	Factory systems. entrepreneurs, partnerships	1780s–1815 1815–1848
Steam-powered mechanisation of industry and transport	Liverpool to Manchester Railway (1831) Brunel's 'Great Western' Atlantic Steamship (1838)	Railways and railway equipment, steam engines, machine tools, alkali industry	Iron, coal	Railways, telegraph, steam ships	Joint stock companies, sub-contracting to responsible craft workers	1848–1873 1873–1895
Electrification of industry, transport and the home	Carnegie's Bessemer Steel Rail Plant (1875) Edison's Pearl St.	Electrical equipment, heavy engineering, heavy chemicals, steel products	Steel, copper, metal alloys	Steel railways, steel ships, telephone	Specialised professional management systems, 'Taylorism', giant	1895–1918 1918–1940

Table 8.1 (continued)

Constellation of technical and organisational innovations	Examples of highly visible, technically successful and profitable innovations	'Carrier' branch and other leading branches of the economy	Core input and other key inputs	Transport and communication infrastructure	Managerial and organisational changes	Approximate timing of the 'upswing' (boom) / 'downswing' (crisis of adjustment)
	New York Electric Power Station (1882)				firms	
Motorization of transport, civil economy and war	Ford's Highland Park Assembly Line (1913) Burton process for cracking heavy oil (1913)	Automobiles, trucks, tractors, tanks, diesel engines, aircraft, refineries	Oil, gas, synthetic materials	Radio, motorways, airports, airlines	Mass production and consumption, 'Fordism', hierarchies	1941–1973 / 1973–
Computerisation of entire economy	IBM 1401 and 360 Series (1960s) Intel micro-processor (1972)	Computers, software, telecommunication equipment, biotechnology	'Chips' (integrated circuits)	'Information Highways' (Internet)	Networks; internal, local and global	??

Source: Freeman and Louçã (2001).

'success' worth billions of dollars before they have actually sold a single item, only to sink a few months later with scarcely a trace. Bubbles, euphoria and panics have been characteristic phenomena of most new technologies in the early stages of their diffusion and ICT is no different in this respect. Early demonstrations of their immense potential for the future and their technical efficiency (Table 8.1) lead to exaggerated expectations of the profits to be made in a variety of applications, all of which have to be explored and tested. Consequently, with a very pervasive technology, such as those listed in Table 8.1, this period of turbulence may last several decades before being followed by a period of greater stability, when the limitations, as well as the achievements of the new technology have become more apparent.

At the level of the individual investment, the findings of empirical studies of innovation are virtually unanimous, they strongly support the view of Keynes and Shackle that investment in new products and processes has an element of true uncertainty, as well as general business uncertainty (Freeman and Perez, 1988, p. 48). However, once a new technological system has become firmly established, many different enterprises have had experience with it, and it is supported by a new infrastructure and a new institutional framework, a rather more confident business environment can emerge. These are the periods of prolonged boom and prosperity, shown in the last right hand column of Table 8.1

Such periods of 'upswing' may last for two or three decades before another major new technology begins, in its turn, to disrupt the established regime. The diffusion of each of these new technologies brings about a crisis of structural adjustment in which the now 'old' institutions are challenged by reformers who seek to adapt the framework to a system more compatible with the next rising technology (Perez, 1983, 1996, 1998). The changes, which are advocated include not only the legal framework, but also education and training systems for new skills and professions, new management systems and new national and international standards. Such institutional changes can be made in a variety of different ways depending on local history, politics and culture; they are the essential substances of most studies of NSI and RSI. Enthusiasts for the 'new economy' tend to believe that these changes have already been made in the United States NSI and that the structural crisis of adjustment for ICT was over in the 1980s. According to this view, the world economy is now taking off for a prolonged upswing, led by the US, comparable to the 1950s and 1960s, or the 1850s and 1860s. However, international comparisons made at the OECD clearly show that most other countries lagged significantly behind the US in the development of the ICT industries in the 1990s (Bassanini et al., 2000; Scarpetta et al., 2000).

As the computer was developed and used on a small scale already in the 1940s and had a pre-history going back to Babbage a century earlier, many people are surprised that it should have taken so long before it became a universal tool. They are even more surprised that it is now taking still longer for the computer *industry* and the Internet to dominate the global economy and to raise productivity in other parts of the economic system. But this is not atypical. The steam engine, the electric motor and the automobile all had a similarly long period of gestation and diffusion before they became the dominant influence in world-wide economic growth (Freeman and Louçã, 2001). It is not just a question of one product and one design but of an evolving combination of products and processes and of industries supplying new materials and components, as well as new skills, software and management systems and a vast investment in new infrastructure. The new industries have to achieve a high *rate* of growth for a long time before they have a big enough *weight* and a strong enough influence on other industries and services to drive the entire world economy into a period of prolonged prosperity. This paper argues that they have not yet reached this point, i.e. that Gates (1995) was right when he said of the ICT Revolution: 'We're experiencing the early days of a revolution in communications that will be long-lived and widespread' (page xii).

Enthusiasts for the 'new economy' take the view that its combined weight and rate are now already sufficient to drive the whole system onwards and upwards for a long time to come. This paper takes the view that it was still 'irrational exuberance' which was sustaining the American stock market in 2000 and that this bubble was inflated by expectations, which could not possibly be fulfilled. Shiller (2000) has given a brilliant exposition of the psychology, which generates and sustains this type of bubble. His book is an invaluable addition to the earlier literature of Kindleberger and Galbraith on euphoria, panics and mania; he thanks his wife, a professional psychologist, for her contribution to the many psychological insights on the nature of the latest bubble.

Before embarking on a discussion of this fundamental question in Sections 4–6, this paper first of all pursues a little further the relationship between the *aggregate* trend in a new technology and in the economy, and the *individual* firms and projects, which together drive that movement.

3. AGGREGATE TRENDS AND INDIVIDUAL FIRMS IN ICT

Even though *individual* firms and individual projects within firms may fail to fulfil the hopes and expectations of entrepreneurs and investors, in the *aggregate* these hopes may nevertheless be fulfilled. The aggregate outcome depends on a combination of varying degrees of success and failure on the part of individual firms and one of the chief claims for the viability of capitalist economies is their ability to create a selective environment in which the more efficient succeed and their weaker competitors fail. The problem for *systems* of innovation, therefore, whether at sectoral, regional or national level, is to establish a selection environment in which various types of entrepreneurs are able and willing to embark on new investment despite the hazards which inevitably accompany such activities.

It has been argued in the preceding section that this is not simply a question of providing *information* about market *prices* more rapidly in all parts of the globe. It is a far more complicated question of creating an institutional framework in which a new technology can flourish. Neither private nor public agencies can possibly foresee or predict the twists and turns in the evolution of a new radical technology and its manifold applications. Although it *was* possible for visionary scientists or engineers more than half a century ago to forecast that computers would transform the economic system, none of them could foresee the advent of the microprocessor, the personal computer or the Internet. Even when the Internet was first developed in the 1960s and 1970s by the United States ARPA (formerly the Agency for military R&D projects) it was for very different purposes than those, which are now being so assiduously exploited. Originally, the main application, which was envisaged was to preserve some level of communications in the event of a breakdown of conventional telecommunication systems as a result of nuclear warfare. Later, the main applications in the 1970s were for the speedy exchange of information between university and other scientific researchers. It was relatively late in the diffusion that the potential *business* applications began to be explored and exploited in the 1980s and 1990s.

Leadership in the development and uses of the Internet is undoubtedly one of the main advantages of the United States national system of innovation. But this advantage is due less to any special foresight or calculation by the US government or private firms than to more general characteristics of the US economy, American industry and technology.

The history of ICT and of other technologies shows that forecasts about the *general* direction of technical change are more reliable than forecasts of the fate of an *individual* project or firm. That many ICT sectors will continue to grow rather rapidly is a fairly safe prediction, even though they may experience cyclical fluctuations and even though individual firms or projects may collapse. Of course, a time will come when even the continued rapid growth of the computer industry or of the telecommunications network will no longer be a safe forecast. Even now, it is hard to forecast the share of *mobile* telephony in the global network. A major uncertainty at the time this paper was being written (2000), was whether the *cost* of mobile phone licences to telecom companies in the forthcoming auctions in various European countries would lead to higher prices for consumers and slower diffusion. This is precisely why research on new technological systems and on innovation systems is so difficult yet so important for policy-making. The early identification of major new waves of technical change and of those features, which may facilitate or hinder their diffusion is the key to effective technology policies and economic policies, whether on the part of public agencies or private firms. The rapid pace of change and its international dimension mean that such policies must be continuously adapted and re-formulated as technology evolves. What are needed for this extremely difficult task of strategic policy-making are not just *information* but *knowledge* and understanding of the relevant systems. It is also essential to take account of the possible need for *political* regulation to limit or prevent undesirable social consequences of any new technology.

General awareness of the *potential* importance of ICT was probably more widespread in the US in the 1950s and 1960s than anywhere else in the world, although individual firms continued to overestimate or underestimate the markets for their own products. Even IBM vastly *under*estimated the future market for electronic computers in the late 1940s and early 1950s (Freeman and Soete, 1997). The markets for transistors and integrated circuits were also disastrously underestimated by incumbent firms in the electronic valve (tube) industry. The need for a new software industry to support the diffusion of hardware was largely unforeseen. Even the word 'software' itself only came into general use in the late 1950s and software could not usually be patented until much later.

Despite these vast uncertainties, the general awareness of the future importance of computers had become very widespread by the 1960s, as was clearly shown by the upsurge of patenting in ICT. A general upsurge of patenting, including ICT, was renewed in the 1980s and 1990s (Figure 8.1) and it has been one of the remarkable features of the US boom in the 1990s (OECD, 2000). For the first time, more patents are being taken out now by West Coast firms and universities than by those in the 'old' North East of the country. This confirms the role of Silicon Valley and other clusters of innovative new firms and universities as analysed by many studies of RSI (for example, Saxenian, 1991). Not all the firms in these clusters succeeded, however; there were many failures too. Despite these failures and the constant uncertainties of forecasting, ICT has been more successful in the USA than anywhere else. Section 4 will discuss some of the emerging outstanding features of the United States NSI, which, at first

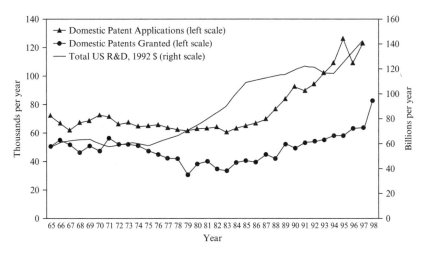

Source: National Science Board (1998), USPTO (1998), Jaffe (2000).

Figure 8.1   Patenting and R&D in the US, 1965–1998

sight, make the 'new economy' thesis seem fairly credible. However, a closer look in Section 5 at what has been happening there, still leaves grounds for scepticism and the evidence from past history discussed in Section 6 reinforces that scepticism.

4.   THE UNITED STATES NATIONAL SYSTEM OF INNOVATION

It was not so long ago that leading American economists were pointing to the *weaknesses* of American industry in the adoption of new technology. The MIT Study 'Made in America' (Dertouzos et al., 1989) argued that American firms were still very often clinging to old ideas about mass production and were reluctant to change their management and production systems to embrace new technologies. The study was made by some of the most competent and knowledgeable specialists in the leading Institute of Technology in the world, who were in close contact with American industry, so that its findings cannot be dismissed as ignorant or ill-informed criticism by ivory-tower academics. What, then, could explain the transition in the 1990s to an economy, which is now universally regarded as the world leader in applications of new technology? Is this leadership now so firmly established that it will give rise to a prolonged boom in the US economy?

These are obviously questions, which have preoccupied anyone interested in national systems of innovation, as well as policy-makers in the US, Japan and other countries. To give a satisfactory answer would require a book rather than a short paper, so what is attempted here is simply to make a few comments and reflections, which may interest those who are seeking a more comprehensive survey.

The weaknesses in several American industries, which were identified in the MIT Report were also attested by many other studies. Mowery and Rosenberg (1993) commented that:

> The recent technological performance of US firms appears to be relatively weak in several areas. US firms have been slower than their counterparts in a number of other industrial economies to adopt new manufacturing technologies and, some observers suggest, do not utilise these technologies (e.g. robotics, computer-integrated manufacturing) as intensively or effectively as foreign firms (p. 30).

Studies of particular industries appeared to confirm these conclusions, most notably the International Motor Vehicle Project (IMVP), which compared the performance of automobile firms in all the leading countries. The IMVP (Womack et al., 1990) showed that Japanese firms had become the world leaders in the 1980s in productivity, in export performance and in shortening the lead times for the introduction of new models. It argued that this huge Japanese success in displacing American leadership, in what had been an industry once completely dominated by US firms, was due to Japanese management concepts pioneered by the Toyota-Ohno system and later known as 'lean production'.

In several other industries, for example, colour TV, semi-conductors and video recorders, a similar story could be told, leading in some cases to restrictions on imports from Japan because of the devastating effects in the American market. However, during the 1990s, there was a remarkable revival of competitive strength on the part of American industry, described by some as 'The Empire Strikes Back'; in a number of industries, American firms regained a position of leadership. Scherer (1992) made a series of case studies in American firms of the response to 'high tech' competition. He found that already in the 1980s, firms in several sectors were responding with aggressive innovative strategies. In the semi-conductor industry in particular, Intel, Motorola and Texas Instruments challenged the Japanese firms for supremacy in technology and productivity. In the automobile industry, partly as a result of the IMVP project, Ford and GM imitated some of the Japanese innovations and established new plants with more advanced production and management systems. But much more important than this relative success was the American performance in all those activities related to the Internet and the software industries. American trade performance in *manufacturing* remained relatively poor, and Japan continued to enjoy a large surplus in trade with the US, but the American economy nevertheless grew rapidly in the 1990s, based on the so-called 'New Paradigm'. Technical change was not of course the only source of the acceleration in growth rate. Higher utilisation of labour played an important role as it did also in some of the smaller OECD countries, such as Ireland and the Netherlands. However, diffusion of ICT was certainly a major factor (OECD, 2000). The confidence of foreign, as well as American investors, grew because of the belief that the new paradigm would bring continuing high growth of productivity and profitability, beyond the late 1990s well into the twenty-first century.

Section 5 will attempt to show that this confidence may not be so well-founded as many investors believe and, in particular, that there are reasons for believing the claims sometimes made for the long-term trend in US productivity may be exaggerated. This section will concentrate on the reasons for those improvements in American technological and economic performance, which have already occurred in the 1990s. There are three features of this American performance, which are clearly related to outstanding characteristics of the US national system of innovation. The first of these features, which has already been briefly mentioned, is the role of new small firms in the American economy; the second is the role of the Federal and local state governments, and the third is the role of universities. Each of these will now be briefly discussed, using a number of notable studies of the NSI made in the 1990s.

In their analysis of the United States NSI, Mowery and Rosenberg (1993, pp. 48–9) emphasised strongly that 'the successive waves of new product technologies that have swept through the post-war US economy . . . have been commercialised in large part through the efforts of new firms' and further that this is in sharp contrast with European countries and Japan. In explaining this special feature of the United States NSI, they point out that 'the large basic research establishments in universities, government and a number of private firms served as important "incubators" for the development of innovations' which were commercialised by individuals who 'walked out of the door' to become innovative entrepreneurs. The private venture capital financial system, stronger in the US than elsewhere, greatly facilitated the efforts of these new small firms. These special features of the United States NSI were further reinforced by the anti-Trust policies of the US government and by US government procurement policies. The extraordinarily rapid growth of such new firms as Cisco Systems, developing equipment for the Internet, and of software firms, such as AOL, provides further impressive supporting evidence for the Mowery–Rosenberg thesis in the most recent period. Not only the growth of Microsoft but also the anti-trust action of the Federal Government against that firm demonstrate that this tradition of the United States NSI continues today.

The role of the US Federal Government in the promotion of ICT has been far from the passive non-interventionist stance sometimes assumed. From the Second World War onwards, the military agencies and other Departments have consistently recognised the extraordinary importance of ICT and of the basic research underlying technological advance. Indeed, they showed greater awareness than private industry. They have also recognised the need to support university research on a large scale and the efforts of industrial firms through both procurement and development contracts. A feature of the US R&D system for a long time has been the exceptionally large part of total R&D expenditures *financed* by the Federal Government but *performed* in industry.

The deep awareness of the importance of ICT for the long-term prosperity of the US, as well as for its military security, has been further demonstrated in the most recent period by the support given to the efforts of many *state* governments to strengthen their local clusters of technological activities both in industry and universities. Tax regimes have been designed and improved to support innovative small firms, while new taxes such as those proposed for the Internet and other ICT-based activities have usually been resisted. In the field of foreign trade, the US government has fought tenaciously and successfully to reduce barriers in foreign markets to the penetration of ICT products and services, to uphold the intellectual property of US firms and, when necessary, to limit penetration of the US market by foreign firms. Nor have direct commercial subsidies to private R&D been completely absent, although less common than in most European countries. Klete et al. (2000), in their study of such subsidies, argue that the 'Sematech' Project, supported by the US government from 1987 to 1996, at the rate of $200 million per annum, achieved its main objectives. It was designed to help 14 US semi-conductor firms sustain their competitive position in world semi-conductor technology.

Last, but by no means least, the US Federal Government and most individual State governments have maintained their support for higher education and university research. The role of this part of the US NSI has consistently been rated as one of its most important, if not *the* most important feature of the system. Already in the nineteenth century, foreign observers remarked on it and Gavin Wright (1999) showed that the education and professional standards of American mining and other engineers were one of the main factors in the huge spurt of growth in the late nineteenth and early twentieth centuries, which enabled the US to overtake all of its competitors in the achieved rate of productivity growth over a long

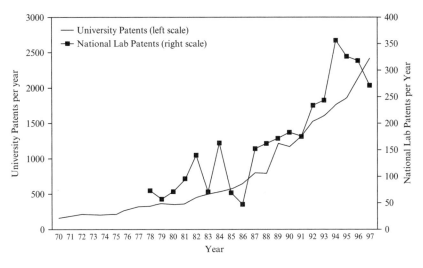

Source: Jaffe (2000).

Figure 8.2   University and national laboratory patents in US

period. In a more detailed study, Rosenberg and Nelson (1994) showed that, in each one of the new engineering disciplines, as they emerged, American universities were not only very quick to start new courses and train postgraduates but were also responsible for a great deal of generic and applied research of immediate practical value to industry. After showing that this was the case in electrical engineering, in chemical engineering and aeronautical engineering, they show that it was also true of computer science and of course of biotechnology. Summing up, they say:

> If we review the history of the development of a number of important engineering disciplines, it seems apparent that engineering education in the US has consistently attempted to provide reference points for inquiry into the details of very practical problems. At the same time, university research has been instrumental in providing an appropriate intellectual framework for training efficient professional decision-makers. (Rosenberg and Nelson, 1994, p. 333).

In the most recent period, these features of the United States NSI have been still further strengthened. University research supported by industry increased in the 1980s and 1990s and patenting by universities themselves has increased considerably (Figure 8.2). National laboratories have also played an important role in this big upsurge of patenting activity in the US, an upsurge that has been particularly remarkable in data processing and molecular biology (Figure 8.3). The *number* of universities involved in

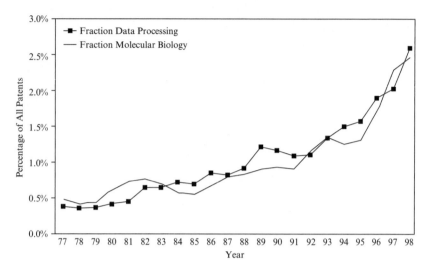

Source: Jaffe (2000), USPTO (1999).

Figure 8.3   Software and biotechnology patents in the US

patenting activities has sharply increased. In 1965, only 30 academic institutions received patents; this had increased to about 150 in 1991 and over
400 by 1997 (Jaffe, 2000, p. 541). Legislative changes accounted for part of
this increase and biotechnology was particularly important. Nevertheless,
these statistics, including those for ICT, do mark an important new development in the United States NSI.

Etzkovitz (1998) goes even further with his 'Triple Helix' theory of the
'Entrepreneurial University' in the US:

> The entrepreneurial university integrates economic development with the uni-
> versity as an academic function along with teaching and research. It is this 'cap-
> italisation of knowledge' that is the heart of a new mission for the university,
> linking universities to users of knowledge more tightly and establishing the uni-
> versity as an economic actor in its own right. (Etzkovitz, 1998, p. 833).

Not all American academics would be happy with this re-definition of
their role and some have pointed to a possible decline in the quality of more
fundamental research, as well as a decline in the *quality* of patents because
of the pressures on universities to 'patent or perish', as well as the older
pressures to 'publish or perish'. Be this as it may, there is certainly evidence
that the American universities in the 1980s and 1990s have played a major
role in the enhanced performance of the United States NSI.

5. THE 'NEW PARADIGM' IN THE USA AND LONG-TERM PRODUCTIVITY GROWTH

The proposition that the upsurge in the US economy from 1995 to 2000 would continue for a long period into the twenty-first century is often supported by references to the characteristics of the NSI outlined in Section 4 above. In particular, of course, the world leadership of US firms and universities in computer technology and the Internet is singled out as a guarantee of future progress and competitive strength. In spite of the fact that he warned more than once against 'irrational' exuberance, the remarks of Alan Greenspan, Chairman of the Federal Reserve, about the 'new paradigm' based on ICT, are often seen as an endorsement of this view. The optimists, particularly among stockbrokers and small investors, brush aside such disquieting features as the asset inflation, the yawning US trade deficit, the growth of corporate and personal indebtedness, the surge of mergers and acquisitions, and the extremely uneven development of the world economy, as well as the remaining problems of institutional change in the US itself. Despite these problems, the view that low inflation, low unemployment and the upsurge of new technology constituted some kind of 'new economy' emerging in the 1990s was very widespread in the US and elsewhere in the world.

To measure the size of the ICT industries is itself quite a difficult problem (Van Ark, 2000). The US Department of Commerce in June 1999 estimated the size of the 'digital economy', including the software industry, as 8% of GDP, but two analysts at Goldman Sachs argued that by including *consumer* electronics, this estimate greatly exaggerated the 'core' ICT industries. They estimated it at only 5% of GDP (*Economist*, 1999c, p. 101). An even bigger problem is the adjustment of the figures for quantitative growth to allow for *quality* and price changes in the output. The Commerce Department now makes generous allowance for this. The *'nominal'* contribution of the 'digital economy' to GDP growth has risen by 14% per annum since 1992 but the estimated *'real'* (adjusted) contribution rose at 40% per annum, according to the Department of Commerce. Whereas the Department estimates that the digital economy contributed 35% of *real* GDP growth from 1995 to 1999, the *nominal* contribution was only 10%. An OECD Working Paper (Scarpetta et al., 2000) recently presented useful estimates of sectoral growth in a number of countries, including the USA.

The difficulties of adjusting for quality change are even greater when it comes to measuring productivity increases and it is not surprising that there has been an intense debate about these measurements. One argument between 'bulls' and 'bears' hinges largely on this debate. If the bulls are right in their highly optimistic vision of the future of the American economy, then not only should there be strong evidence of steep rises in productivity in the digital economy, but these should be widely apparent elsewhere in the system. Otherwise, there is no way in which the current prices for US Stocks could be justified.

It is true that, in the past, each technological revolution has at first demonstrated a productivity 'miracle' only in a few industries. In these industries (cotton, iron, railways, steel, electricity, automobiles, oil, computers) there was indeed an astonishing spurt of growth based on rapidly rising productivity, falling prices and a huge increase in demand (Freeman and Louçã, 2001). Whilst the rate of growth in these industries, and a few others closely related to them, was sufficient to impart a healthy push to the aggregate growth of the economy as a whole, their weight in the system was not yet sufficient to sustain this growth through a long period of prosperity, lasting several decades.

For this to occur, two things historically were needed. First of all, the limits to the diffusion of each new technology in the rest of the economic system had to be overcome through a combination of changes in the institutional and social framework (Perez, 1983, 1985, 1998) and productivity increases in other industries. Secondly, worldwide diffusion of the new technology had to be on such a scale that aggregate demand could sustain a worldwide boom and not just an expansion in one or two countries.

Whilst there has been abundant evidence of rapid productivity growth in the 'core' ICT industries in the USA, i.e. computers, microelectronics and telecommunications, there has until recently been little such evidence of increased productivity growth elsewhere in the economy (Figure 8.4). Revisions to the earlier statistics have now shown some evidence of such growth for the period 1995–1999, so that the rise in the ICT industries has been supported by some increases elsewhere in the economy (Economist, 2000d). However, Robert Gordon, who has made an intensive study of US long-term productivity growth (Gordon, 2000), maintains that after allowance for cyclical factors, the increase in productivity growth outside the ICT industries was still only 0.4% per annum in the late 1990s. Moreover, this increase is confined to durables; in services and in non-manufacturing industry, there has been either stagnation or decline in total factor productivity, i.e. in the greater part of the American economy. Gordon concludes that the new paradigm story for the US economy has been greatly exaggerated despite the evidence of the revised figures. The productivity increases in earlier periods of expansion, such as the 1960s, were significantly greater after allowance for cyclical factors in the 1990s (Figure 8.4)

Other American economists who have expressed varying degrees of scepticism about the 'new paradigm' story in relation to the American economy include Krugman (*The Ponzi Paradigm*, 2000) and Dale Jorgensen. The

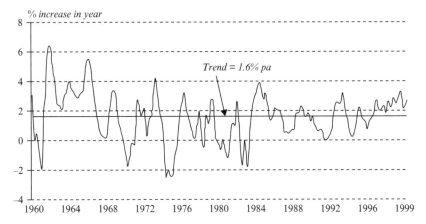

Source: Lloyds TSB Economic Bulletin (1999).

Figure 8.4   US productivity growth, whole economy

Fed. has argued that Gordon underestimates the increase in total factor productivity in the non-ICT economy because of his method of calculating the cyclical adjustment for the late 1990s. Jorgensen and Stiroh (2000) also argue that Gordon has under-estimated the TFP gains in the 1990s but nevertheless endorse his main conclusion:

> Gains in TFP growth can be traced in substantial part to information technology industries. . . . the evidence is equally clear that computer-using industries like finance, insurance, real estate and other services have continued to lag in productivity growth. Reconciliation of massive high-tech investment and relatively slow productivity growth in service industries remains an important task for proponents of the new economy position. (*Economist*, 2000c, p. 130)

One of the main areas in which the Internet was widely supposed to have revolutionary effects was retail trade. Sales made over the Internet were often forecast to grow at an astronomical rate and the demise of the shopping mall, the high street and the corner shop were all foreseen. 'E-Tail', as it became known, has indeed grown very rapidly and most big retail companies have taken precautionary steps to get a foot in the door (if that is the right expression). However, the experience of the headlong E-tail expansion itself in the late 1990s has raised many new doubts about its future. E-dot.com companies, which were floated in 1998 and 1999 and experienced a meteoric rise in their share prices before they had actually sold any goods, often suffered a collapse in the Spring of 2000. Even those companies such as Amazon, which had become the largest on-line retail company in the

World and had undertaken massive investment in new distribution facilities, suffered some loss of confidence in the market ('Amazon shares tumble amid sales and credit fears', *Financial Times*, 2000). Methods of payment, as well as of distribution, although they had apparently been very well managed by Amazon and other leading companies in the *book* trade, caused increasing anxieties in such areas as clothing and groceries.

However, all of this scepticism did not deter a huge number of both American and foreign investors from continuing to put their faith in the 'new economy'. Even the sharp drop in the NASDAQ stock market index, based mainly on ICT companies, in the Spring of 2000 did not lead to a more serious cyclical downturn in the economy. Indeed, some commentators actually maintained that the business cycle itself had become a thing of the past even if there were some fluctuations in stock market prices. *Newsweek* magazine confronted Robert Rubin himself on this point (Rubin was formerly a senior economic advisor to President Clinton):

> *Newsweek* – As you know, there are people who believe that new technology and globalisation have repealed the business cycle.
> *Robert Rubin* – There are people who believe that, and it may turn out that that's true. But there is another possibility, which is that all of human history may turn out to be true instead. And you just have to decide which you think is more likely. (Robert Rubin, interview to *Newsweek*, special issue December 1999–February 2000, p. 61).

The complexity of the issues and the uncertainties involved are so great, that it is likely that only the unfolding of events themselves will resolve these disagreements and it is not possible here to review 'all of human history'. In any case, historical evidence can never be wholly convincing because history is a unique set of events and the proponents of the 'new economy' school simply maintain that the US economy today is indeed 'new' and that therefore analogies and warnings from past experience are simply irrelevant. Nevertheless, this paper takes the view that something can be learned from the last major boom, which took off in the US in a rather similar way in the 1920s. Section 6 deals with the lessons of this boom.

6.   THE AUTOMOBILE BOOM IN THE US IN THE 1920s AND THE LESSONS OF HISTORY

Although the original inventions of the internal combustion engine and the Diesel engine were made in France and Germany, it was in the US that large-scale production of automobiles took off, with Ford's Model T, before the First World War. It sold 15 million units before it was discontinued in 1927 and Ford was making profits of 300% per annum at one time. The technology of mass production, pioneered by Ford and soon followed by those firms who combined together in General Motors, enabled the US industry to dominate the world automobile market in the 1920s. By 1929, North America accounted for nearly 90% of total world production and for over 80% of world exports of automobiles. The US also dominated the world tractor market and the production of most other consumer durables where the techniques of mass production could easily be applied – refrigerators, washing machines, vacuum cleaners and so forth. Led by these industries and by induced growth in roads, service stations and suburban construction, the US economy grew rapidly after the recession of 1920–1921. Unemployment fell to less than 4% of the labour force and inflation was low except for Stock market prices. The US economy in the late 1920s in fact resembled in many respects the economy of the late 1990s and generated very similar ideas about enduring prosperity.

The general view of the US economy in the late 1920s was extremely optimistic. President Coolidge's State of the Union message to Congress on 4 December 1928 claimed that: 'No Congress of the US ever assembled, on surveying the State of the Union, has met with a more pleasing prospect than that which appears at the present time. In the domestic field there is tranquillity and contentment . . . and the highest record of years of prosperity' (Galbraith, 1954, p. 30).

Academics and business forecasters were hardly less optimistic. The highly respected National Bureau of Economic Research was commissioned to prepare a study on 'Recent Economic Changes' for the President's Conference in 1929. In their summary of the 'Characteristics of the Years 1922–1929', they reported that 'something distinctly different was taking place', agreed upon by numerous visitors from abroad:

> . . . the unprecedented utilisation of power and its wide dispersion by automobile and tractor, in which this country leads the way, is a new addition to the economic potentiality of our resources. With the general increase in wealth, the growth in the number of millionaires has been accompanied by a remarkable rise in the real wages of industrial workers, and a wide diffusion of investments. . . . The strength and stability of our financial structure, both governmental and commercial is of modern growth. The great corporate development of business enterprise, . . . has gone on to new heights. It may be creating, as some think, a new type of social organisation. (Hoover Report, 1929, pp. 6–7).

Euphoric ideas about a 'new economy' have a rebirth with each great technological revolution. While there is some justification for such ideas in relation to technology, there is less justification for underestimation of the economic turmoil accompanying these changes. Even in October and

November 1929, during and after the Wall Street crash, there were constant assurances that the 'fundamentals' of the economy were sound. Among those who gave such assurances late in October 1929 were not only President Hoover, the Assistant Secretary of Commerce and Mr Catchings of Goldman Sachs, but also John D. Rockefeller, who issued a statement on 29 October, 1929, saying: 'Believing that the fundamental conditions of the country are sound . . . my son and I have for some days been purchasing common stocks' (Galbraith, 1954, p. 140).

Of course, these statements could all be regarded as orchestrated efforts to steady the ship and prevent further panic falls on the stock market. However, even in November 1929 and in the Spring of 1930, the *Newsletter* of the Harvard Economic Society constantly repeated the view that 'the present recession . . . is not the precursor of business depression' and forecast early recovery and vigorous growth in the third quarter of 1930. Other academic economists also reiterated these views; none foresaw the Depression of the 1930s and until late in 1930, many did not even worry about prices on the Stock Exchange. For example, in a famous statement, Lawrence had argued that 'stocks are not at present over-valued', and even Irving Fisher, regarded by many as the greatest American economist, argued that 'stock prices have reached what looks like a permanently high plateau' (Galbraith, 1954, p. 95).

At the end of his life, Fisher broke away from monetary theories of the business cycle and developed an original theory of depressions (Fisher, 1932). In this theory debt-financed Schumpeterian innovations fuel a boom, followed by a recession, which can turn into a depression via an unstable interaction between excessive real debt burdens and deflation (Tobin, 1987). Later on, while other more orthodox economists denounced the public works investments in Roosevelt's New Deal, Fisher gave it strong support in speeches, pamphlets and personal talks with the President. However, Shiller (2000, p. 106) points out that in the immediate aftermath of the Wall Street crash, in his book *The Stock Market Crash and After* (Fisher, 1930), Fisher was still optimistic, because he thought that the merger movement would facilitate scale economies and because, in his view, technical change was more rapid than ever before. Moreover, he maintained that the advantages of the automobile were only just beginning to be exploited, with the development of a new network of highways. Finally, more sophisticated management techniques, including planning methods, meant that American corporations could sustain increases in productivity and earnings. Only bankers like Paul Warburg warned of the 'unrestrained speculation' (Shiller, 2000, p. 107).

This story of the 1920s boom and its collapse does not of course show that the same thing is bound to happen in the next few years. There were some very important differences between the US economy of the 1990s and that of the 1920s, as well as some important similarities. The events of the Great Depression are themselves a factor inducing greater caution on the part of the banks and other financial institutions, including the Federal Reserve, which now has greater powers to regulate the system, and has shown its willingness to use them to make credit available in the event of recession before a downward spiral gained momentum. However, the Fed. now has a somewhat different problem, how to slow or stop the asset inflation without bringing about a serious recession. This dilemma is the main theme of Section 7.

7.   CONCLUSIONS

The story of the 1920s is a salutary reminder that euphoria during a boom can distort judgement even of very well informed observers and participants. However, it is still open to 'new economy' enthusiasts to argue that the 1990s boom did indeed have some unique new features. Even though the US price/earnings ratio was at times nearly 40% higher in the Spring of 2000 than in 1929 and higher than at any time since the 1880s (Figure 8.5), this was apparently the view of Alan Greenspan. He appears to believe that even the revised statistics still underestimate the productivity increase in the American economy in the 1990s and has been remarkably relaxed about the inflation of stock market prices, despite his earlier statement about 'irrational exuberance' in 1996. In a speech delivered on 6 March, 2000 (Martin Wolf, *Financial Times*, 2000), this is how he summed up the situation:

Source: Wolf (2000).

Figure 8.5   The US price/earnings ratio 1881–2000

In the last few years, it has become increasingly clear that this business cycle differs in a very profound way from the many other cycles that have characterised *post-Second World War* America. Not only has the expansion achieved record lengths, but it has done so with economic growth far stronger than expected. Most remarkably, inflation has remained largely subdued. A key factor behind this extremely favourable performance has been the resurgence in productivity growth (emphasis added).

As we have seen in Section 5, there is considerable disagreement about the measurement of US productivity increases and their significance. The *Economist* magazine has been consistently sceptical about the size of the digital economy and about the productivity increases, as well as the whole 'new economy' story (*Economist*, 1998, 1999a, 1999b, 2000a, 2000b, 2000c, 2000d). For this reason, it has also been critical of the policy stance of Alan Greenspan and the Federal Reserve: '. . . if, like this newspaper, your sums tell you that shares are over-valued even on the most bullish interpretation of America's remarkable economic performance, and its future productivity prospects, then you should be worried – seriously so' (*Economist*, 2000b, p. 17).

The private sector's financial deficit reached 5% of GDP in 1999, but in the earlier 50 years, it was never above 1%. Both households and firms are on a borrowing spree, but discussing these problems of corporate and household debt, the *Economist* remarks that this is unlikely 'in and of itself, to bring on a calamity. Its significance is that it makes it now very unlikely that, if or when a downturn comes, it will be a soft or painless one'.

The situation may be even worse than the *Economist* suggests, because there are also disquieting features in the global economy outside the US. The Bank for International Settlements has repeatedly drawn attention to these problems but perhaps the most disturbing commentary came from Joseph Stiglitz, chief economist at the World Bank from 1996 to 1999. After describing how the IMF dealt with the financial crises in East Asia and in Russia, and the secrecy surrounding both the IMF's activities and the Treasury Department, which dominated them, he concluded:

> The Treasury Department is so arrogant about its economic analysis and prescriptions that it often keeps tight – much too tight – control over what the President sees. Open discussion would have raised profound questions that still receive very little attention in the American press . . . Most importantly, did America and the IMF push policies because we, or they, believed the policies would help East Asia or because they would benefit financial interests in the US and the advanced industrial world? And if we believed our policies were helping East Asia, where was the evidence? As a participant in these debates, I got to see the evidence. There was none (Stiglitz, 2000).

Taking into account the extremely uneven development of the world economy, and the inevitability of new financial crises in various parts of the world in the years ahead, it is difficult to be sanguine about the prospects either for the US or the global economy. Developments in Argentina, in Turkey and in Korea are all examples of events, which can give rise to considerable anxiety in various regions of the world.

No one can predict the future course of events with certainty. Neither the evidence about long-term productivity changes in Section 4, nor the historical reflections in Section 5, nor the scale of corporate and household debt discussed in Section 6, nor calculations of the possible future rate of returns on ICT investments, can conclusively show that there will be a hard landing for the US economy. Nevertheless, taken together, they should give cause for serious reflection. Fasten your seatbelts.

NOTE

* This paper is a slightly amended version of a contribution to the project Local Productive Clusters and Innovations Systems in Brazil: new industrial and technological policies (www.ie.ufri.br/gei/gil), financed by FINEP and BNDES, published in Cassiolato et al. (2003).

REFERENCES

Andersen, E.S. (1999). 'National Innovation Systems in the context of multi-sectoral growth and development', presented at DRUID Conference on National Innovation Systems, Rebild, Denmark, June.

Balaguer, A. (2000). 'Learning to grow in organised markets: a commodity chain perspective of petrochemical development in Taiwan', Ph.D. Thesis, Murdoch University, Perth.

Bassanini, A., Scarpetta, S. and Visco, I. (2000). 'Knowledge, Technology and Economic Growth: recent evidence from OECD countries', OECD Working Paper n. 259, OECD, Paris.

Cassiolato, J., Lastres, H. and Maciel, M. (eds.) (2003). *Systems of Innovation and Development: Evidence from Brazil*. Edward Elgar, Cheltenham, UK and Northampton, MA, USA, pp. 119–40.

Dertouzos, M., Lester, R. and Solow, R. (eds) (1989). *Made in America. Report of the MIT Commission on Industrial Productivity*. MIT Press, Cambridge, MA.

Economist (1998). 'America's bubble economy: the Fed needs to pop it and the sooner the better', 18 April, p. 14.

Economist (1999a). 'The new economy: work in progress', 24 July, p. 19.

Economist (1999b). 'Trapped by the bubble', 25 September, p. 13.

Economist (1999c). 'Exaggeration: the digital economy is much smaller than you think', 30 October, p. 101.

Economist (2000a). 'Goldilocks pursued by a bear', 8 January, p. 81.

Economist (2000b). 'A tale of two debtors', 22 January, pp. 17–18.
Economist (2000c). 'Productivity focus: productivity on stilts', 10 June, p. 130.
Economist (2000d). 'Economics focus: performing miracles', 17 June, p. 118.
Edquist, C. and McKelvey, M. (eds) (2000). *Systems of Innovation: Growth, Competitiveness and Employment*, 2 volumes. Edward Elgar, Cheltenham, UK and Northampton, MA, USA.
Etzkovitz, H. (1998). 'The sources of entrepreneurial science: cognitive effects of the new university-industry linkages', *Research Policy* 27 (8), 823–835.
Financial Times (2000). 'Amazon shares tumble amid sales and credit fears', 24 June.
Fisher, I. (1930). *The Stock Market Crash and After*. Macmillan, New York.
Fisher, I. (1932). *Booms and Depressions*. Adelphi, New York.
Freeman, C. and Louçã, F. (2001). *As Time Goes By: From the Industrial Revolutions to the Information Revolution*. Oxford University Press, Oxford.
Freeman, C. and Perez, C. (1988). 'Structural crises of adjustment, business cycles and investment behaviour'. In: Dosi, G., Freeman, C., Nelson, R., Silverberg, G. and Soete, L. (eds), *Technical Change and Economic Theory*. Pinter, London.
Freeman, C. and Soete, L.L.G. (1997). *The Economics of Industrial Innovation*. Third edn, Pinter, London.
Galbraith, J.K. (1954). *The Great Crash*. Penguin, Harmondsworth Edition 1962.
Gates, B. (1995). *The Way Ahead*. Viking, London Revised edition, 1996.
Gordon, R.J. (2000). 'Interpreting the 'One Big Wave' in US Long-term Productivity Growth'. Working Paper 7752, National Bureau of Economic Research, Washington, DC.
Hoover Report (1929). 'Report of the Committee on recent economic changes of the President's Conference on Unemployment', National Bureau of Economic Research, Washington, DC.
Jaffe, A.B. (2000). 'The US patent system in transition: policy innovation and the innovation process'. *Research Policy* 29 (4), 531–559.
Jorgensen, D. and Stiroh, K.J. (2000). 'Raising the speed limit: US economic growth in the information age'. In: *Brookings Papers on Economic Activity*, vol. 1, 125–211.
Keynes, J.M. (1936). *General Theory of Employment, Interest and Money*. Macmillan.
Klete, T.J., Moen, J. and Griliches, Z. (2000). 'Do subsidies to commercial R&D reduce market failures? Microeconometric evaluation studies'. *Research Policy* 29 (4), 471–497.
Krugman, P. (2000). 'The Ponzi Paradigm', *New York Times*, 12 March.
List, F. (1841). *The National System of Political Economy*. Longman, London, English Edition, 1904.
Lloyds TSB Economic Bulletin (1999). 'New paradigm or old wine in new bottles?', No. 31, December.
Lundvall B-Å (ed.) (1992). *The National System of Innovation*. Pinter, London.
Mowery, D.C. and Rosenberg, N. (1993). 'The US National Innovation System?'. In: Nelson, R.R. (ed.), *National Innovation Systems: A Comparative Analysis*. Oxford University Press, Oxford.
National Science Board (1998). 'Science Indicators – 1998'. US Government Printing Office, Washington, DC.
Nelson, R.R. (ed.) (1993). *National Innovation Systems: A Comparative Analysis* Oxford University Press, Oxford.
Niosi, J. (2000). *Canada's National System of Innovation*. McGill-Queen's University Press, Montreal.

OECD (2000). 'A New Economy? The Changing Role of Innovation and IT in Economic Growth', Background report for Ministerial Meeting, June, OECD, Paris.

Perez, C. (1983). 'Structural change and the assimilation of new technologies in the economic and social system'. *Futures* 15 (5), 357–375.

Perez, C. (1985). 'Microelectronics, long waves and world structural change: new perspectives for developing countries'. *World Development* 13 (3), 441–463.

Perez, C. (1996). 'New technologies and socio-institutional change'. Paper presented at the International Conference on 'Long Wave Theory and its Practical Applications'. Lindenthal Institute, Cologne, September.

Perez, C. (1998). *Desafíos Sociales y Políticos del Cambio de Paradigma Tecnológico.* Universidad Catolica, Venezuela.

Poh-Kam Wong (1999). 'National Innovation Systems for rapid technological catch-up: an analytical framework and a comparative analysis of Korea, Taiwan and Singapore'. In: DRUID Conference on National Innovation Systems, Industrial Dynamics and Innovation Policy, Rebild, Denmark, June.

Rosenberg, N. and Nelson, R.R. (1994). 'American universities and technical advance in industry'. *Research Policy* 23 (3), 323–349.

Rubin, R. (1999), 'Interview', *Newsweek*, special issue December 1999–February 2000, p. 61.

Saxenian, A. (1991). 'The origins and dynamics of production networks in Silicon Valley'. *Research Policy* 20 (5), 423–439.

Scarpetta, S., Bassanini, A., Pilat, D. and Schreyer, P. (2000). 'Economic Growth in the OECD Area: recent trends at the aggregate and sectoral level', OECD Working Paper n. 248, OECD, Paris.

Scherer, F.M. (1992). *International High Technology Competition.* Harvard University Press, Cambridge, MA.

Shiller, R. (2000). *Irrational Exuberance*, Princeton University Press, Princeton, NJ.

Stiglitz, J. (2000). 'What I learned of the world economic crisis', *The New Republic*, 17 April.

Tobin, J. (1987). 'Irving Fisher'. In: *New Palgrave Dictionary of Economics*, vol. 2. Macmillan, London.

Van Ark, B. (2000). 'The Renewal of the Old Economy: Europe in an Internationally Comparative Perspective', paper presented at the Annual Meeting of the Netherlands Royal Economic Society, December.

US Patent and Trademark Office (1998). 'Forecasting Office of Technology Assessment and Forecasting. Number of utility patent applications filed in the US by country of origin, 1965–present', July.

US Patent and Trademark Office (1999). 'Forecasting Office of Technology Assessment and Forecasting. Patent counts by class by year, January 1977–December 1998', March.

Wolf, M. (2000). 'Growing too fast for comfort', *Financial Times*, 5 April.

Womack, J.T., Jones, D.T. and Roos, D.T. (eds) (1990). *The Machine that Changed the World.* Rawson Associates, New York.

Wright, G. (1999). 'Can a nation learn? American technology as a network phenomenon'. In: Lamoreaux, N.R., Raff, D.M.G. and Temin, P. (eds), *Learning by Doing in Markets, Firms and Countries.* NBER, University of Chicago Press, Chicago, IL, pp. 295–326.

9. 'Catching up' and innovation systems: implications for Eastern Europe[1]

I

Abramovitz (1986) coined the expression 'social capability' to describe that capacity to make institutional changes which is so essential for long-term economic growth. He was himself one of the pioneers of 'growth accounting' but, as he cogently pointed out, the accumulation of capital and increase in the labour force are not in themselves sufficient to explain varying rates of economic growth. The huge divergence in growth rates which is so obvious a feature of long-term economic growth over the past two centuries must be attributed in large measure to the presence or absence of social capability for institutional change, and especially for those types of institutional change which facilitate and stimulate a high rate of technical change. Nowhere has this been more apparent than in Eastern Europe.

Many historians and economists had of course always emphasized these aspects of the growth process, for example, Landes (1970) or Supple (1963). Indeed, going back to the early development of economic theory, Friedrich List (1841) had strongly criticized Adam Smith and other classical economists for what he perceived as their neglect of technology and skills.

The main concern of List was with the problem of Germany catching up with England and for underdeveloped countries (as the German states then were in relation to England); he advocated not only protection of infant industries but a broad range of policies designed to accelerate, or to make possible, industrialization and economic growth. Most of these policies were concerned with learning about new technology and applying it.

After reviewing the changing ideas of economists about development in the years since the Second World War, the World Bank (1993) concluded that it is intangible investment in knowledge accumulation that is decisive rather than physical capital investment, as was at one time believed (pp. 33–5). The Report cited the 'New Growth Theory' (Romer, 1986; Grossman and Helpman, 1991) in support of this view but the so-called 'New' growth theory has, in fact, only belatedly incorporated into neo-classical models the realistic assumptions which had become commonplace among economic historians and neo-Schumpeterian economists. Indeed, it could just as well have cited Friedrich List (1841), who in criticizing a passage from Adam Smith said: 'Adam Smith has . . . forgotten that he himself includes [in his definition of capital] the intellectual and bodily abilities of the producers under this term. He wrongly maintains that the revenues of the nation are dependent only on the sum of its material capital' (p. 183). And further:

> The present state of the nations is the result of the accumulation of all discoveries, inventions, improvements, perfections and exertions of all generations which have lived before us: they form the intellectual capital of the present human race, and every separate nation is productive only in the proportion in which it has known how to appropriate those attainments of former generations and to increase them by its own acquirements. (p. 113)

List's clear recognition of the interdependence of domestic and imported technology and of tangible and intangible investment has a decidedly modern ring. He saw too that industry should be linked to the formal institutions of science and of education:

> There scarcely exists a manufacturing business which has not relation to physics, mechanics, chemistry, mathematics or to the art of design, etc. No progress, no new discoveries and inventions can be made in these sciences by which a hundred industries and processes could not be improved or altered. In the manufacturing State, therefore, sciences and arts must necessarily become popular. (p. 162)

The recent literature on 'national systems of innovation' (for example, Lundvall, 1992; Nelson, 1993; Mjøset, 1992; Freeman and Soete, 1997) could be described as an attempt to come to terms more systematically with the problems of social capability for technical change. However, List's book on *The National System of Political Economy* might just as well have been entitled 'The National System of Innovation' since he anticipated many of the concerns of this contemporary literature. The main purpose of this paper is to discuss the relevance of these ideas to developments in Eastern Europe in the twentieth century and, in particular, the growth rate of those economies in different periods.

In discussing the problems of social capability for efficient innovation, in relation to Eastern Europe from 1950 to 1990, and in the case of Russia and most other former constituent states of the USSR from 1917 onwards, it should be noted first of all that their governments were well aware of the importance of both tangible and intangible investment for their ambitious growth objectives. From their earliest days these regimes claimed that one of the principal advantages of a centrally planned economy was that it would permit a high rate of capital accumulation and of investment in science, education and training and they all set out to achieve this. Neither could their efforts be regarded as wholly unsuccessful. They generally did have high rates of tangible capital investment in relation to GDP, especially in the period from 1950 to 1970 (and in the case of the USSR much earlier) and they also enjoyed moderately high rates of economic growth. Some catch-up did take place in this period.

A more notable feature of the centrally planned economies of Eastern Europe was their relatively large investment in research and development, in technical education and in other scientific and technical services. There are considerable difficulties in establishing comparable definitions and measurements (Borowy, 1967; Freeman and Young, 1965) between Eastern and Western Europe for the period from 1950 to 1990, but it seems that by 1965 the ratio of gross expenditure on research and development to gross domestic product – GERD/GDP – ratio was higher for most East European countries than the OECD average and that the USSR even had a higher ratio than the United States (Table 9.1). A high ratio may of course be attributed to a low denominator (GDP) rather than a high enumerator (GERD) and in absolute terms the United States had a far higher expenditure on R&D than the old Soviet Union. Nevertheless the persistently high ratios did indicate a strong policy commitment to the expansion of the R&D system since they depended almost entirely on public investment and started from a low level, with the possible exceptions of Hungary and Czechoslovakia.

Almost all analysts agree therefore that, whatever the problems may have been with respect to the post-war growth of the East European economies, they were not problems of sheer lack of quantitative investment, whether

Table 9.1   Estimated gross expenditure on R&D as a fraction of GNP (GERD/GNP ratio), 1934–83

	1934	1967	1983	1983***	2000
USA	0.6	3.1	2.7	2.0	2.7
EC*	0.2	1.2	2.1	1.3	1.9
Japan	0.1	1.0	2.7	2.7	3.0
USSR**	0.3	3.2	3.6	1.0	1.1

Notes: Year 1983: Civil R&D only.
*   Estimated weighted average of 12 EC countries, for 2000: European Union.
**   Data for 2000 are for Russian Federation.
***   Civil R&D only.

Sources: Author's estimates based on Bernal (1939) adapted to 'Frascati' Definitions (OECD, 1963), OECD statistics and adjustments to Soviet statistics based on Freeman and Young (1965). Data for 2000 from OECD.

in tangible or intangible capital. Indeed many speak of 'over-investment' both in physical capital and in R&D (e.g., Auriol and Radosevic, 1996). This, however, is when serious disagreement begins.

For the majority of economists it was the lack of capitalist institutions which led to the slowdown of the growth rate in the East European economies in the 1980s and indeed to their eventual collapse. This explanation now appears so obvious and is echoed so continuously in the media that it appears to most people as a straightforward *fact*, rather than a possible and plausible explanation. It underlies almost all the policy advice given by numerous American and West European economists and by international institutions over the past decade. The central plank of this advice has almost always been to accelerate privatization, free trade and other 'free market' institutions and to scrap any remnants of 'socialism' as rapidly as possible. In this, of course, it resembles the essentially similar advice given to all developing countries. It is the high tide of neo-liberalism sweeping all before it. Some of its most enthusiastic proponents evidently expected (and many still expect) that the wave of privatization and opening up of the East European economies to foreign investment and consultancy would be sufficient in themselves to transform them into European 'Tigers' achieving the very high GDP growth ratios of between 6 and 8 per cent *per annum* characteristic of a number of Asian economies over the past two or three decades. There is little sign of this and the Russian negative growth has been especially disappointing in the 1990s even though some time lags were inevitable.

Although this mainstream explanation of events in Eastern Europe is now so much an established orthodoxy that it often goes completely unchallenged, this paper will argue that it is grossly over-simplistic and fails to account for many major features of the East European experience both before and after 1990. Moreover, insofar as the advice is unconditionally accepted it may lead to consequences which are in important respects the opposite of those intended. The pressures to reduce government expenditures have already led to a massive reduction in GERD/GNP ratios throughout Eastern Europe (Tables 9.2 and 9.3). Some of this reduction may well be essential, especially in military R&D, but it will be argued that the central problem is not one of 'over-investment' or of public control of research institutions but rather one of structural change in these institutions, of fundamental changes in their mode of operation and of stimulating enterprise-level R&D in the enterprises themselves.

The literature on 'national systems of innovation' (NSI) makes a distinction between NSI in a *narrow* sense and in a *broad* sense. The NSI in a narrow sense embraces those institutions which are directly involved in R&D and the dissemination of the results of R&D. The NSI in a broad

Table 9.2   Gross domestic expenditure on R&D as a percentage of GDP

	1990	1992	1994	1996	1998	2000	2002
Czech Republic*	2.19	1.83	1.1	1.04	1.24	1.33	1.30
Hungary**	1.60	1.07	0.89	0.65	0.68	0.80	1.01
Poland***		0.83	0.84	0.8	0.72	0.70	0.67
Slovak Republic****	1.75	1.88	1.01	0.94	0.79	0.67	0.59
Romania		0.85	0.77	0.71	0.49	0.37	0.38
Russian Federation	2.03	0.78	0.82	0.97	1.00	1.05	1.24

Notes: Defence R&D not included, except for Russia 1994 and Romania.
*   Total expenditure of the R&D base, depreciation costs not excluded.
**   Until 1993, including purchase of licences, know-how and so on; break in series in
          1991 due to changing methodology for calculating GDP.
***   Until 1993, capital expenditure in enterprises and the higher education sector not
          included, depreciation costs not excluded. Data for 2001.
**** Until 1993, total expenditure of the R&D base, depreciation costs not excluded.

Source: OECD (1996).

Table 9.3   Total R&D personnel

	1990	1992	1994	1998	2000	2002
Czech Republic*	107828	60292	37779	22740	24198	26032
Hungary**	36384	24192	22008	20315	23534	23703
Poland**			74819	84510	78925	78027
Slovak Republic***	51641	30284	17256	16461	15221	13631
Romania****		59174	56455	52454	33892	32799
Russian Federation****	1943400	1532600	1106300	967499	1007257	986854

Notes: Defence R&D personnel not included, except for Romania.
*   Average recalculated number of full-time personnel in the R&D base.
**   In full-time equivalent (FTE).
***   Until 1993, average recalculated number of full-time personnel in the R&D base; in
          1994, full-time equivalent (FTE).
**** In head counts; in Russia, higher education teaching personnel working as part-time
          researchers excluded.

Source: OECD (1996).

sense is a far wider concept equivalent to List's *The National System of Political Economy* since it attempts to describe the social, economic and political context of technical and organizational innovation. It quite justifiably points out that the way in which enterprises conduct innovation is not simply a matter of R&D but is also dependent on the way in which markets operate and production is organized, as well as on the legal and cultural norms of society. Lundvall (1992) and his colleagues rightly insisted that much discussion of the relationship between R&D and rates of economic growth ignored the broad NSI and was therefore misleading. A high rate of *intangible* investment can no more be considered as an adequate explanation of a high rate of economic growth than a high rate of *tangible* investment.

Obviously, the view that economic growth cannot take place successfully without the universal predominance of capitalist institutions is a 'broad' NSI theory and its proponents frequently ignore the functioning of the 'narrow' NSI. This is also dangerous because the narrow NSI is not typical of the way in which other capitalist institutions normally function. The collapse of the narrow NSI over much of Eastern Europe is not likely to be remedied by privatization alone but, as elsewhere in the world, will require deliberate public policies which address the specific problems of research institutions, their management and control. Both the broad and narrow NSI need to be analysed in considering the nature of social capability for innovation in Eastern Europe.

Some of the main weaknesses of the East European national innovation systems were attributable not so much to the prevalence of public ownership and control per se as to the peculiar nature of that public ownership and control. Many of the most successful institutions promoting and supporting innovation in the leading capitalist economies have in fact also been wholly or partly in the public sector. One has only to think of the experience of agricultural research worldwide, including most recently the 'Green Revolution', to recognize this fact. Equally impressive has been the role of public institutions in medical research and biotechnology such as the National Institute of Health in the United States or the Medical Research Council in Britain and many similar institutions in other countries. Economists of almost all persuasions have accepted that there are strong theoretical arguments justifying the investment of public funds in both research and education (Arrow, 1962; Nelson, 1959). Consequently the narrow NSI almost everywhere are 'hybrid' systems embodying complex public/private interdependencies (Nelson, 1959).

It is actually unlikely that the universities, academies of science and a variety of other 'narrow' institutions will all be privatized in Eastern Europe or indeed anywhere else in the world. Consequently the governments of Eastern Europe are having to learn how to manage these hybrid systems and in doing so have to take account of some peculiar features of the narrow NSI systems which they have inherited. The following sections of this paper, therefore discuss some of the main weaknesses in the historical development of *both* the broad and the narrow NSI in Eastern Europe.

Section II discusses the way in which the militarization of R&D and of the economy interacted with a totalitarian political system to inhibit original thinking and experimental work. Section III discusses why the centrally planned economies were particularly vulnerable in the pervasive wave of technical change represented by information and communication technology. A brief final section draws some conclusions.

II

One of the major characteristics of the East European NSI from the accession to power of communist-led governments until about 1990 was the absolute priority given to military R&D and to military production. This was, of course, above all true of the former Soviet Union but it was true to a lesser extent of all those regimes and was indeed one aspect of Soviet hegemony in the whole Eastern bloc. This was not simply a question of the *scale* of military R&D but of the ideological norms which accompanied the militarization of the entire system.

Although Western intelligence services had made their own assessments of the scale of Soviet R&D, before, during and after the Second World War, it was only after the collapse of the regime that the sheer size of the military R&D was firmly established and some of its main characteristics more clearly delineated. Official statistics of the breakdown between civil and military R&D, comparable to those published for OECD countries, were of course not published. What has now become clear is that many of the Western guesses, whether made by academics, or by intelligence agencies, underestimated the share of the military in the Soviet system. Many whole towns and districts were completely turned over to military R&D and production, while even part of the civil R&D was actually conducted *within* the military sector. Probably about three quarters of the total R&D was conducted directly for military objectives (Table 9.1), varying a little with the exigencies of the Cold War and the strategies pursued by various United States administrations. A precise estimate is not possible because of the overlap between civil and military objectives in areas such as space and nuclear research. What is certain is that the militarization of Soviet R&D far exceeded that of the United States or any other OECD country. This was indeed the only way in which a relatively poor country could compete in the strategic arms race in fairly exotic weapons systems as well as in conventional weapons. Whether or not the Reagan administration in the 1980s set out deliberately to weaken the Soviet economy through its Star Wars strategy, or simply to achieve military technological leadership in the arms race, the burden of military expenditures did prove to be one of the main problems for the entire system.

Controversy still continues about the possible 'spin-off' effects of military R&D in the United States and other OECD countries, especially Britain and France. Economists generally have been suspicious of the technology spin-off arguments used by military and space agencies to bolster their large R&D expenditures. On the other hand there are clear examples of a positive stimulus to some sectors, such as the civil aircraft industry or satellite communication systems or, in earlier times, the scaling up effects in the US semiconductor industry from military procurement orders. In more recent times the divergence between civil and military technologies in the electronic industries and elsewhere appears to have reduced the scale of any possible beneficial spin-off (Walker, 1991) to civil technology. Be this as it may, it is obvious that the burden of military expenditures in purely economic terms is far greater in a relatively poor country such as the Soviet Union still was in the 1980s, than in a very wealthy country, such as the United States. However any argument for a kind of 'military Keynesianism' of the type pursued by Schacht in the Hitler regime in the period of high unemployment, hardly applied to the USSR. Any possible spin-off effects could have been achieved more easily in a more relaxed atmosphere in which considerations of national security did not dominate all communication and all technology transfer within the system as well as all publications.

The long-term political, cultural and ideological consequences of the militarization of East European R&D were probably even more serious than the purely economic resource-allocation effects of the arms race. These features, which were embryonic in the earliest days of the young Soviet government, later hardened into a rigid system of cultural norms, political persecution, ideological straitjackets, bureaucratic control systems and, in the darkest days of Stalinism, sheer terror in the intellectual community. Both science and technical innovation depend for their advance on a continuous process of experiment and debate in which the possibilities for the expression of alternative opinions and disagreements is absolutely essential. In many countries the scientific community has succeeded in establishing institutions governing the norms of publication, debate, conferences and so on, which protect this freedom but these norms were already disrupted in the USSR in the 1920s and were completely swept away from the 1930s onwards, culminating in the Lysenko episode in genetics and similar episodes in other scientific disciplines. Paradoxically and with extraordinary dramatic irony, it was Stalin (1951) himself who intervened in the linguistics controversy to insist on the importance of freedom of expression. In phrases which echoed John Stuart Mill he argued that no science could advance without freedom of criticism and condemned 'the Arakcheyev regime' established by supporters of one academician Marr, in the linguistics community. Why Stalin should have intervened in this particular way to condemn a clique and a mode of repression (Arakcheyev was a former Tsarist Minister of the Interior), which he had himself far outdone, may be left to the psychologists and historians. What this and similar episodes illustrate is the extraordinary and bizarre nightmare of ideological conformism which descended on the Soviet Union and was imposed on the other East European countries in the 1950s.

This nightmare was not simply the result of militarization or indeed of socialism. It was rather the end result of a *political* process of extreme concentration of power in the hands of one party and ultimately of one man. It was a process which was already clearly foreseen as early as 1918 by both liberal and Marxist critics of Bolshevism. Both Bertrand Russell and Rosa Luxembourg, from their different standpoints, argued that the suppression of other political parties and factions would ultimately lead, via the further concentration of power in the Central Committee and the Secretariat of the Communist Party, to a repressive dictatorial regime.

These criticisms were primarily based on the *political* tendencies towards totalitarianism. What the *militarization* of the economy did in later years was greatly to reinforce this political totalitarianism and to make it extraordinarily difficult for opponents of the totalitarian trend to resist it. Not only Trotsky and his supporters but almost all other critics were routinely condemned as agents of foreign powers and in the notorious trials of the 1930s and 1950s were sentenced to death on the grounds of this alleged involvement. The nightmare quality of this process has best been illustrated by novels such as Koestler's *Darkness at Noon* or the work of Solzhenitsyn.

What it meant so far as the process of technical change was concerned is extraordinarily difficult to measure in quantitative terms. Irma Adelmann, in her discussion of models of economic growth, used the formula (1963, p. 9):

$$Y_t = f(K_t N_t L_t S_t U_t)$$

where
K_t denotes the amount of the services of the capital stock at time t
N_t stands for the rate of use of natural resources
L_t represents the employment of the labour force
S_t represents 'society's fund of applied knowledge'
U_t represents the 'social-cultural milieu within which the economy operates'

It is difficult enough to measure 'S_t' although some progress has been made in this direction but Adelman accepted that it is even more difficult and perhaps impossible to measure U_t. However, the fact that some of these variables cannot be quantified satisfactorily does not mean that they can simply be ignored. In his famous debate with Tinbergen in the 1930s, Keynes already pointed to the danger of ignoring variables which could not be easily quantified in econometric analysis (Louçã, 1997). East European experience has amply confirmed his reservations.

There can be little doubt that the combined effects of militarization and political totalitarianism did have some retarding effect on economic growth in Eastern Europe. The stifling of original ideas, the sheer physical removal of many capable intellectuals and the inefficiencies generated by bureaucratic conformism throughout the system must all have taken their toll. However, it will be argued in the following sections that the negative effects were far greater in the long term than in the short term. So long as the catch-up process was mainly one of imitation of fairly well-established technologies and the simple expansion of the share of manufacturing within the GDP, fairly rapid growth was still quite possible and clearly did occur in the 1950s and 1960s throughout Eastern Europe. It was only in the 1970s and 1980s when global technologies were changing towards the predominance of information technology and biotechnology that the widespread negative consequences of decades of bureaucratic conformism and militarization became universally apparent. Hierarchical management systems and even command systems were typical of mass production technologies from Henry Ford onwards, so that the determined Soviet efforts to imitate Fordism and Taylorism were certainly not fruitless.

III

Voznesensky was one of the leading economic planners in the USSR in the late 1940s who recognized very early the enormous potential of semiconductor and electronic computer technology for the future development of the Soviet economy. He was supported by a group of planners who advocated special measures to foster the growth of these industries. More significantly, he had a vision of the decentralized application of computers by the management of each enterprise. In this he anticipated some of the ideas of Stafford Beer, which the ill-fated Allende regime attempted to introduce much later in Chile. However, the tone and direction of the Voznesensky reforms were not compatible with the type of regime described above in Section II and, like so many other would-be reformers before them, Voznesensky and his colleagues disappeared together with their ideas in the early 1950s.

This was a fateful turning point in the evolution of the post-war Soviet economy, whose full significance became apparent only decades later. It meant not only that the development of these technologies was retarded but their application, including software development, was largely confined to the military industrial complex under centralized controls. The parallel ideological attack on cybernetics was less significant than the weakening of enterprise-level R&D, of management initiatives and organizational innovation throughout the civil economy which their decisions implied.

Here the social context of Voznesensky's defeat and banishment is all-important. A major weakness of the Soviet narrow NSI from the 1950s through to the 1980s was the relatively low amount of *enterprise-level* R&D, indeed its nonexistence in many sectors. Starting with very limited resources in scientific and technical personnel in the 1920s and 1930s the central planners took the understandable decision to set up research institutes and project design organizations for each *industry*, rather than to encourage or initiate R&D in each *enterprise*. Similar tendencies have been apparent in most countries in the early stages of industrialization and the growth of new technologies. But whereas in the United States and most West European countries this phase was soon displaced by the rapid growth of enterprise-financed and enterprise-controlled R&D (Hughes, 1989; Mowery, 1980) in the Soviet Union the centralized industry institutes continued to conduct by far the greater part of industrial R&D and a large part of the technology import for plant designs. This type of narrow NSI structure was widely imitated throughout Eastern Europe from the 1950s onwards and led to a serious lack of enterprise-level capacity for technical change since communication was often poor and innovation took insufficient account of the problems of plant-level production and of the market. These weaknesses were increasingly recognized in official pronouncements and policies in the 1960s and 1970s. Many measures were introduced, such as contract research subsidies and still later 'industry enterprise-research associations' to improve communication and cooperation but they were not very successful for many reasons related to the lack of initiative and flexibility in management at industry and plant level (Amann et al., 1979; Barker and Davies, 1965).

The difficulties affecting technical and organizational innovation in industry were greatly exacerbated by some features of the planning system which have been well described by Gomulka (1990). The setting of *quantitative* targets for production diminished the incentives for product innovation and for model changes and improvements. Again, the attempts at reform were largely negated by bureaucratic inertia and incompetence.

Another important feature of the Soviet and later of other East European narrow NSI was the concentration of most fundamental research activities in specialized research institutes controlled by the various academies of science in the USSR. Universities played a much smaller part in fundamental research than has been the norm in Western Europe and North America and were mainly teaching institutions. This was much less true of Czechoslovakia, Poland and Hungary, which had long-established and fairly strong universities accustomed to working in the West European tradition but everywhere in the Eastern bloc the Soviet model was influential. The big disadvantages of this academy system were the lack of mobility between the fundamental research institutions and industry, the tendency to gerontocracy in the academy institutes and the weak relationships between teaching and research. As in the case of the industry research institutes, these were major problems of communication within the system and again the various attempts at reform were too little and too late (Amann et al., 1979; Hanson and Pavitt, 1987).

So far as the operation of the narrow NSI is concerned an interesting contrast can be made between Japan and the USSR during the period from 1950 to 1990 (Table 9.4). Both were countries in the later stages of industrialization and recovering from very considerable war damage. Both had

Table 9.4   Contrasting national systems of innovation of Japan and USSR, 1960s–70s

Japan	USSR
High GERD/GNP ratio (2.5%) Very low proportion of military/ space R&D (<2% of R&D)	Very high GERD/GNP ratio (c. 4%) Extremely high proportion of military/space R&D (>70% of R&D)
	Low proportion of total R&D at enterprise level and company-financed (<10%)
Strong integration of R&D, production and import of technology at enterprise level	Separation of R&D, production and import of technology and weak institutional linkages
Strong user–producer and subcontractor network linkages, including R&D	Weak or nonexistent linkages between R&D, marketing, production and procurement
Strong incentives to innovate at enterprise level involving both management and workforce	Some incentives to innovate made increasingly strong in 1960s and 1970s but offset by other negative disincentives affecting both management and workforce
Intensive experience of competition in international markets	Weak exposure to international competition except in arms race
Increasing amount of fundamental research in industry itself as well as in universities and government institutes	Fundamental research concentrated in academy institutes with poor communications with industry

quite well-developed education systems with large numbers of young people studying science and technology. Both imported much technology from Western Europe and the United States although restrictions on technology transfer were a more serious problem for the USSR. Both had ways of generating long-term visions for the science and technology system. However, despite some basic similarities the contrasts were even more striking (Table 9.4). Most observers of the Japanese system stress the integration of R&D, production and marketing *at the enterprise level* as its most striking characteristic (Takeuchi and Nonaka, 1986; Baba, 1985; Clark and Fujimoto, 1989; Womack et al., 1990). This integration within the firm and close coupling with external sources which was so important in Japan and other OECD countries was very weak or nonexistent in the Soviet case. The one big exception was the aircraft industry and other defence industries. They are the exception that proves the rule. They were very small indeed in Japan (although of growing importance now) but they were the most successful part of the Soviet economy both because of the high priority given to military objectives and the far closer linkages between enterprises, customers (the armed forces) and research and design organizations.

In the case of the smaller East European economies, a similar contrast can be made for the later period with the East Asian 'Tigers'. Two features of the South Korean, Taiwanese and Singapore economies are especially significant: first, their successful shift from an NSI with little enterprise-level R&D and STS to one in which enterprise performed R&D accounts for the greater part of the total; second, government and university R&D continued to grow while this transition was taking place, as illustrated for South Korea in Table 9.5.

The incentives given to enterprises through the fiscal system, bank loans, protection and political pressures all played an important part (Wade, 1990) in strengthening their ability to invest heavily in modern plant and in new technology. Hobday (1995) has shown how their enterprises gradually improved their autonomous technological capability to move from dependence on imported technology, via joint ventures of various kinds to independent product innovation, learning all the time from the world market.

This evolutionary process at the enterprise level spurred on by government policies and infrastructural developments enabled many Asian countries to take full advantage of the numerous new opportunities opened up by information and communication technology. Whilst the World Bank (1993) in its report on the *East Asian Miracle* rightly stresses the export incentives and achievements of the 'Tigers' it fails to point out that both they and Japan have an extraordinarily high proportion of their total exports in the field of ICT products, equipment and systems. These are by far the fastest-growing commodity group in world trade and world

Table 9.5   South Korea: science and education indicators, 1953–87

	1953	1970	1987
	22	89	99
Middle school (12–14%)	21	53	99
High school (15–17%)	12	29	83
College/University (%)	3	9	26
Scientists/Engineers	4 157	65 687	361 920
Corporate R&D labs	–	1	455
Researchers			
Government RIs	–	2 477	9 184
Universities	–	1 918	17 415
Private industry	–	925	26 104
TOTAL	–	5 320	52 783
R&D/GNP (%)	0.1	0.3	1.9

Sources: UNESCO Statistical Yearbook (1980); OECD, MSTI (1992); and KNSO (1990).

production. The East European economies and most developing countries lacked the capability in the 1970s and 1980s to move on a large scale into these markets and to keep up with the extremely rapid pace of technical change and of international standards.

The East European failure in ICT was not just a failure to develop new branches of industry, such as the semiconductor industry, the computer industry or the software industry. Most East European countries did succeed in starting production of some commodities and all had R&D activities in this domain. Russian computers and software were good enough to sustain a competitive challenge in the military-space area. Where the East European systems conspicuously failed was in the *application* of successive new generations of computers, software and components in the everyday activities of firms both within the electronic industry and everywhere else in the economy. Management at the enterprise level was not flexible enough and lacked the innovative capability and external networks to introduce and to modify and update the new equipment efficiently. Consultancy organizations and the narrow NSI were not able to provide the technical and management support necessary to overcome these problems. In the older technologies of mass production and large-scale output of basic commodities such as steel, the hierarchical structure of the management systems did offer some advantages but with ICT, decentralized flexibility is the name of the game (Perez, 1985). The long-term consequences of Voznesensky's defeat over decentralization reforms came home to roost.

IV

The conclusion from the previous analysis is not that the East European economies suffered from 'over-investment' in R&D, STS or technical education, nor even necessarily that they suffered from public ownership. They certainly suffered from the militarization of their societies including both the broad and narrow NSI and from a greatly over-centralized system of planning. The crucial weakness of the narrow NSI was the failure to develop R&D at enterprise level. This weakness is a common one in most developing countries but is not necessarily an inherent weakness of a predominantly socialist society characterized by various forms of public and cooperative ownership. Many publicly owned enterprises have operated quite successfully and continued efficient R&D in West European countries.

Simply to privatize enterprises will not necessarily generate management which is capable of introducing those technical and organization innovations necessary for catch-up in the present world economy. This requires a fairly prolonged process of knowledge accumulation and sustained investment in R&D by the enterprises. The evidence so far is inconclusive but it appears to indicate rather little take-off at the enterprise level with the possible exceptions of some sectors in Poland, the Czech Republic and Hungary. The wholesale decline of R&D activities which occurred between 1990 and 1994 appears to have slowed down and university research appears to have been the least damaged by this decline. The greatest reduction in expenditures occurred in the industry institutes. If this involves a transfer of qualified and experienced people to the enterprises or the start-up of new enterprises, as in software, it may have considerable benefits but insofar as it is simply a shut-down the opposite is true. Moreover, these institutes not only had accumulated considerable tacit and formal knowledge, they were often useful sources of information and technical advice to enterprises within the overall constraints of the system. This role could now be greatly enhanced and there are some indications that this is beginning to take place, both at the level of the institutes and of individual members of staff moonlighting as consultants. Some academy institute staff members also appear to be offsetting their drastic fall in salaries by private consultancy and teaching. The reduction in *expenditure* of both academy and industrial institutes is almost everywhere greater than the reduction in *personnel*. The severe salary drop, although very painful for the individuals affected and hardly conducive to long-term efficiency, may have the short-term benefit of increasing mobility and improving communication within the narrow NSI.

What is now needed is to reinforce these positive tendencies and early green shoots in the enterprises with very positive policies designed to overcome those specific structural weaknesses identified in Section III and to continue the transfer of resources from the military to the civil sector.

It is of course possible to argue that *all* public investment and expenditure on R&D is damaging both to science and to the economy. This is the extreme position taken up by the biochemist Terence Kealey (1996) but his view has found little support from Western economists (Pavitt, 1996). So far the Kealey position has not been seriously endorsed in Eastern Europe either so that long-term damage is more likely to occur through neglect and the general effects of cuts in government expenditure than from a straightforward ideological opposition to any role for positive public policies. Obviously, where uncertainty necessarily prevails, as in R&D activities, problems in the allocation of resources are inevitable whether in the public or the private sector. The evidence of catch-up so far, whether in Europe, Asia, Latin America or Africa is that catch-up does require rather deliberate long-term strategies for science, technology and innovation, including above all the strengthening of enterprise capability for innovation. Obviously too the content of such policies and their mode of operation must vary with the evolution of technologies, but they have become more important rather than less important with the growing complexity of new technologies and their increasingly scientific content.

A more fundamental argument than that of Kealey is the argument of Hayek (1944) in his celebrated book on *The Road to Serfdom*. Hayek argued that a socialist-planned economy necessarily leads to a totalitarian dictatorship because of the centralization of decision-making and the imperative need of the planners to mobilize political support for their targets. In Hayek's view the negative features of the East European economies described in Sections II and III were the inevitable outcome of the departure from capitalist institutions with their decentralized and to some degree anonymous decision-making. However, Hayek's argument too suffers from ideological over-statement.

First of all, some capitalist countries have also most certainly had totalitarian regimes. Second, the degree of centralization and the authoritarianism of the USSR and other East European regimes was not so much an outcome of a socialist agenda as of war-time circumstances and the associated militarization. It had not actually been the original objective of the Bolsheviks to nationalize all industry in 1917. It was in the period of the wars of intervention and so-called 'War Communism' from 1918 to 1922 that the peculiar system of controls and management first evolved. Very different types of ownership, management, decentralized institutions and indicative planning could have emerged in more favourable circumstances in a less backward and beleaguered country.

However, the arguments of Hayek as well as the entire East European experience do undoubtedly demonstrate and reinforce traditional liberal arguments for civil liberties and pluralism in political institutions, as well as for pluralistic institutions in the economy and the science-technology system. That this means universal privatization and a minimalist night-watchman state has not been shown. All catching up and industrializing countries have used a variety of state-led institutions and policies to facilitate their catch-up, including state ownership and protection (Reinert, 1994) and the East European experience has not yet demonstrated that this will not be the case there too. Neither can a laissez-faire regime resolve the increasingly acute problems of inequality in income distribution which threaten the social stability of the entire region.

NOTE

1.   The term Eastern Europe refers here to all countries of Central and Eastern Europe.

BIBLIOGRAPHY

Abramovitz, M. (1986) 'Catching Up, Forging Ahead, and Falling Behind', *Journal of Economic History*, 46, 385–406.
Adelman, I. (1963) *Theories of Economic Growth and Development*, Stanford, CA, Stanford University Press.
Amann, R., M. Berry and R.W. Davies (1979) *Industrial Innovation in the Soviet Union*, Newhaven, CT, Yale University Press.
Archibugi, D. and M. Pinta (1992) *The Technological Specialisation of Advanced Countries*, report to the EC on International Science and Technology Activities, Dordrecht, Kluwer.
Arrow, K. (1962) 'The Economic Implications of Learning by Doing', *Review of Economic Studies*, 29, 155–73.
Auriol, L. and S. Radosevic (1996) *R&D and Innovation Activities in Central and East European Countries: Analysis Based on S and T Indicators*, Budapest and Paris, OECD and Hungarian National Committee for Technological Development (OMFB).
Baba, Y. (1985) 'Japanese Colour TV Firms. Decision-making from the 1950s to the 1980s', D.Phil. dissertation, Brighton, University of Sussex.
Barker, G.R. and R.W. Davies (1965), 'The Research and Development Effort of the Soviet Union', in C. Freeman and A. Young, *The Research and Development Effort in Western Europe, North America and the Soviet Union*, Paris, OECD.
Bernal, J.D. (1939) *The Social Function of Science*, London, Routledge.
Borowy, M. (1967) 'Expenditures on Research and Development in Poland 1961 to 1965', *Minerva*, V (3), 357–71 and 'Comment' (C. Freeman), 371–5.
Clark, K.B. and R. Fujimoto (1989) 'Lead Time in Automobile Product Development: Explaining the Japanese Advantage', *Journal of Engineering and Technology Management*, 6, 25–58.

David, P. (1997) 'From Market Magic to Calypso Science Policy: A Review of T. Kealey's Economic Laws of Scientific Research', *Research Policy*, 26, 229–55.

Freeman, C. (1987) *Technology Policy and Economic Performance: Lessons from Japan*, London, Pinter.

Freeman, C. (1994) 'The Economics of Technical Change: A Critical Survey Article', *Cambridge Journal of Economics*, 18(5), 463–514.

Freeman, C. and L. Soete (1997) *The Economics of Industrial Innovation*, 3rd edn, London, Pinter/Cassell.

Freeman, C. and A. Young (1965) *The Research and Development Effort in Western Europe, North America and the Soviet Union*, Paris, OECD.

Gomulka, S. (1990) *The Theory of Technological Change and Economic Growth*, London, Routledge.

Grossman, G. and E. Helpman (1991) *Innovation and Growth in the Global Economy*, Cambridge, MA, MIT Press.

Hanson, P. and K. Pavitt (1987) *The Comparative Economics of Research Development and Innovation in East and West: A Survey*, London, Harwood.

Hayek, F. (1944) *The Road to Serfdom*, Chicago, IL, University of Chicago Press.

Hobday, M. (1995) *Innovation in East Asia: The Challenge to Japan*, Aldershot, UK and Brookfield, US, Edward Elgar.

Hughes, T.P. (1989) *American Genesis*, New York, Viking.

Irvine, J. and Martin, B.R. (1984) *Foresight in Science: Picking the Winners*, London, Pinter.

Kealey, T. (1996) *The Economic Laws of Scientific Research*, London, Macmillan.

KNSO (1990) *Statistics Yearbook of Korea*, Seoul, Korea National Statistical Office.

Landes, D.S. (1970) *The Unbound Prometheus: Technological and Industrial Development in Western Europe from 1750 to the Present*, Cambridge, Cambridge University Press.

List, F. (1841) *The National System of Political Economy*, English edn, London, Longman, 1904.

Louçã, F. (1997) *Turbulence in Economics*, Aldershot, UK and Brookfield US, Edward Elgar.

Lundvall, B.Å. (1985) 'Product Innovation and User-producer Interaction', *Industrial Development Research Series*, 31, Aalborg, Aalborg University Press.

Lundvall, B.Å. (1988) 'Innovation as an Interactive Process: From User-producer Interaction to the National System of Innovation', in G. Dosi, C. Freeman, R.R. Nelson, G. Silverberg and L.L.G. Soete (eds), *Technical Change and Economic Theory*, London, Pinter.

Lundvall, B.Å. (ed.) (1992) *National Systems of Innovation: Towards a Theory of Innovation and Interactive Learning*, London, Pinter.

Miyazaki, K. (1993) 'Dynamic Competence Building in Japanese and European Firms: the case of opto-electronics', D.Phil. thesis, University of Sussex.

Mjøset, L. (1992) *The Irish Economy in a Comparative Institutional Perspective*, Dublin, National Economic and Social Council.

Mowery, D.C. (1980) 'The Emergence and Growth of Industrial Research in American Manufacturing 1899–1946', Ph.D. dissertation, Stanford University.

Mowery, D.C. (1983) 'The Relationship between Intrafirm and Contractual Forms of Industrial Research in American Manufacturing 1900–1940', *Explorations in Economic History*, 20(4) October, 351–74.

Nelson, R.R. (1959) 'The Simple Economics of Basic Scientific Research', *Journal of Political Economics*, 67(3), 297–306.

Nelson, R.R. (ed.) (1993), *National Innovation Systems: A Comparative Analysis*, Oxford, Oxford University Press.

Nelson, R.R. (1996) *The Sources of Economic Growth*, Boston, MA, Harvard University Press.

OECD (1963) *Frascati Manual: The Proposed Standard Practice for Survey of Research and Experimental Development*, Paris, OECD.

OECD (1992) *Main S&T Indicators*, Paris, OECD.

OECD (1996) *Statistics*, Paris, OECD.

Pavitt, K. (1996) 'Road to Ruin', *New Scientist*, 3 August.

Perez, C. (1985) 'Microelectronics, Long Waves and World Structural Change', *World Development*, 13(3), 441–63.

Reinert, E. (1994) 'Symptoms and Causes of Poverty: Under-development in a Schumpeterian System', *Forum for Development Studies*, 5, 71–111.

Romer, P. (1986) 'Increasing Return and Long Run Growth', *Journal of Political Economy*, 94, 1002–37.

Soete, L. and B. Verspagen (1993) 'Technology and Growth: The Complex Dynamics of Catching Up', in D. Pilat, E. Szirmai and B. van Ark (eds), *Explaining Economic Growth*, Amsterdam, Elsevier, 101–27.

Stalin, J. (1951) *Marxism and Linguistics*, Moscow, Foreign Language Publishing House.

Supple, B. (ed.) (1963) *The Experience of Economic Growth*, New York, Random Publishing House.

Takeuchi, H. and Nonaka, I. (1986) 'The New Product Development Game', *Harvard Business Review*, January/February, 285–305.

UNESCO (1980) *UNESCO Statistical Yearbook*, Paris, UNESCO.

Wade, R. (1990) *Governing the Market: Economic Theory and the Role of Government in East Asian Industrialization*, Princeton, NJ, Princeton University Press.

Walker, W. (1991) 'The Triad and the New World Order', *Science and Public Policy*, 18(6), 401–6.

Womack, J., D. Jones and D. Roos (1990) *The Machine that Changed the World*, New York, Rawson Associates (Macmillan).

World Bank (1993) *East Asian Miracle*, Washington, DC, World Bank.

10.   The ICT paradigm

1.   INTRODUCTION

During the 1990s, the use of the expression 'change of paradigm' to describe the advance of information and communication technology (ICT) became commonplace. This fashionable change in language can be explained by three main events. First, in the intellectual world, a debate was initiated by the publication of a provocative new book, which made the concept of paradigm change familiar to both natural and social scientists (Kuhn 1970). Secondly, in the real economy, the production and extremely widespread sale by Intel of a cheap microprocessor encouraged a focus on ICTs. Finally, the use of the expression by Greenspan, the then Chairman of the US Federal Reserve, drew the financial world's attention to the potential and hazards of ICTs.

By the end of the twentieth century it was already clearly evident that the new leading ICT industries (computers, software, electronic components, and telecommunications equipment) were firmly established as the leading sectors of the economy in the US. Indeed, although they still accounted for a relatively small proportion of aggregate production and employment, their rate of growth was so high that they accounted for over half of total growth in the US economy in the 1990s, and gave rise to a huge financial bubble early in the next century.

The second section of this chapter deals with the origins and definition of the paradigm concept; the third with the formation and collapse of the Bubble; and the final section with a critique of some myths that have attended diffusion of the ICT paradigm which were (and to some extent still are) the intellectual counterpart of the financial bubble. Among them were the supposed decline and even possible disappearance of some familiar institutions, such as the large firm and the nation state. How wrong they were.

2.   ORIGINS OF THE EXPRESSION 'CHANGE OF PARADIGM'

Dictionaries (for example, the *Oxford English Dictionary* 1965) trace the word paradigm to both Greek and Latin derivations and distinguish the emergence of two distinct meanings of the word. In the first place, a paradigm was an *observed pattern* and later came to mean an *exemplary pattern* of human behaviour. Not surprisingly, the latter sense was characteristic of religious literature in the Middle Ages. This chapter will discuss both uses of the word, but only in relation to recent literature in the social and the natural sciences.

In terms of economics, a new pattern may be construed as a new basic *structure* of the economy, and a new exemplary pattern as a set of principles designed to guide the behaviour of managers, firms, government organizations, and others, which are striving to understand, to develop, and to modify or adapt to such a newly emerging structure of the economy.

Although historians have consistently emphasized the revolutionary changes in technology in the leading economies ever since the British industrial revolution in the late eighteenth century, there are many still who argue that the ICT revolution surpasses the industrial revolution itself in terms of the breadth of its applications and the depth of its social consequences. ICT not only affects every industry and every service, but also every function within these industries and services. Not only production, but also design, distribution, and marketing are all profoundly affected by ICT. Multinational entities enjoy a new freedom in the location of these functions and in the networks that provide them. Moreover, eBay's new trading market brings together the greatest collection of small buyers and sellers in history. These and other remarkable features of the new ICTs have led some enthusiasts for the expression 'paradigm' to adopt missionary zeal with respect to its characteristics and diffusion, and to exaggerate its exemplary aspects.

The expression 'change of paradigm' was not widely used in the social sciences before the 1970s and not at all in economics. The main stimulus for its more widespread use was undoubtedly the debate among historians of science, which followed the publication of Thomas Kuhn's (1970) book on *The Structure of Scientific Revolutions*. Although certainly controversial, this work made familiar the concept of a paradigm as a commonly agreed theoretical approach, based on a set of principles and methods, which might however periodically be challenged by new ideas, derived from discoveries and evidence not consistent with this received theory. In Kuhn's view the accumulation of such anomalies led discontented (and usually younger) scientists within a discipline to rebel against the established norms, and ultimately to develop and propagate a revolutionary new paradigm, which would become in its turn a new orthodoxy of normal science.

Some historians and philosophers of science never accepted Kuhn's theory and strongly criticized his use of the paradigm concept as inaccurate and misleading (see, for example, Lakatos and Musgrave 1970; Fuller

2004). Nevertheless, partly because of this controversy, Kuhn's book did serve to popularize the idea of a paradigm and paradigm change among both scientists and historians. It was not long before economists and technologists took the fairly obvious step of applying some of these ideas about the history of science to the history of technology. The notion of a dominant design was one advanced in various branches of technology and was in some ways analogous to Kuhn's theory of normal science. The stretching of robust and dominant designs may be compared with normal scientific work within an established paradigm (Gardiner and Rothwell 1985).

In his pioneering comparison of scientific and technological paradigms, Norman Clark (1985) pointed to some significant differences, as well as similarities. In his view, technological paradigms show greater structural heterogeneity because of the variety of inter-industry linkages and the complexity of socio-economic relationships. He cited Constant's (1973, 1980) study of the origins of the turbojet revolution to illustrate this point. The transition from propeller-driven engines to jet engines required not only a major change among designers and producers of aero-engines and manufacturers of aircraft, but also changes in the attitudes and behaviour of airlines, airports, and regulatory authorities.

It was a paper by Giovanni Dosi (1982) that brought the concept of technological paradigms explicitly to the attention of a wider circle of economists and other social scientists. He systematically related such paradigm changes to changes in the structure of specific industries and in particular the electronics industry. Defining a technological paradigm as 'an outlook, a set of procedures, a definition of the relevant problems and of the specific knowledge related to their solution' (Dosi 1982: 148), he argued that new paradigms could not emerge simply from changes in market demand or in consumer tastes.

A new paradigm could emerge only as a result of an interplay between economic pressures and new developments in technology and in science. In this early phase, new, small 'Schumpeterian' firms often played an important role together with public agencies and a variety of technological and scientific institutions. As the new paradigm became dominant, normal incremental technological change would often correspond to a phase of oligopolistic maturity in the relevant industry.

Dosi was primarily concerned with paradigm change in specific industries and did not attempt to identify or analyse paradigm changes which might affect a large number of industries and services, or even the entire economy. However, he did hint at the possibility that 'broad new technological trajectories' could influence economic cycles in the wider economy (Dosi 1982: 160) in rather the same way as Nelson and Winter (1977) had spoken of 'generalized natural trajectories' of technology, such as electrification.

Quite independently of the discussion on paradigm change, economists and sociologists had become familiar with the notion of a general structural change in the economy arising simply from the large increase in the proportion of the total labour force engaged in information or knowledge production and distribution. Although they did not use the expression paradigm change, several studies (for example, Bernal 1939) analysed this trend even before World War II. In the post-war period, among the most influential works published were those of Machlup (1962) on *The Production and Distribution of Knowledge* and Daniel Bell (1973) on *The Coming of Post-Industrial Society*, and, in the management literature, Peter Drucker's (1945) concept of the corporation.

In contemporary discussion, the ICT paradigm is generally taken to refer to electronic technologies, but neither Machlup nor Bell spoke of paradigms, nor did they assign a central role to electronics in their analysis of the knowledge economy and structural change. A survey of research and development (R&D) in the electronic capital goods industry (Freeman et al. 1965) did however already show that by the early 1960s, the general view among those active in research was that the telephone communications network would increasingly depend on new electronic exchanges and that this network would be used for massive data transmission as well as voice telephony. The extraordinarily rapid growth of data processing in the computer industry would be complemented by a corresponding growth of the links between computers. Thus, the basic elements of a new pattern, or ICT paradigm, were present and observed long before the expression was coined and came into general use. The key industries in this newly emerging pattern were the computer industry, storing, processing, and transmitting vast quantities of information, the telecommunications network enabling worldwide and very rapid communication between these computers, and the micro-electronics industry supplying large numbers of cheap reliable components. This was, however, not yet regarded as an exemplary pattern, except by a few visionaries at, or near, the leading edge among researchers in science and technology policy, such as Diebold (1952, 1990).

It was especially the work of Carlota Perez (1983, 1985, 2002) that brought into general use both of the original meanings of paradigm. While the new pattern of very rapid growth of the core electronics industries could be fairly easily observed in the US, it was by no means so clear how far the new technologies could be developed in other industries and services beyond the early applications, and in other countries beyond the shores of the US. Working at this time in California, but with a background in the oil industry of her native Venezuela, Carlota Perez was particularly well qualified to recognize and study the problems of change of paradigm in industries hitherto dominated by an older technological style – the paradigm of oil-intensive mass production. She became convinced that there were potential profitable applications of ICT in every industry and service. Intel's development, production and sale of an extremely cheap but efficient 'computer on a chip' made computing universally accessible. Similarly to Dosi, she recognized the importance of the intense interaction between technology and economic pressures, which is why she used the expression 'techno-economic paradigm'. But like Kuhn, she recognized the strength of the resistance to change from those who were accustomed to a different way of thinking. Hence her insistence on the exemplary aspect of paradigm change and on the process of institutional change as an essential condition for successful diffusion. The specific characteristics of the new technologies meant that organizational changes had to accompany and facilitate technical change.

In later work Perez (2002) distinguished two phases in the diffusion of a new technological paradigm. In the first phase, which she designated as installation, investment in a new infrastructure and in new core industries are the dominant features. In the later phase, designated as deployment, it is the applications of the technological revolution in all the other industries and service activities and in many other countries that characterize the period. Clearly, in this conceptualization of the second phase the exemplary features of the new paradigm, and the institutional changes needed to establish its hegemony everywhere, are the predominant characteristics of social, economic, and technical change. While experimental and early applications of new technology would of course already be made during the installation phase, it is only after major institutional changes that the incremental process innovations in every part of the economy and in many countries can be fully deployed.

In her model, exceptional importance attaches to the role of infrastructural change, especially the communications infrastructure, in propagating the exemplary paradigm, since this can reach almost all potential actors. Only when the economic and technical advantages of the new technologies have been clearly demonstrated far beyond the industries of early applications can the paradigm become a meta-paradigm and generate widespread increases in productivity. Recognition of the potential profitability and universal applicability of the new paradigm would be driven by many events, experiments, and experiences but frequently in the past history of paradigm change one particular event had been especially significant, designated by her as a 'big bang'. For the ICT paradigm this big bang was the Intel microprocessor; in earlier times for another paradigm, the Liverpool to Manchester railway trials played the role of a big bang for the age of railways and steam power (see Table 10.1).

Systems of innovation

Table 10.1   Five successive technological revolutions, 1770s to 2000s

Technological revolution	Popular name for the period	Core country or countries	Big-bang initiating the revolution	Year
First	The Industrial Revolution	Britain	Arkwright's mill opens in Cromford	1771
Second	Age of steam and railways	Britain (spreading to Continent and US)	Test of the 'Rocket' steam engine for the Liverpool-Manchester railway	1829
Third	Age of steel, electricity and heavy engineering	US and Germany forging ahead and overtaking Britain	The Carnegie Bessemer steel plant opens in Pittsburgh, PA	1875
Fourth	Age of oil, automobile and mass production	US (with Germany at first vying for world leadership), later spreading to Europe	First Model-T Ford plant in Detroit, MI	1908
Fifth	Age of information and telecommunication	US (spreading to Europe and Asia)	The Intel microprocessor is announced in Santa Clara, CA	1971

Source: Adapted from Perez (2002: 11).

It was the extent of opposition and scepticism that in the early days retarded the growth of infrastructural investment and other related investments. But once the dam was breached the opposite situation began to prevail. Local flash floods occurred because of the rush to invest in new projects. Finance capital became hyperactive in the desire to stimulate this investment. Some kind of investor mania was characteristic of canals and railways as it was of the Internet in the 1990s. The flood of new investment became so great that it often exceeded for some time the real possibilities of profitable application, both in the case of the ICT paradigm and of earlier changes of paradigm (see Table 10.1). A salutary reminder of the excesses comes when bubbles burst, but not before a vitally important new infrastructure and other facilities had been established by the wave of investment that has been labelled as a spell of 'irrational exuberance'.

Alan Greenspan was not the first to use this expression to describe the surge of expansion in the ICT industries in the 1990s and the later associated Internet Bubble (Shiller 2000). Nor of course was he the first to speak of the new paradigm in connection with the new economy, and with the surge of growth in the ICT industries in mind. But his status and reputation as Chairman of the US Federal Reserve were such that, from 1996 onwards, the expression *paradigm change* entered common parlance far beyond the investor community, the economics profession or scientific research. The ICT paradigm had become both an established pattern and an exemplary pattern.

Among professional economists and historians, the notion of periodic revolutionary changes in technology, and periods of dominance of specific technologies, gained currency not only through the concept of paradigm change, but also through Bresnahan and Trajtenberg's (1995) work on General Purpose Technologies (GPT), which influenced many industries and services over long periods.

3.   THE ICT PARADIGM AND THE REAL ECONOMY

As a new pattern or structure of the economy, the ICT paradigm was clearly established by the end of the twentieth century in the US. The leading producing industries of the ICT paradigm were also growing very rapidly in Europe, in Japan, and in East and South-East Asia, influencing other industries. The rise of the Internet spawned new forms of transacting business in many of these other industries and services, including retail and wholesale distribution, travel and tourism, financial services, auctioneering and gambling, as well as publishing and information services. Of course, the penetration of e-commerce, as these new methods became known, was not instantaneous and was very uneven, but it was sufficient to fuel Internet mania in all of the numerous service activities, listed by Machlup (1962) as being those affected by the growth of the knowledge economy. These could all be transacted now, at least partly and sometimes preponderantly, by electronic means.

Obviously, changes of this magnitude could not possibly pass unnoticed by almost the entire population and expressions such as the Information Revolution, the Computer Revolution, or the Internet Revolution had become commonplace by the end of the century. Many exaggerated estimates were made about both the scale and the speed of the transformation that was occurring although, as *The Economist* (2004) observed in its *Survey of E-Commerce*, the changes that were actually occurring in the real economy were sometimes not those predicted by exuberant speculation during the heady years of the expansion of the Internet Bubble.

Among the services most deeply affected was retail distribution, and according to the US Department of Commerce, online retail sales rose to

$56 billion in 2003, but this was still only 1.7 per cent of total retail sales.[1] Although the annual rate of increase at this time was 26 per cent, the biggest change was not so much in total sales as in the behaviour of consumers, and whether they bought online or not. For example, buyers of cars, armchairs, electrical appliances, or other large items, frequently did research online even if they made the final purchase offline. They came in to buy, armed with information from the Internet. The interplay between shops, showrooms online, and offline information was transformed so that a potential buyer might often go to a shop or a showroom, ask for a demonstration, but then make some excuse and get more information from the Internet, and finally make the purchase in a different shop. *The Economist Survey of E-Commerce* (2004) described this as the 'unbundling' of product information from the transaction, an expression first used by Professor Sawhney of the Kellogg School of Management in Chicago (Sawhney and Parkh 2001).

Most shops will probably not disappear as a result of the e-commerce revolution, even though the American statistics actually under-estimated the extent of the change. Travel, tourism, and auctioneering were some of the areas excluded from the Department of Commerce estimates, although they were very fast-growing e-businesses. Moreover, many shops and showrooms are changing their product range and the ways in which they operate. For example, bookshops may turn themselves also into cafes or snackbars, where potential customers may peruse books or journals in comfort before they buy them. What will eventually emerge is probably a new form of co-existence of shops, showrooms, and Internet. University of Michigan Surveys of consumer satisfaction showed a slightly higher rating for e-tail than traditional retail, but the difference was not great and traditional shopping offers advantages of personal interaction, physical exercise, and neighbourly contact so often underestimated by conventional cost-benefit techniques.[2]

Wholesale and retail distribution are of course by no means the only service industries to be deeply affected by the ICT change of paradigm, but they are among the most important and provide a good illustration of the type of structural change facilitated by the ICT paradigm. Two good examples of the ways in which firms could grow and prosper, taking advantage of new possibilities afforded by new infrastructures, were given by Fields (2004). PC's Limited, later to become Dell Computer Corporation, only began operations in 1984 in a hall of residence at the University of Texas at Austin, but by 2001 it had gained the largest share of any company in the world market for personal computers (PCs). The elimination of the retailer by direct sales over the Internet was one, but by no means the only one, of the business innovations introduced by Dell Computer to fuel its meteoric rise. The organization of production in several sites in different parts of the world was also very important. Fields makes an extremely interesting comparison with the rise of G.F. Swift in the US meat-packing industry in the late nineteenth century. In this case too, the new communication and transport infrastructure (the railways) made possible the radical transformation of both distribution and production in a major industry.

During the period around the end of the twentieth century, when e-business was taking off and the Internet Bubble was being inflated, the new information infrastructure was often referred to as The Information Highway or, using the distinctively American phraseology, as The Super-Highway. Even before the arrival of broadband technology it was capable of conveying and processing vast quantities of information at very high speeds. Broadband technology accelerated this speed by at least an order of magnitude. Not surprisingly the future of the Internet became the subject of heated political debate as well as e-business investment. The candidate for the Democratic Party in the US election for the Vice-Presidency in 1996 emphasized the crucial role of government in ICT research in his contribution to a 1991 special issue of the *Scientific American*: 'Federal policies can make a difference in several key areas of the computer revolution . . . most important we need a commitment to build the high-speed data highways. Their absence constitutes the largest single barrier to realizing the potential of the information age' (Gore 1991: 150).

Although some of his Republican opponents also advocated more active policies to build the super-highways, not everyone was in favour of such proactive government policies, either then or later. A good example of a more sceptical standpoint was *The Economist* magazine which, in a characteristically sharp article in 1995, entitled 'Let the Digital Age Bloom' argued that: 'Apart from imposing a few familiar safeguards, the cleverest thing that governments can do about all these changes is to stand back and let them happen' (*The Economist* 1995: 16). However, later in the same article under the sub-heading 'The case for watering and a little weeding', *The Economist* conceded that 'governments cannot ignore cyber-space altogether. There are some regulating functions which governments have to perform, at least for the foreseeable future, even if they wish to disengage as much as possible'.

Controversy over the role of government in the ICT paradigm has continued to this day and is likely to continue indefinitely since ICT cannot and does not resolve of itself the most fundamental problems of political life, which have persisted for several thousand years (Aristotle 330BC [English translation 1905]). One of the most difficult issues involving the role of government is the whole question of access to the Internet (Alexander 1999; Kruger and Gilroy 2001; see also Cabinet Office 2005) and another is control over the content. These issues are dealt with at length in Parts III and IV of this handbook. Here it will suffice to note that the policy of non-intervention prescribed by *The Economist* was never consistently followed even in the US; in some Asian countries, notably the so-called Tigers, a more radical attitude prevailed and ten years later they were ahead of the US in numbers of broadband connections as a proportion of the population and of Internet users. How far this rapid catch-up could be ascribed to a little judicious watering and weeding by governments was a matter of intense debate (Wade 1990; Hobday 1995), but the changes in the real economy were now a matter of established fact.

Yang (2004) lamented that the US had fallen behind in the world league of broadband connections from third place in 2000 to tenth place in 2004. In her article entitled 'Behind in Broadband: New policies are needed to help the US catch up', she explained the relative decline of the US in terms of insufficient market competition. Whereas the leaders, especially South Korea, forced the incumbent companies to let start-ups use their networks at reasonable, government-set prices, and these start-ups drove speeds up and prices down, in the US the regional Bell companies prevailed in their long battle to stop this happening there. According to Yang, the US was 'in dire need of stronger leadership in broadband. The country is alone among developed nations in not having a comprehensive broadband plan' (Yang 2004: 70; see also Fransman 2006). Controversy on government policy in the US was further stimulated by the 'Brand X' decision of the Supreme Court affecting both access and content (Mossberg 2005; Supreme Court of the US 2005a, b). It was not only in broadband diffusion that catch-up of the US lead was taking place. In mobile telephony too, the erstwhile leader of the technological revolution had fallen behind.

Mobile telephones, as they evolved, also began to perform many of the functions performed by computers, television sets, and cameras. Some commentators even spoke of another change of paradigm. A big change *within* the ICT paradigm is probably a more accurate description. In this case, the competition came not only from Asia, but from Northern Europe too. However, the fact that firms in these and other countries have overtaken and often surpassed American firms in particular sectors, does not mean the end of US domination in general. The leadership of the US was based on some more enduring factors including military power, strong fundamental research, and higher education (Rosenberg and Nelson 1994).

It had at one time seemed probable that Japan would take the lead in the introduction of the ICT paradigm. In the 1970s and 1980s Japanese firms out-competed their American rivals in consumer electronics and established a worldwide lead in such areas as robotics, leading to some pessimism among American economists about the capacity to shake off the habits of the old mass production paradigm and move on to a new paradigm in the US (Dertouzos et al. 1989). However, the Internet, the American advances in micro-electronics, computers, and software – the most basic elements of the new paradigm – combined with the enduring strengths in basic research to re-establish American hegemony. Hicks et al. (2000) used patent statistics to demonstrate the depth of industrial leadership by American ICT firms. In this period too, the Japanese economy suffered from the explosion of a different type of bubble, based not on over-investment in the new paradigm, but on a huge rise in the price of land and financial assets. Whereas in the previous (mass production) bubble of the 1920s, bubbles in land prices were intimately associated with the growth of new transport infrastructure, this was no longer the case with ICT.

It took a fairly long time to make the necessary reforms in the Japanese financial system (and in the political system) before many Japanese firms were in a strong enough position to strike back again, but according to some observers (for example, Kunii and Tashiro 2004) they were doing so by the early years of the twenty-first century after substantial restructuring. Their renewed expansion was mainly in the 'high end' of the world markets for digital cameras, digital video disc players, plasma television, and camera phones. Here they were soon faced with intense competition from other Asian countries.

The broadband connections of the millions of computers in the information highways were of course very different from the highways of earlier technological paradigms, such as railways and motor highways. Nevertheless, the expression 'highway' is itself revealing of the ways in which the economy receives and digests new technological systems. The information highway and the earlier highways all have certain features in common despite their completely different technological characteristics. All of them facilitated the performance of a vast range of other industrial and service activities and changed the ways in which their business affairs were conducted. The railways changed the pattern of livestock breeding in Scotland, and meat marketing in London, just as fundamentally as they allowed for the transformation of the meat-packing industry in the US, described by Fields (2004), or the activities of the publishing industry that were transformed by the Internet. In poor countries, diffusion was accelerated by the use of Internet cafés. Following Korea's experience of rapid growth in the number of Internet cafés, China had an estimated 2 million cafés by 2005.

No less important, although more familiar, have been the changes in the computer and software industries themselves that have made PCs available in almost every firm, laboratory, school, office, hospital, and home. Technical change and competition constantly lead to the introduction of new models of computers while organizations are themselves constantly changing too. Finally, networks of organizations and links with the Internet are also continuously forming, re-forming, and dissolving. All of this leads to continual new requirements for software. Crime too strives to keep up with technology so that one of the main demands on the software industry is for new encryption and security methods (Giarratana 2004; Grow 2005). Military organizations engender the same or even greater pressures.

The future of the ICT paradigm depends, on the one hand, on the continuation of this enormous process of 'normal' technical change within the now well-established paradigm and, on the other hand, on the continuing extension and deployment of the new industries, services, and activities to all parts of the world (Mansell 2002; Perez 2002). Heated controversy has surrounded the worldwide deployment of the ICT paradigm. The technology undoubtedly facilitates and accelerates communication between all parts of the world as well as interception of those communications, but there are many different possible outcomes of this global deployment and big problems of institutional change.

In a capitalist economy it is mainly market competition that drives the world deployment process; but, as is evident from the foregoing, there is scope for considerable variation in the ways in which the exemplary paradigm is interpreted, modified, and applied. Moreover, it is not only the dominant firms whose interaction is determining the outcome. As was clearly recognized in the European Commission's (1997) High Level Expert Group report *Building the European Information Society for Us All*, government policies and the general culture of society are also extremely influential. Nor is it only those countries that dominated the world economy in the twentieth century that will continue to dominate it through the twenty-first century. In their book *New Technologies and Global Restructuring*, Brundenius and Göransson (1993), and more recently, Baskaran and Muchie (2006) in *Bridging the Digital Divide*, illustrate how rapidly catch-up countries such as Brazil, China, India, and South Africa are closing the gap, and how varied are the circumstances and strategies of these and other catch-up countries. Uneven development is the rule both within and between countries, despite some counter-tendencies towards convergence and the more extreme view that the spread of the ICT paradigm involves the disappearance of the nation state.

4.   MYTHS AND REALITY IN THE DEPLOYMENT OF THE ICT PARADIGM

Corresponding to the irrational exuberance that fuelled the Internet Bubble, the early period of installation of the ICT paradigm was accompanied by various myths about the economic and social consequences of its diffusion. Among these were some that related to such basic institutions of contemporary society as the state and the large firm.

There were indeed big changes in the real economy and in social institutions in the last quarter of the twentieth century and it was not surprising that some of these were so impressive that they were exaggerated and extrapolated into the future. One extreme example was Ohmae (1990: xii) who argued in his book *The Borderless World* that the 'interlinked economy' was now becoming so powerful that 'it has swallowed most consumers and corporations, made traditional national borders almost disappear and pushed bureaucrats, politicians and the military towards the status of declining industries'. More recent accounts would use the expression globalized economy rather than interlinked economy, but many others have emphasized the decline of the nation state and have postulated a close connection between the ICT paradigm and globalization.

Among the reasons for such beliefs were obviously the sheer speed and facility of global communications using ICT. These in their turn may plausibly be held to have facilitated both intra-firm and inter-firm connections on a worldwide basis, as well as inter-governmental communications, and all kinds of inter-personal communications. The rise of the multinational corporation (MNC) cannot in itself be directly attributed to the spread of the ICT paradigm, since it began much earlier. Nevertheless, most ardent opponents and enthusiasts for globalization do tend to associate them (Friedman 1999).

Critics of a strong globalization thesis often point out that there was an earlier period of globalization in the late nineteenth century which was brought to an end by the First World War and the Great Depression (Hirst and Thompson 1999; Held et al. 1999). It is even claimed that in that earlier period, globalization went further than it has today. However, Krugman (1995) is one of several well-known economists who forcefully argued that globalization has recently gone much further than in any earlier period. While not accepting all of Krugman's arguments on the nature and extent of the increase in international trade, Eichengreen (1996) in a balanced and careful survey did accept some of his main points. The change in the composition of trade in manufactures and the huge increase of trade in services occurred mainly in the 1980s and 1990s (Bordo et al. 1999), that is, when the ICT paradigm had clearly taken off and when the speed advantages of that paradigm were already obvious. The relative decline in the purely physical volume of production and trade had given rise to the expression 'weightless economy' to describe the impact of ICT. Thus, there were reasonable grounds for associating ICT with some prominent aspects of globalization.

Eichengreen placed even greater emphasis on the recent reduction in trade barriers and obstacles to the flow of capital, and contrasted this with what Williamson (1998) called the 'globalization backlash' of the late nineteenth and early twentieth centuries, when tariffs were often increased and pressures to restrict migration of both labour and capital were increasing in the US and other countries. While there were certainly some indications of a similar backlash early in the twenty-first century, the formal commitments in the international community to the Washington Consensus and their embodiment in the World Trade Organization and the International Monetary Fund may constitute a stronger movement towards globalization. This was the clear-cut conclusion of Bordo et al. (1999: 56) that 'the globalization of commodity and financial markets is historically unprecedented. Facile comparisons with the late nineteenth century notwithstanding the international integration of capital and commodity markets goes further and runs deeper than ever before.'

The weightless ICT paradigm made some significant contribution to this unprecedented degree of globalization, but this is a long way from the Ohmae thesis on the decline and disappearance of the nation state. On the contrary, there are still many good reasons for maintaining that in spite of and even because of financial and trade globalization, the nation state has actually become more important. This somewhat paradoxical argument was forcefully presented by Michael Porter (1990: 19) when he said that:

> Competitive advantage is created and sustained through a highly localised process. Differences in national economic structures, values, cultures, institutions and histories contribute profoundly to competitive success. The role of the home nation seems to be as strong or stronger than ever . . . the home nation takes on growing significance because it is the source of the skills and technology that underpin competitive advantage.

At first sight, the ICT paradigm might appear to undermine these national advantages since ICT can facilitate international flows of scientific and technical information as well as financial information. Indeed, Rothwell's (1992) study of the 'electronification' of design and development in MNCs appears to lend support to this proposition. He pointed out that MNCs were already locating specialized aspects, or stages of product and process design, in their subsidiary operations or related organizations abroad. In fact, even before electronification of design, it was quite a normal feature of the activity of large multinational chemical engineering firms, to take advantage of the huge cost differences, to locate various parts of their design activities in different international locations. Electronification (that is, application of the ICT paradigm) offered the possibility of greatly accelerating this process as well as lowering the cost, but it did not initiate the globalization of design, or the demise of the large firm.

One of the major advantages of ICT is indeed that it facilitates and accelerates all kinds of networking arrangements, both inter-firm and intra-firm (see, e.g. Callon 1992; Coombs et al. 1992; Coombs et al. 1996; Dertouzos 1991; Chesnais 1996; Green et al. 1999; Mansell and Steinmueller 2000; Weiser 1991). This is surely one of the main exemplary features of the new paradigm. But the subcontracting of some parts of design activities, or their transfer, under exchange agreements with other independent firms, did not necessarily weaken the role of the large multi-national firm itself.

Just as some economists construed ICT and globalization to signify the malaise and impending death of the nation state, others have construed the rapid growth of networking activities in the late twentieth century to foreshadow the displacement of the firm by the network. One of the best and most comprehensive studies of the information society (Castells 1996: 198; 1997, 1998) argues that 'the basic unit of economic organization' is no longer the entrepreneur, the family, the corporation, or the state, but a network composed of a variety of organizations. This network is held together by the 'spirit of information', which is a cultural code 'informing and enforcing powerful economic decisions at every moment in the life of the network'. Castells makes an analogy with Weber's spirit of accumulation and enterprise in the rise of capitalism, suggesting that the 'spirit of informationalism' is 'the culture of creative destruction accelerated to the speed of the opto-electronic circuits that process its signals, Schumpeter meets Weber in the cyberspace of the network enterprise' (Castells 1996: 199).

This analogy with Weber is reminiscent of the notion of a paradigm in its secondary meaning as an exemplary pattern, but neither Weber nor Castells saw either the spirit of accumulation or the spirit of information in quite this prescriptive way. Speaking of the last stage of the cultural development of capitalism, Weber referred to the possibility of 'mechanical petrification, embellished with a sort of convulsive self-importance' represented by 'specialists without spirit' and 'sensualists without heart', who imagine that they have attained a level of civilization never before achieved (Castells 1996: 200, quoting from Weber's *Protestant Ethic and the Spirit of Capitalism*). Although never so contemptuous as Weber, Castells nevertheless recognizes that the networking information society can develop in a variety of different directions, not all of them easily recognizable as a 'culture of creative destruction'.

This too is very much the attitude of Perez (2002) who envisages a wide range of possibilities for the future of the techno-economic paradigm of

ICT, depending on the selective strength of contending political and cultural forces and the process of institutional change within each country and in the international arena. The fact that some social scientists were very optimistic about the future of democratic ideals within the ICT paradigm reflected to some degree the relatively early stage of development of the information society, when Utopian ideals had more currency.

It is reasonable to express some scepticism about the notion that the 'network' is displacing, or soon will displace, the large firm as the basic unit of economic organization in the capitalist economy. Whereas in the early days many economists and sociologists stressed the role of small- and medium-sized firms in the new economy, and the huge new opportunities offered to them by the Internet, after the collapse of the Internet Bubble the emphasis has been swinging back to demonstrating the advantages of the very large global firm, itself becoming a giant network. Nor have the numerous networks in which these large firms undoubtedly participate (Hagedoorn and Schakenraad 1992) shown the durability and purposeful strategic direction characteristic of some of these large firms.

It is of course true that the ICT revolution did actually weaken, or even destroy, the monopolistic power of the old telecommunication utilities, which were often state-owned or at least closely regulated. This did facilitate the rapid development of many new services and new technologies as well as many new firms. Moreover, the former mass production paradigm was frequently accompanied by a marked trend towards centralization of economic decision making and often by extensions of public ownership. This has certainly not been the case so far during the diffusion of the ICT paradigm. On the contrary, there was a wave of privatization and a repudiation, not only of socialism, but even of Keynesian or dirigiste state economic policies. Thus it is hardly surprising that many commentators should see this latter trend as characteristic of the paradigm itself.

However, neither privatization nor deregulation are necessarily permanent features of ICT, and neither does this paradigm necessarily lead to the disappearance of either large oligopolistic firms or the nation state. In their analysis of the changing population of the 200 largest US-manufacturing firms, Louçã and Mendonça (1999) show that the picture has been rather one of a new set of oligopolies establishing themselves side by side with the old oligopolies of the twentieth century. Right at the heart of the Internet, the new service providers have been described by Javary and Mansell (2002) as an 'emerging Internet oligopoly'.

Neither the electronification of design, nor the undoubted rapid growth of technology exchange and partnership agreements are unimportant developments. Both do reflect aspects of the diffusion of the ICT paradigm, but it is difficult not to reject the conclusion that their significance has been exaggerated. Qualitative analysis of the transnational activities of large MNCs shows that most of it is either local design modification to meet local regulations, or monitoring of local scientific and technological activities (Brundenius and Göransson 1993). However, both in the drug and in the electronics industry, there are important exceptions (Reddy and Sigurdson 1994) and these are sufficient to merit continuous re-examination of the distribution of MNC R&D activities in relation to national systems of innovation. This is especially important in view of the determined efforts of some erstwhile 'under-developed' third world countries to use science and technology, and especially the ICT paradigm, to aid their struggle to overcome poverty, ill health, and economic backwardness. It is at this point that the myth of the disappearance of the nation state connects with the myth of the displacement of the firm in the ICT paradigm.

Far from mythical is the rise of the two most populous countries in the world – China and India – in their share of world production and world trade, based to a considerable extent on their capability in the ICT paradigm. Regrettably, their extraordinary economic growth has led to a polarization of income distribution and ownership of wealth, which, however, has been a general trend in the world economy, including both North and South America, East and West Europe, and Africa. Kuznets (1930) suggested that such long-term swings in inequality may well be associated with the absorption of technological and demographic changes in the world economy, and there are many reasons to think that those who are the quickest and most proficient in the adoption of this ICT paradigm will gain at the expense of the laggards. Such a widening of inequality has been characteristic of the emerging ICT paradigm, both at the international level between countries, and within each country. The European Commission's Expert Group on *Building the European Information Society for Us All* (European Commission 1997) analysed the influence of the gap between the 'information rich' and the 'information poor' households and individuals, and advocated various policies to reduce this new dimension of poverty, including both fiscal proposals and much wider social and educational policies (see also Graham 2002; ILO 2004; Burrows et al. 2005).

Perez (2002) has argued that the inequality effects of the early stages of installation of ICT are not so much inherent characteristics of the paradigm, as features of its cyclical development and deployment. It is not unreasonable, therefore, to hope that in the later stages they may be at least partly reversed, as occurred in the case of the deployment of the mass production paradigm. Whether or not such a reversal does occur is a matter of political and social policies and conflicts, but Reinert (2004) and his colleagues are probably right in their contention that there would have to be a massive change in social justice on a global scale if such a golden age is to emerge from the deployment of the ICT paradigm. In the period of installation of the new industries and infrastructure, the pressures towards polarization of income and wealth are very strong because of the exceptionally high monopoly profits won by the innovators due to the bubble phenomena, and acute skill shortages for developing and using the new processes and products. These things persist for quite a long time and can easily be reinforced by government policies or inertia. The need for strong countervailing policies, especially for expansion in the less developed countries, was first articulated by Tylecote (1985) and has been strongly re-emphasized by Mansell (2002) and Perez (2002). It is to be hoped that such policies prevail to aid the expansion of the world economy, as well as to promote social justice worldwide.

NOTES

1. See http://www.census.gov/eos/www/papers/2003/2003finaltext.pdf, accessed 5 May 2006.
2. See 'E-Commerce Customer Satisfaction Outpaces Most Other Industries, New Report Shows', University of Michigan, http://www.foreseeresults.com/Press_ACSIFeb2004.html, accessed 5 May 2006.

REFERENCES

Alexander, D.L. (1999). *Internet Access: Government Intervention or Private Innovation?* Mackinac Center for Public Policy, http://www.mackinac.org/archives/1999/s1999-08.pdf, accessed 5 May 2006.

Aristotle, (330BC, English translation 1905). *The Politics* (trans. B. Jowett). Oxford: Clarendon Press.

Baskaran, A. and Muchie, M. (2006). *Bridging the Digital Divide: Innovation Systems for ICT in Brazil, China, India, Thailand and Southern Africa.* London: Adonis & Abby.

Bell, D. (1973). *The Coming of Post-Industrial Society: A Venture in Social Forecasting.* New York: Basic Books.

Bernal, J.D. (1939). *The Social Function of Science.* London: Routledge.

Bordo, M.D., Eichengreen, B. and Irwin, D.A. (1999). 'Is Globalization Really Different Than Globalization a Hundred Years Ago?' *Brookings Trade Policy Forum*, Washington DC, 15–16 April.

Bresnahan, T.E. and Trajtenberg, M. (1995). 'General Purpose Technologies: "Engines of Growth"?' *Journal of Econometrics*, 65(1): 83–108.

Brundenius, C. and Göransson, B. (1993). *New Technologies and Global Restructuring.* London: Taylor Graham.

Burrows, R., Ellison, N. and Woods, B. (2005). 'Neighbourhoods on the Net: The Nature and Impact of Internet-based Neighbourhood Information Systems'. Report for the Joseph Rowntree Foundation, Bristol: The Policy Press, http://www.jrf.org.uk/bookshop/eBooks/1861347723.pdf, accessed 5 May 2006.

Cabinet Office (2005). 'Connecting the UK: The Digital Strategy', Prime Minister's Strategy Unit, March, http://www.strategy.gov.uk/downloads/work_areas/digital_strategy/digital_strategy.pdf, accessed 5 May 2006.

Callon, M. (1992). 'The Dynamics of Techno-Economic Networks', in R. Coombs, P. Saviotti and V. Walsh (eds), *Technological Change and Company Strategies: Economic and Sociological Perspectives*. London: Academic Press, 72–102.

Castells, M. (1996). *The Information Age: Economy, Society and Culture Volume I: The Rise of the Network Society*. Oxford: Blackwell.

Castells, M. (1997). *The Information Age: Economy, Society and Culture Volume II: The Power of Identity*. Oxford: Blackwell.

Castells, M. (1998). *The Information Age: Economy, Society and Culture Volume III: End of Millennium*. Oxford: Blackwell.

Chesnais, F. (1996). 'Technological Agreements, Networks and Selected Issues in Economic Theory', in R. Coombs, A. Richards, P. Saviotti and V. Walsh (eds), *Technological Collaboration: The Dynamics of Cooperation in Industrial Innovation*. Cheltenham, UK and Brookfield, US: Edward Elgar, 18–33.

Clark, N. (1985). *The Political Economy of Science and Technology*. Oxford: Basil Blackwell.

Constant, E.W. (1973). 'A Model for Radical Technological Change Applied to the Turbojet Revolution'. *Technology and Culture*, 14(4): 553–72.

Constant, E. (1980). *The Origins of the Turbojet Revolution*. Baltimore, MD: Johns Hopkins University Press.

Coombs, R., Richards, A., Saviotti, P. and Walsh, V. (eds) (1996). *Technological Collaboration: The Dynamics of Cooperation in Industrial Innovation*. Cheltenham, UK and Brookfield, US: Edward Elgar.

Coombs, R., Saviotti, P. and Walsh, V. (eds) (1992). *Technological Change and Company Strategies: Economic and Sociological Perspectives*. London: Academic Press.

Dertouzos, M. (1991). 'Communications, Computers and Networks'. *Scientific American*, 265(3): 62–71.

Dertouzos, M. Lester, R. and Solow, R. (eds) (1989). *Made in America: Report of the MIT Commission on Industrial Productivity*. Cambridge, MA: MIT Press.

Diebold, J. (1952). *Automation: The Advent of the Automatic Factory*. New York: Van Nostrand.

Diebold, J. (1990). *The Innovators: The Discoveries, Inventions and Breakthroughs of our Time*. New York: Dutton.

Dosi, G. (1982). 'Technological Paradigms and Technological Trajectories – A Suggested Interpretation of the Determinants and Directions of Technological Change'. *Research Policy*, 11(3): 147–208.

Drucker, P. (1945). *The Concept of the Corporation*. New York: Mentor.

Economist, The (1995). 'Let the Digital Age Bloom'. *The Economist*, 25 Feb.: 16–17.

Economist, The (2004). 'A Perfect Market: A Survey of E-Commerce'. *The Economist*, 15 May.

Eichengreen, B. (1996). *Globalizing Capital: A History of the International Monetary System*. Princeton, NJ: Princeton University Press.

European Commission (1997). *Building the European Information Society for Us All*. Final Policy Report of High-Level Expert Group, Directorate-General Employment, Industrial Relations and Social Affairs, Luxembourg: OOPEC.

Fields, G. (2004). *Territories of Profit: Communications, Capitalist Development and the Innovative Enterprises of G.F. Swift and Dell Computer*. Stanford, CA: Stanford University Press.

Fransman, M. (ed.) (2006). *Global Broadband Battles: Why the US and Europe Lag While Asia Leads*. Stanford, CA: Stanford Business Books.

Freeman, C., Fuller, J.K., Harlow, C.J. et al. (1965). 'Research and Development in Electronic Capital Goods'. *National Institute Economic Review*, No. 34, November, 40–91.

Friedman, T.L. (1999). *The Lexus and the Olive Tree: Understanding Globalization*. New York: Farrar, Straus Giroux.

Fuller, S. (2004). *Kuhn Versus Popper*. London: ICOM.

Gardiner, P. and Rothwell, R. (1985). 'Tough Customers: Good Designers'. *Design Studies*, 6(1): 7–18.

Giarratana, M.S. (2004). 'The Birth of a New Industry: Entry by Start-ups and the Drivers of Firm Growth: The Case of Encryption Software'. *Research Policy*, 33(5): 787–806.

Gore, A. (1991). 'Infrastructure for the Global Village: Does the Information Highway Need Government Investment? *Scientific American*, 265(3): 150 ff.

Graham, S. (2002). 'Bridging Digital Divides? Urban Polarisations and ICT'. *Urban Studies*, 39(1): 33–56

Green, K., Hull, R., McMeekin, A. and Walsh, V. (1999). 'The Construction of Techno-Economic Networks vs. Paradigms'. *Research Policy*, 28(7): 777–92.

Grow, B. (2005). 'The Hacker Hunters'. *Business Week*, 6 June, 46–54.

Hagedoorn, J. and Schakenraad, J. (1992). 'Leading Companies and Networks of Strategic Alliances in Information Technologies'. *Research Policy*, 21(2): 163–91.

Held, D., McGrew, A., Goldblatt, D. and Perraton, J. (1999). *Global Transformations*. Stanford, CA: Stanford University Press.

Hicks, D., Breitzman, T. and Olivastro, D. (2000). *Innovations in IT in the United States – A Portrait Based on Patent Analysis*. Haddon Heights, NJ: CHI Research Inc.

Hirst, P. and Thompson, G. (1999). *Globalization in Question* (2nd edn). Cambridge: Polity Press.

Hobday, M. (1995). *Innovation in East Asia: The Challenge to Japan*. Aldershot, UK and Brookfield, US: Edward Elgar.

International Labour Office (ILO) (2004). *A Fair Globalization: Creating Opportunities For All*. Report of the World Commission on the Social Dimension of Globalization. Geneva: ILO, 108.

Javary, M. and Mansell, R. (2002). 'Emerging Internet Oligopolies: A Political Economy Analysis', in E.S. Miller and W.J. Samuels (eds), *An Institutionalist Approach to Public Utilities Regulation*. East Lansing, MI: Michigan State University Press, 162–201.

Kruger, L.G. and Gilroy, A.A. (2001). 'IB10045: Broadband Internet Access: Background and Issues', CRS Issue Brief for Congress, 18 May, http://www.ncseonline.org/NLE/CRSreports/Science/st-49.cfm?&CFID=4942178&CFTOKEN=85462795#_1_1, accessed 5 May 2006.

Krugman, P. (1995). 'Growing World Trade, Causes and Consequences'. *Brookings Papers on Economic Activity*, 1: 327–62.

Kuhn, T.S. (1970). *The Structure of Scientific Revolutions*. Chicago, IL: Chicago University Press.

Kunii, I.M. and Tashiro, H. (2004). 'Japan's Tech Comeback'. *Business Week*, 9 Feb.: 38–9.

Kuznets, S. (1930). *Secular Movements in Production and Prices*. Boston, MA: Houghton Mifflin.

Lakatos, I. and Musgrave, A. (1970). *Criticism and the Growth of Knowledge*. Cambridge: Cambridge University Press.

Louçã, F. and Mendonçã, S. (1999). 'Steady Change: The 200 Largest US Manufacturing Firms in the Twentieth Century'. Working Paper No. 14, CISEP/ISEG, UTI, Lisbon.

Machlup, F. (1962). *The Production and Distribution of Knowledge in the United States*. Princeton, NJ: Princeton University Press.

Mansell, R. (ed.) (2002). *Inside the Communication Revolution: Evolving Patterns of Social Interaction*. Oxford: Oxford University Press.

Mansell, R. and Steinmueller, W.E. (2000). *Mobilizing the Information Society: Strategies for Growth and Opportunity*. Oxford: Oxford University Press.

Mossberg, W.S. (2005). ' "Wireless Carriers" Veto over how Phones Work Hampers Innovation', Personal Technology – Walt Mossberg, 2 June, at http://ptech.wsj.com/archive/ptech-20050602.html, accessed 5 May 2006.

Nelson, R.R. and Winter, S.G. (1977). 'In Search of a Useful Theory of Innovation'. *Research Policy*, 6(1): 36–76.

Ohmae, K. (1990). *The Borderless World*. New York: Harper.

Oxford English Dictionary (1965). Shorter Third Edition. Oxford: Oxford University Press.

Perez, C. (1983). 'Structural Change and the Assimilation of New Technologies in the Economic and Social System'. *Futures*, 15(4): 357–75.

Perez, C. (1985). 'Microelectronics, Long Waves and World Structural Change: New Perspectives for Developing Countries'. *World Development*, 13(3): 441–63.

Perez, C. (2002). *Technological Revolutions and Financial Capital: The Dynamics of Bubbles and Golden Ages*. Cheltenham, UK and Northampton, MA, US: Edward Elgar.

Porter, M. (1990). *The Competitive Advantage of Nations*. New York: Free Press.

Reddy, A.S.P. and Sigurdson, J. (1994). 'Emerging Patterns of Globalisation of Corporate R&D and Scope for Innovation Capability Building in Developing Countries'. *Science and Public Policy*, 21: 283–99.

Reinert, E.S. (ed.) (2004). *Globalization, Economic Development and Inequality*. Cheltenham, UK and Northampton, MA, US: Edward Elgar.

Rosenberg, N. and Nelson, R.R. (1994). 'American Universities and Technical Advance in Industry'. *Research Policy*, 23(3): 323–48.

Rothwell, R. (1992). 'Successful Industrial Innovation: Critical Factors for the 1990s' *R&D Management*, 22(3): 221–39.

Sawhney, M. and Parkh, D. (2001). 'Where Value Lives in a Networked World'. *Harvard Business Review*, Jan.: 79–86.

Scientific American (1991). 'Computers, Networks and Public Policy [Introduction to articles on US Government ICT Policy]'. *Scientific American*, 265(3): 150.

Shiller, R. (2000). *Irrational Exuberance*. Princeton, NJ: Princeton University Press.

Supreme Court of the United States (2005a). 'National Cable and Telecommunications Association, et al., Petitioners v. Brand X Internet Services et al. (04–277); Federal Communications Commission and United States, Petitioners v. Brand X Internet Services et al. (04–281) on Writs of Certiorari to the United

States Court of Appeals for the Ninth Circuit', 27 June, http://wid.ap.org/scotus/pdf/04-277P.ZO.pdf, accessed 5 May 2006.

Supreme Court of the United States (2005b). 'J. Scalia dissenting, National Cable & Telecommunications Association, et al., Petitioners v. Brand X Internet Services et al.; (04-277); Federal Communications Commission and United States, Petitioners v. Brand X Internet Services et al. (04-281) on Writs of Certiorari to the United States Court of Appeals for the Ninth Circuit, 27 June', http://wid.ap.org/scotus/pdf/04-277P.ZD.pdf, accessed 5 May 2006.

Tylecote, A. (1985). 'Inequality in the Long Wave: Trend and Cycle in the Core and Periphery'. *European Association of Development Institutes Bulletin*, 1: 1–23.

Tylecote, A. (1992). *The Long Wave in the World Economy: The Current Crisis in Historical Perspective*. London: Routledge.

United States Department of Commerce (2003). 'E-Stats' http://www.census.gov/eos/www/papers/2003/2003finaltext.pdf, accessed 5 May 2006.

Wade, R. (1990). *Governing the Market: Economic Theory and the Role of Government in East Asian Industrialisation*. Princeton, NJ: Princeton University Press.

Weber, M. (1930). *The Protestant Ethic and the Spirit of Capitalism*. London: George Allen and Unwin.

Weiser, M. (1991). 'The Computer in the 21st Century'. *Scientific American*, 265(3): 94 ff.

Williamson, J.G. (1998). 'Globalisation, Labour Markets and Policy Backlash in the Past'. *Journal of Economic Perspectives*, 12(1): 51–72.

Yang, C. (2004). 'Behind in Broadband: New Policies are Needed to Help the US Catch Up'. *Business Week*, 6 Sept.: 70–71.

11. A Schumpeterian renaissance?

I INTRODUCTION

This chapter endeavours to address three main questions. First, has there actually been a 'Schumpeterian renaissance'? Second, if so, which of the main features of this renaissance have been especially influential? Finally, which of these features has been particularly contested and what has been the outcome of these debates?

Early work on the economics of invention and innovation often commented on the lack of attention to these topics in the mainstream literature, or indeed, in any of the published literature, e.g. Jewkes *et al.* (1958) or Rogers (1962). In his book *Diffusion of Innovations* (1962), Rogers reported that he could find only one study of diffusion of industrial innovations in the economics literature and as late as 1973, in a major survey article, Kennedy and Thirlwall still complained at the lack of attention to innovation.

The same complaint certainly could not be made today and this is indeed one indication that there has been a Schumpeterian renaissance in the late twentieth century, continuing to this day. Rogers (1986) himself in his later work on diffusion of innovations commented on the rapid proliferation of studies in this field in the 1970s and 1980s. A more general indication of the upsurge of interest in the economics literature as well as in the related management literature is provided by the appearance of a number of new journals in the 1980s and 1990s (Table 11.1). This change is also evident in the numbers of papers dealing with Schumpeterian topics in such major journals as the *Economic Journal, The American Economic Review*, the *Journal of Economic Literature* and the *Harvard Business Review*.

In the period just after his death, much of the literature concentrated on one rather narrow aspect of Schumpeter's legacy – the role of large monopolistic firms in innovation (see Kamien and Schwartz, 1975, for a summary of this debate). This was sometimes erroneously construed as Schumpeter's main contribution to economics and described as the Schumpeterian theorem. As with several similar debates, it has been largely resolved by various contributors to the Schumpeterian renaissance, who have shown that in the early phases of a technological revolution typically many small firms compete, although one or a few of these may enjoy temporary monopolistic positions and earn exceptionally high profits.

Table 11.1   The Schumpeterian heritage: journals dealing mainly with innovation and management of innovation

Title	Date of inception
Technological Forecasting and Social Change	1965
Research Policy	1971
Science and Public Policy	1973
Economics of Innovation and New Technology	1980
Structural Change and Economic Dynamics	1989
Journal of Evolutionary Economics	1991
Industrial and Corporate Change	1991
Industrial Innovation	1993
Technovation	1980
International Journal of Technology Management	1983
Technology Analysis and Strategic Management	1988
International Journal of Innovation Management	1997
International Journal of Entrepreneurship and Innovation	1999

Recent evidence has confirmed abundantly Schumpeter's theory of 'bandwagon' effects in which these high profits are eroded and competed away by new entrants, not before, however, some of them have grown into very large successful firms. In the later stages of rapid diffusion, these profits may confer exceptional advantages in market power, incremental innovation and scale of R&D, as has evidently been the case with Microsoft, to take only one example from recent history. An evolutionary view of changing technology and market structure resolves many such problems despite the complexities of the turbulent competitive struggles and occasionally of government intervention. Attention to the high degree of uncertainty about the outcome of such struggles and depth of empirical analysis of their evolution has been one of the main achievements of the Schumpeterian renaissance.

Schumpeter's main point that competition from the new or improved product, process or organization is a more devastating form of competition than non-innovative competition has been abundantly confirmed, absorbed and disseminated by numerous case studies of management in almost every industry. (See, for example, Crépon *et al.* (1998) for a statistical approach to productivity gains from innovation, or Christensen and Rosenbloom (1995) for the case of competition *between* innovative firms.) So, too, has his point that there are phases in this struggle when large monopolies do enjoy some advantages, despite the persistent dogmatic insistence of some of his critics that they are always harmful to technical progress and economic efficiency. Perhaps the stronger evidence of the Schumpeterian renaissance is in the attention paid to management of innovation in management courses, schools and textbooks (see, for example, Tidd *et al.*, 1997, and Porter, 1990, for competition in innovation between nations). Lundvall (2004) has reported that Google came up with 5000 references to 'national systems of innovation'.

Historians still wrestle with the definition and evaluation of the Renaissance in Italy six centuries ago, so that it is hardly surprising that the contemporary evaluation of the Schumpeterian renaissance is controversial. Bibliometric evidence, although it is quite persuasive of a considerable growth of interest in some of Schumpeter's main ideas, does not in itself demonstrate that any of his ideas became dominant in the economics profession, nor which of his ideas have had the greatest influence beyond this profession.

Consequently, the viewpoint of this chapter is a purely personal one and certainly would not claim to be definitive. It is however based on about 50 years of research and discussion from the time of Schumpeter's death (1950) until the present day. This has been sufficient to convince this author that Schumpeter's central ideas – that innovation is the crucial source of effective competition, of economic development and the transformation of society – have become very widely accepted. They were, of course, neither original to Schumpeter, nor unusual for Germany in the nineteenth and twentieth centuries. Reinert (1995, 2002) has argued convincingly that they were actually quite widespread among German economists both before and during the *Methodenstreit*. Schumpeter himself acknowledged his debt both to Marx and to Schmoller, while other ideas, such as the expression 'Creative Destruction' have been traced to Sombart.

The formulation of the young Marx and Engels in their exuberant *Communist Manifesto* (1848) has scarcely been improved upon by either Schumpeter or his followers, as a succinct summary of some of the most significant features of capitalist economies:

> The bourgeoisie cannot exist without constantly revolutionising the instruments of production and thereby the relations of production and with them the whole relations of society . . . Constant revolutionising of production, uninterrupted disturbance of all social conditions, everlasting uncertainty and agitation, distinguish the bourgeois epoch from all earlier ones.

Despite their total disagreement on the source and role of profit and ownership under capitalism, Schumpeter derived his theory of the erosion of profit margins during diffusion of innovations also from Marx.

It should be noted that Schumpeter took the side of Menger in the *Methodenstreit* and repeatedly during his lifetime insisted on the value of

Walrasian equilibrium theory (Freeman and Louçã, 2001: 43–4). This has caused some of his biographers and critics to describe his theory and indeed his whole life as a paradox (Allen, 1991: 4). Nevertheless, it is quite understandable that Rosenberg (1994: 41) should insist on his point that Schumpeter made a more radical challenge to neoclassical orthodoxy than any other twentieth-century economist. Although his work was indeed paradoxical, the renaissance of his influence in the last 20 years has certainly not been based on equilibrium theory but on his evolutionary dynamics. Several recent authors have emphasized that Schumpeter's method was a pluralistic combination of the historical institutional perspective of Schmoller with the use of formal analytical techniques (Ebner, 2000; Shionoya, 1991). This combination is believed to be in the tradition of Schmoller himself. The discussion is partly semantic but, be this as it may, the Schumpeterian renaissance derives from his evolutionary ideas. And as Dahmen (1984) put it: 'Schumpeterian dynamics is characterised by its focus on economic transformation' (p. 25).

II   INFLUENTIAL FEATURES OF THE SCHUMPETERIAN RENAISSANCE

However, the Schumpeterian renaissance has not simply been based on a more widespread recognition of the importance of innovation. Although this was certainly a major feature of most of Schumpeter's work, if it had been the only one, then others would deserve more credit than him. His distinctive contribution was based on his recognition of some special features of the innovative process in the evolution of capitalist societies, notably the clustering of innovations and the explosive growth of new firms and industries based on these clusters. He described this evolution as a succession of industrial revolutions and it is the recognition of this historical process which has characterized the Schumpeterian renaissance, just as Dahmen (1984) foresaw in his theory of structural change and development blocks.

The clustering of inventions and innovations, of the inputs and the outputs of research and development activities, has been apparent from all the work on measurement of scientific and technical activities which has proliferated since Schumpeter's death. Early work was mainly concerned with the measurement of inputs into innovative projects and indirect measures of inventive output, especially patent statistics, which had of course been available for centuries but seldom used much by economists until the proceedings of the first major conference on 'The rate and direction of inventive activity' became available. This conference was a herald of the Schumpeterian renaissance and was followed by a brilliant demonstration by Schmookler (1966) of the use of patent statistics for economic analysis. He maintained that the appearance of clusters of patents in various industries after major productive investment in those industries demonstrated that invention and innovation were generally demand-led and not technology-led. This initiated a fruitful debate among Schumpeterians, even though the most influential paper concluded that Schmookler's interpretation of clustering was mistaken (Mowery and Rosenberg, 1979) since the clustering measured the numerous follow-through inventions of the rapid diffusion phase of innovation rather than the crucial original inventions and innovations.

This debate and several others in the 1960s and 1970s also began to make use of the newer statistics of science and technology which were becoming available, culminating in the systematic measurement of innovations themselves (Arundel *et al.*, 2003). Before these most recent developments surrogate measures of innovative activities, such as R&D statistics, provided a valuable additional impetus to the new wave of Schumpeterian research in such areas as the relationship between innovation and economic growth, innovations and international trade performance or innovations and profitability.

Even long before official innovation surveys, much painstaking work on individual industries had already provided convincing evidence of clustering and explosive growth directly related to these clusters (e.g. Hufbauer, 1966). On a broader canvas, historians too had used economic statistics to confirm some of Schumpeter's points, especially on the growth of leading industries in technological revolutions (Table 11.2). In the most recent period the semiconductor industry and the computer industry in several countries both had growth rates which far exceeded those of other industries. As in previous revolutions, this rate was several times more rapid than the average growth rate of industrial output (Table 11.2).

Table 11.2   Estimated growth rates of leading industries and firms in technological revolutions

Industry	Period	Growth rate per annum
Cotton (UK)	1770–1801	8%
Railways (UK)		
Freight	1837/46–1866/74	13%
Passengers		9%
Steel (USA)	1880–1913	11%
Automobiles (USA)		
Ford Model-T	1908–1927	14%

Source: Author's estimates based on data in Freeman and Louçã (2001).

This last point reminds us that the actual course of events in the real economy has probably been more persuasive than any theoretical arguments or historical statistics. The effects of the diffusion of information and communication technology (ICT) have been so obvious to almost everyone that it has become quite difficult for opponents of Schumpeter's theory of successive technological revolutions to sustain their argument, at least in this case. The successive spurts of innovation and growth in the electronics industry, the telecommunication industry, the computer industry and the Internet have made the ICT revolution a commonplace and the expressions 'information society' and 'knowledge economy' have passed into general use (e.g. Castells, 1996, 1997, 1998). The numerous books and papers on this topic are testimony to the Schumpeterian renaissance, whether or not they acknowledge his direct or indirect influence.

Whilst there are relatively few people who would be ready to defend the proposition that there has not been an ICT revolution, surprisingly there are still a few who cling to the notion that there never was an industrial revolution in Britain in the first place, although the evidence of contemporary observers, of artists and writers, of artefacts and of economic statistics is almost as strong as in the contemporary revolution. However, some of the most authoritative and best-known historians have used and defended an essentially Schumpeterian framework, particularly with respect to the first industrial revolution (Hobsbawm, 1962, 1964; Landes, 1969, 1993). The compelling evidence of the industrial statistics is discussed in Freeman and Louçã, 2001: 24–31. Schumpeter himself confronted early exponents of the idea that there never was an industrial revolution and whilst conceding that there was a little substance in their ideas, nevertheless gave them a clear if gentle rebuff (Schumpeter, 1939, vol. 2: 253–5).

Whilst to speak of a 'Schumpeterian renaissance' does imply that the general spirit of his work and his main ideas have become a significant influence on the general climate of ideas, it certainly does not imply that every one of his propositions and theories have been accepted. Nor is that what he himself would have wished. On the contrary, he was quite emphatic that he did not want a 'school' of disciplined followers, but expected that further research on innovation, while enriching and reinforcing some of his ideas, would falsify others. This has indeed been the general outcome of the Schumpeterian renaissance, which has usually been marked by a lack of dogmatism and a readiness to accept the evidence of new empirical research studies.

An example of this spirit is the reassessment of the role of incremental innovation by most scholars in the Schumpeterian renaissance. Schumpeter himself drew a sharp distinction between 'entrepreneurs' who were responsible for innovations, as acts of 'will not intellect', and managers who were 'mere' imitators. He did however recognize that, during the diffusion of an innovation, further significant improvements could be made in both product and process, as well as financial and organizational innovations, necessary for opening new markets and introducing the product to new countries. Thus, he remarked with respect to the automobile that it would never have diffused so widely if it had remained the same product as at its inception, and if it had not transformed its own environment. Moreover, his strictly functional definitions of 'entrepreneurs', 'capitalists', 'owners' and the 'mere head or manager of a firm' (Schumpeter, 1939, vol. 1: 102–9) left room for the designation of any individual as an entrepreneur (innovator). In his terminology, an entrepreneur might have any official job title and he himself argued that the leaders of R&D groups in the large German electrical firms were 'entrepreneurs' in his sense of the word. The function could be temporary in the course of a career so that the same individual could be innovator, manager, owner or capitalist, sequentially or all together.

Researchers in the Schumpeterian renaissance have made use of his definitions to distinguish the role of a 'product champion' (Schon, 1973) as the individual who struggles to push an innovation through to its launch against various obstacles, by an 'act of will'. Other researchers, for example, Project SAPPHO (Rothwell, 1992; Freeman, 1994) made a distinction between 'technical innovators' and 'business innovators' and examined the role of each in various industries. In some industries, the same person often performed both functions; in others, they were usually different people with the 'business innovator' being that person in the management and organizational structure who acted as the champion for the technical innovator.

All of this was very much in Schumpeter's tradition, but the results of research demonstrated increasingly that the role of incremental innovations was extraordinarily important and that users of innovation played a key role in this process of incremental improvement. Schumpeter's remarks about the automobile would apply even more to the computer and to other products of the earlier revolutions as well (see, for example, Mowery and Nelson, 1999).

Studies such as that of Hollander (1965) on the source of productivity gains in the rayon industry, in successive generations of Du Pont plants showed that incremental process innovations were just as important as incremental product innovations. These perceptions were further enhanced by the research of Lundvall and his colleagues at Aalborg on user-producer interactions and innovations (Lundvall, 1985). Arrow's (1962) seminal paper on the economic implications of learning by doing and the Aalborg work on learning by user–producer interaction led to the general acceptance of these ideas by the economics profession and management theorists.

Lundvall himself extended his theory to the study of another sphere of influence of the Schumpeterian renaissance – the 'national system of innovation' (see Chapter 54 of the present work [Hanusch and Pyka, 2007]).

So influential was the evidence of the empirical research on innovation that it led some scholars to argue for the abandonment of the distinction between incremental innovations and more radical innovations, as well as between innovations and their diffusion (Silverberg, 2002) and between invention and innovation. However, even though these boundaries are difficult to draw, Schumpeter's distinctions have proved valuable in conceptual terms, especially in relation to inventions.

III   THE OUTCOME

Already during his lifetime, Schumpeter's theory of business cycles was strongly contested (Kuznets, 1940) and he was disappointed by the reception accorded to what he thought of as his major contribution to economic theory – his two volumes on business cycles (1939). During the Schumpeterian renaissance his work on this topic has continued to be the subject of heated controversy. As is well known, it was Schumpeter who introduced the expression 'Kondratieff cycles' into the literature to designate those long-term fluctuations in economic growth which the Russian economist, Nikolai Kondratieff had identified and analysed in the 1920s. Schumpeter's contribution was to explain these cycles in terms of successive technological revolutions. Unfortunately, he failed to analyse satisfactorily either the timing and the phases of the technological revolutions or the timing of the related, but necessarily later, phases of the associated business cycles. Treating them as synchronous has led to a great deal of confusion.

Since his death, while his theory of successive technological revolutions has been very influential, his attempt to defend the nature and periodicity of the Kondratieff cycle has encountered continuous strong criticism (e.g. Solomou, 1987; Rosenberg and Frischtak, 1984; and see Louçã and Reijnders (1999) for a set of papers on the statistical debate). Although it has been prolonged and sometimes heated, this debate has also been an important part of the Schumpeterian renaissance and has led to some fruitful outcomes as well as to the refutation of some of Schumpeter's own ideas about business cycles. In the early days of the econometrics movement, Kondratieff was welcomed into the Econometric Society and his work was taken very seriously by leaders of the movement, such as Frisch and Tinbergen, as well as by Schumpeter. Partly because of Schumpeter's efforts, his work gave a lasting impetus to qualitative and historical research

Table 11.3   Three types of analysis of long-term economic fluctuations

Model analysis	Statistical and econometric analysis		Historical analysis
	Kondratiev		
	Oparin		Trotsky
	Kuznets		
	Imbert		
	Dupriez		
	Duijn	Mandel	Maddison
Forrester	Kleinknecht	SSA	
Sterman	Menshikov	Gordon	Regulation Schools
Mosekilde	Hartman	Aglietta	
	Metz	Boyer	Freeman
Mensch	Reijnders		Perez
	Ewijk	Reati	Tylecote
	Zwan	Kuczynski	Fayolle
Silverberg		Shaikh	
		Entov	Bosserelle
		Poletayev	
		Moseley	
	(others: Sipos, Chizov, Craig/Watt, Glismann, Taylor, Nakicenovic, Marchetti)		(others: Braudel, Wallerstein, Modelski)

Source: Freeman and Louçã (2001), p. 97.

on long-term fluctuations in economic development, as well as the purely quantitative analysis which preoccupied many of his critics.

The same is true of Schumpeter's own work on business cycles despite the heavy criticism which it has encountered. In their discussion of the numerous contributions to long wave theory, Freeman and Louçã (2001) distinguish three main streams of analysis: model analysis, statistical and econometric analysis and historical analysis (Table 11.3). Whilst they themselves believe that a synthesis of the historical approaches is likely to be the most fruitful for evolutionary economics, they nevertheless emphasize the positive stimulus which the whole Schumpeterian debate on business cycles has given to economic theory as well as to the elucidation of appropriate statistical techniques in the analysis and modelling of economic fluctuations.

Recent new work with the Cambridge Growth Model suggests that there may still be valuable results to be achieved by a synthesis of the various techniques shown in Table 11.3. This work further indicates the increasing need to integrate the environmental dimension with long-term analysis of this kind. This could help to remedy a major weakness of the Schumpeterian renaissance: lack of sufficient attention to this dimension of economic and structural change.

Finally, there has been a major positive development arising from the recent Schumpeterian work on long wave analysis: new work on financial capital and technological revolutions (Perez, 2002). The work of Perez not only makes a major contribution to the resolution of several of the major problems arising in the prolonged debate about the timing of 'technological revolutions' and business cycles, it also provides for the first time a set of ideas which fill one of the major gaps in the Schumpeterian renaissance: the role of credit creation in Schumpeterian evolution. Neither Schumpeter nor the neo-Schumpeterians had hitherto related the evolution of credit creation to the evolution of new technologies (see Perez, 2002, and Chapter 49 of the present work [Hanusch and Pyka, 2007]).

CONCLUSIONS

Like Fagerberg (2003), this chapter concludes that the 'Schumpeterian renaissance' has been a real phenomenon. Its main feature has been the resurgence of ideas about innovation, including industrial revolutions. Although it has led to heated debates, these have themselves been a constructive contribution of the renaissance and have enriched evolutionary theory in economics. Fagerberg was justified in his view that the ideas of the 'neo-Schumpeterian' evolutionary economists, although departing in some respects from Schumpeter's own ideas, were nevertheless strongly influenced by the Schumpeterian renaissance.

REFERENCES

Allen, R. (1991). *Opening Doors: The Life and Work of Joseph Schumpeter* (2 vols). New Brunswick: Transaction Books.
Arrow, K.J. (1962). Economic welfare and the allocation of resources for invention, in R. Nelson (ed.), *The Rate and Direction of Innovative Activity: Economic and Social Factors*. Washington, DC: National Bureau of Economic Research.
Arundel, A., Boodoy, C., Hollanders, H., Nesta, L. and Patel, P. (2003). *The Future of the European Innovation Scoreboard (EIS)*. Policy Benchmarking Workshop, Luxembourg, 24 Feb.
Castells, M. (1996, 1997, 1998). *The Information Age: Economy, Society and Culture* (3 vols). Oxford: Blackwell.

Christensen, C.M. and Rosenbloom, R.S. (1995). Explaining the attacker's advantage: technological paradigms, organisational dynamics and the value network, *Research Policy*, **24**: 233–59.

Crépon, B.E., Duguet, E. and Mairesse, J. (1998). Research, innovation and productivity: an econometric analysis at the firm level, *Economics of Innovation and New Technology*, **7**: 115–58.

Dahmen, E. (1984). Schumpeterian dynamics: some methodological notes, *Journal of Economic Behaviour and Organisation*, **5**: 25–34.

Ebner, A. (2000). Schumpeter and the 'Schmollerprogramm' integrating theory and history in the analysis of economic development, *Journal of Evolutionary Economics*, **10**: 355–72.

Fagerberg, J. (2003). Schumpeter and the revival of evolutionary economics: an appraisal of the literature, *Journal of Evolutionary Economics*, **13**(2): 125–59.

Freeman, C. (1994). The economics of technical change: a critical survey, *Cambridge Journal of Economics*, **18**: 463–514.

Freeman, C. and Louçã, F. (2001). *As Time Goes By*. Oxford: Oxford University Press.

Hanusch, H. and Pyka, A. (eds) (2007), *Elgar Companion to Neo-Schumpeterian Economics*. Cheltenham, UK and Northampton, MA, USA: Edward Elgar.

Hobsbawm, E. (1962). *The Age of Revolution*. London: Weidenfeld and Nicolson.

Hobsbawm, E. (ed.) (1964). *Labouring Men*. London: Weidenfeld and Nicolson.

Hollander, S. (1965). *The Sources of Increased Effciency: A Study of DuPont Rayon Plants*. Cambridge, MA: MIT Press.

Hufbauer, G.C. (1966). *Synthetic Materials and the Theory of International Trade*. London: Duckworth.

Jewkes, J., Sawers, D. and Stillerman, J. (1958). *The Sources of Invention*. London: Macmillan.

Kamien, M.I. and Schwartz, N.L. (1975). Market structure and innovation, *Journal of Economic Literature*, **13**: 1–37.

Kennedy, C. and Thirlwall, A.P. (1983). *Technical Progress, Surveys of Applied Economics*, vol.1. London: Macmillan.

Kuznets, S. (1940). Schumpeter's business cycles, *American Economic Review*, **30**: 257–71.

Landes, D. (1969). *The Unbound Prometheus: Technological and Industrial Development in Western Europe from 1750 to the Present*. Cambridge: Cambridge University Press.

Landes, D. (1993). The fable of the dead horse: or the industrial revolution revisited, in J. Mokyr (ed.), *The British Industrial Revolution*. Boulder, CO: Westview Press.

Louçã, F. and Reijnders, J. (1999). *The Foundations of Long Wave Theory* (2 vols). Cheltenham, UK and Northampton, MA, USA: Edward Elgar.

Lundvall, B.-Å. (1985). Product innovation and user–producer interaction, *Industrial Development Research Series*, vol. 31. Aalborg: Aalborg University Press.

Lundvall, B.-Å. (2004). 'Introduction' to C. Freeman, Technological infrastructure and international competitiveness, *Industrial and Corporate Change*, **13**(3): 531–9.

Marx, K. and Engels, F. (1848). *Manifesto of the Communist Party*. Republished in many editions, e.g. in Marx, *Selected Works*, vol. 1, Moscow, 1935.

Mowery, D.C. and Nelson, R.R. (eds) (1999). *Sources of Industrial Leadership: Studies of Seven Industries*. Cambridge: Cambridge University Press.

Mowery, D.C. and Rosenberg, N. (1979). The influence of market demand upon innovation: a critical review of some recent empirical studies, *Research Policy*, **8**: 102–53.

Perez, C. (2002). *Technological Revolutions and Financial Capital: The Dynamics of Bubbles and Golden Ages*. Cheltenham, UK and Northampton, MA, USA: Edward Elgar.

Porter, M. (1990). *The Competitive Advantage of Nations*. New York: Free Press, Macmillan.

Reinert, E.S. (1995). Competitiveness and its predecessors: a cross-national perspective, *Structural Change and Economic Dynamics*, **6**: 223–42.

Reinert, E.S. (2002). Schumpeter in the context of two canons of economic thought, *Industry and Innovation*, **9**: 23–39.

Rogers, E.M. (1962). *Diffusion of Innovations*. New York: Free Press of Glencoe.

Rogers, E.M. (1986). Three decades of research on the diffusion of innovations: progress, problems, prospects. Paper at the DAEST Conference, Venice, April.

Rosenberg, N. (1994). Joseph Schumpeter: radical economist, in Y. Shinoya and M. Perlman (eds), *Schumpeter in the History of Ideas*. Ann Arbor, MI: University of Michigan Press, pp. 41–57.

Rosenberg, N. and Frischtak, C.R. (1984). Technological innovation and long waves, *Cambridge Journal of Economics*, **8**: 7–24.

Rothwell, R. (1992). Successful industrial innovation: critical factors for the 1990s, *R&D Management*, **22**(3): 221–39.

Schmookler, J. (1966). *Invention and Economic Growth*. Cambridge, MA: Harvard University Press.

Schon, D.A. (1973). Product champions for radical new innovations, *Harvard Business Review*, **5**, March/April.

Schumpeter, J.A. (1939). *Business Cycles: A Theoretical, Historical and Statistical Analysis of the Capitalist Process*. (2 vols). New York: McGraw-Hill.

Shionoya, Y. (1991). Schumpeter on Schmoller and Weber: a methodology of economic sociology, *History of Political Economy*, **23**: 193–219.

Silverberg, G. (2002). The discrete charm of the bourgeoisie: quantum and continuous perspectives on innovation and growth, *Research Policy*, **31**(8–9): 1275–91.

Solomou, S. (1987). *Phases of Economic Growth, 1850–1979: Kondratieff Waves and Kuznet Swings*. Cambridge: Cambridge University Press.

Tidd, J., Bessant, J. and Pavitt, K. (1997). *Managing Innovation: Integrating Technological, Market and Organisational Change*. Chichester: Wiley.

12. Conclusions: a 'theory of reasoned history'

To some extent the eleven previous essays have illustrated the evolution of the concept of 'national systems of innovation', although they were not written specifically with that purpose in mind. Not surprisingly, since they are dealing with innovation, they lay stress on technology and on science. However, they generally tried to avoid a simplistic technological determinism by also stressing the interdependence of technology, the economy and the political process. From the time in 1983 when I first collaborated with Carlota Perez (Chapter 3), we coincided on the emphasis on institutional innovations in the diffusion of new technologies and in shaping some of the main features of national systems of innovation in each country. I was also persuaded by her conception of 'techno-economic paradigms' emerging with each major technological revolution (Chapter 10).

A belief in the enduring political strength and power relationships of many nation states led me to reject Ohmae's theory of the supposed disappearance of nation states and their armed forces (Chapter 10). Consequently, when I came to collaborate with my colleague Francisco Louçã in writing a joint book, *As Time Goes By*, on the history of successive technological revolutions (Freeman and Louçã, 2001) we were looking to develop a theory of history which would take into account the relative autonomy of various sub-systems of society. In his work on the history of economic thought, Francisco Louçã was particularly impressed by the way in which J.M. Keynes had stressed the relative autonomy of the economic and political sub-systems of society as well as their interdependence.

Working together, we developed that Keynesian notion to embrace five distinct sub-systems and their interaction. These five sub-systems were: science, technology, economy, politics and general culture. In our joint book, we attempted to show the co-evolution of these sub-systems in the course of the major technological revolutions since the late eighteenth century. I believe that the most appropriate way to wrap up the approach underlying the present collection of essays is to reproduce an excerpt from the Conclusions to Part I of *As Time Goes By*. That chapter shows the various ways in which our theory of 'reasoned history' differs from Schumpeter and from other earlier efforts to explore the relationship

between technical and social change, such as those of Marx and his immediate successors (for example, Kautsky, 1906).

I hope that the ideas developed therein, especially the critique of
Popper's theory of 'unintended consequences', will explain to a small
extent why I remain fundamentally an optimist about the future of the
human species (Chapter 1).

EXCERPT FROM Freeman and Louçã (2001), *As Time Goes By*, pp. 124–34.

The theory put forward here resembles many earlier explanations of economic growth. For example, Marx's materialist conception of history
stressed the tensions between 'forces of production', 'relations of production', and 'superstructure' as a source of social and political change or of
stagnation in economic growth. Many other historians and economists (e.g.
Veblen, Mokyr, von Tunzelmann, Galbraith, Perez) have stressed in particular the interaction between technical change and organizational change
within firms, as well as political and institutional change at other levels in
society. Our approach differs from most of them in two respects. First, it
attaches greater importance to science and to general culture. In this, it
resembles the theories of scientists such as Needham and Bernal and some
historians, such as Margaret Jacob, Maxine Berg and Kristine Bruland.
Second, it does not attempt to assign primacy in causal relationships to any
one of the five spheres at this level of analysis, whereas most other theories
assign primacy to technology or to the economy, or to both. It emphasizes
rather the relative autonomy of each of the five spheres, based on the division of labour and, most important, each with its own selection environment. It is this co-evolution that generates the possibility of mismatch
between them and, periodically, of radical institutional innovations, which
attempt to restore better coordinated development. Such coordination in
new regimes of regulation, however, is not necessarily favourable to economic growth, which is not the only objective pursued by human beings.
'Congruence' that is favourable to economic growth must be distinguished
from other types of congruence, for example to achieve and maintain military conquest.

However, our analysis here is concerned primarily with economic growth
and with those societies in which this objective has been of major importance. A theoretical framework for the history of economic growth should
satisfy four main requirements. First, it should provide a plausible explanation and illumination of the stylized facts, which summarize the main features of the growth of the world economy, especially over the last two

centuries, but ideally for a much longer period. Second, it should do this for the three main categories identified by Abramovitz (1986): forging ahead, catching up, and falling behind. Third, it should identify the major recurrent phenomena in each category to pave the way for generalizations, which should of course be constantly tested against new historical evidence, as well as newly unfolding events. Finally, it should provide a framework for analysing and reconciling the research data, case studies, and generalizations emerging from the various sub-disciplines of history: the history of science and of technology, economic history, political history, and cultural history. As a first step in an inevitably ambitious and hazardous undertaking, the following definitions are tentatively proposed for the subject matter that is of interest, and from which the evidence is drawn for explanations of economic growth.

1. *The history of science* is the history of those institutions and sub-systems of society that are primarily concerned with the advancement of knowledge about the natural world and the ideas of those individuals (whether working in specialized institutions or not) whose activity is directed towards this objective.
2. *The history of technology* is the history of artefacts and techniques and of the activities of those individuals, groups, institutions, and sub-systems of society that are primarily concerned with their design, development, and improvement, and with the recording and dissemination of the knowledge used for these activities.
3. *Economic history* is the history of those institutions and sub-systems of society that are primarily concerned with the production, distribution, and consumption of goods and services and of those individuals and institutions concerned with the organization of these activities.
4. *Political history* is the history of those individuals, institutions and sub-systems of society that are primarily concerned with the governance (legal and political regulation by central, local or international authorities) of society, including its military affairs.
5. *Cultural history* is the history of those ideas, values, artistic creations, traditions, religions and customs that influence the behavioural norms of society and of those individuals and institutions that promote them.

Finally, human beings share with other animals the *natural environment*, and this too has its own history and largely independent evolution. Although this is not usually studied by historians, but is left to geologists, ecologists, astronomers, meteorologists, physicists, and others, it is nevertheless an important influence on human history and is certainly reciprocally influenced by industrialization and economic growth. Moreover, it is now possible that ecological factors may predominate in determining the rate and direction of economic growth during the course of the twenty-first century. However, in view of the special factors involved in this discussion, this aspect of economic growth is not further developed here. On the basis of these conclusions, we will now attempt briefly to justify the use of these five sub-divisions for conceptual and analytical purposes while accepting of course that people make only one history, and recognizing that in real life the five streams overlap and intermingle. However, the use of sub-divisions is not simply a matter of convenience in handling an extremely complicated topic, nor is it just a question of following the academic departmentalization and specializations, that have emerged in the twentieth century. These two factors do play some part, and the academic specialization does provide some indication of the importance of the independent consideration of each sphere. Moreover, the establishment of separate sub-disciplines reflects the sense of dissatisfaction felt especially by scientists, technologists and economists that their special interests were being neglected within the wider rubric in which they were contained. 'History' was often felt to be mainly the story of kings, queens, emperors, empresses, presidents, constitutions, parliaments, generals, ministers and other agents of the state (i.e. 'political history' in terms of the above definitions) or, at most, political and cultural history. The editor of the *Encyclopaedia of the History of Technology* was certainly not alone in protesting at the neglect of technology in this approach (McNeil 1990).

However, these five sub-divisions are proposed here for far more fundamental reasons. In the first place, they are proposed because each one has been shown to have some semi-autonomous, and certainly not insignificant, influence on the processes of economic growth, varying in different periods and different parts of the world. Finally, and most important of all, it is precisely the *relative* autonomy of each of these five process that can give rise to problems of lack of synchronicity and harmony or, alternatively, of harmonious integration and virtuous circle effects on economic growth. It is thus essential to study both the relatively independent development of each stream of history and their interdependencies, their loss of integration, and their reintegration.

The study of 'out-of-synch' phenomena and of the positive or negative interaction between these five different streams is as essential for the understanding of Abramovitz's (1979; with P.A. David 1994) distinction between 'potential' for growth and realized growth as it is for Leibenstein's (1957) 'X' inefficiency.

Anyone who has debated with historians of *science* brought up in the Lakatos tradition must have been impressed by their strong attachment to the 'internalist' view of their subject and their resistance to 'externalist' ideas about the influence of the economy or of political events on the development of science. For them, the 'selection environment' that operates for novel scientific hypotheses and theorems consists purely of the criteria and methods of the scientific community itself. They are wrong to ignore the 'external' influences, but so too are those historians who belittle or ignore the 'internal' selection environment of the scientific community.

Similarly, with the history of *technology*, studies of the evolution of the ship, of the hammer, of flints for tools and weapons, of the harnessing of the horse, and of the steam engine or the plough emphasize alike the relative autonomy of the improvements that were made over the centuries to these artefacts, so essential for human civilization. The same point emerges from the recent impressive volume on *Technological Innovation as an Evolutionary Process* (Ziman 2000). The selection environment, which interests, inspires and constrains engineers, designers, inventors and mechanics and many historians of technology is primarily the technical environment, the criteria of technical efficiency and reliability and of compatibility with existing or future conceivable technology systems.

The reciprocal influence of science and technology upon each other has been demonstrated in numerous studies and is indeed obvious in such fields as computer technology and biotechnology today as well as in earlier developments, such as thermodynamics and the steam engine. Technology has to take account of the laws of nature and hence of science. Nevertheless, Derek Price (1984), Nathan Rosenberg (1969, 1974, 1976, 1982), Keith Pavitt (1995) and many others have produced cogent arguments for recognizing the special features of each sub-system precisely in order to understand the nature of their interaction. Nor does this refer only to recent history, as the massive contributions of Needham (1954) to the history of Chinese science and technology clearly illustrate.

Historians of technology, such as Gille (1978) and Hughes (1982), have amply demonstrated the *systemic* nature of technologies and analysed the interdependencies between different elements in technology systems. Both they and Rosenberg (1969, 1982) have also shown that the technological imperatives derived from these systemic features may serve as focusing devices for new inventive efforts. Such efforts are of course also often powerfully influenced by economic advantages and rewards. Finally, in their seminal paper 'In Search of Useful Theory of Innovation', Nelson and Winter (1977) drew attention to the role of *technological trajectories*, both those specific to particular products or industries and general trajectories, such as electrification or mechanization affecting a vast number of processes and industries. They rightly identified the combination of such trajectories with scaling up in production and markets as one of the most powerful influences on economic growth, as we hope to show in every chapter of

Part II [Freeman and Louçã, 2001]. These ideas were further developed by Dosi (1982) in his work on technological trajectories and technological paradigms, in which he pointed to the relative autonomy of some patterns of technological development by analogy with Kuhn's paradigms in science. Despite the obvious close interdependence between technology and the economy or technology and science, it is essential to take into account these relatively autonomous features in the history of technology.

A satisfactory theory of economic growth and development must take account of these reciprocal interdependencies, but it should also recognize that the *relative* autonomy of evolutionary developments in science and technology justifies some independent consideration. In terms of growth models, there is a strong justification for the procedures adopted by Irma Adelman (1963: 9) in separating S_t from U_t in her production function $(Y_t = f(K_t, N_t, L_t, S_t, U_t)$ where K denotes the services of the capital stock at time t, N_t stands for the rate of use of natural resources, L_t represents the employment of the labour force, S_t represents society's fund of applied knowledge, and U_t represents the socio-cultural milieu within which the economy operates.

An essentially similar argument applies to economic change. No one can seriously doubt the importance of capital accumulation, profits, changes in company organization, and the behaviour of firms and banks for the evolution of industrial societies over the past two centuries. Economic institutions too have some relative autonomy in the cycles of their development. We may fully accept Supple's critique of the treatment of capital accumulation in growth models, but still pay attention to such variables as the share of investment of GDP, business cycles, the trend of the capital–labour ratio, the capital–output ratio, and so forth. This also applies to the growth of the labour force, levels of employment and demographic trends, and the availability of land and natural resources, although all of these are also influenced by cultural and political trends as well as by technology. Explanations of economic growth must pay especially close attention to the interdependencies between economic history and technological history. This has inspired much of our account in Part II [Freeman and Louçã, 2001]. It is precisely the need to understand the changing nature of this interdependency that leads us to study 'out-of-synch' phases of development, when, for example, changes in technology may outstrip the institutional forms of the production and market system, which may be slow to change or impervious to change for relatively long periods. The reverse may also occur, providing impetus to new technological developments, as with the assembly line or factory production.

Some of these out-of-phase synchronicity problems may be on such a scale that they affect the entire *political* and *legal* organization of society. An obvious example was the institution of serfdom in medieval Europe.

Most historians and economists would argue that mobility of labour was one of the essential preconditions for the emergence of capitalist industry. It would appear on almost all lists of 'stylized facts' about the Industrial Revolution. In his six 'major characteristics' of modern economic growth, Simon Kuznets (1971) points to the rapid shift from agricultural to non-agricultural occupations, and most historians agree that the exceptionally early relaxation of the obligations of serfdom in medieval Britain was one of the main factors contributing to Britain's later 'forging ahead' in the Industrial Revolution. By the same token, the tightening up of the 'Second Serfdom' in Eastern Europe and other institutional constraints on the mobility of labour are often advanced as one of the main reasons for the retarded economic growth in Russia and some other East European countries (Dobb 1947), although there is continuing debate on the sequence of events that led to this retardation. These points apply even more to the institution of slavery. Even though, as shown in Chapter 1 [Freeman and Louçã, 2001], we disagree profoundly with the a-historical approach adopted by the cliometricians to slavery in the United States, we could certainly accept the necessity to study this institution in order to understand the development of the American economy.

Finally, *cultural* change is generally accepted as an important influence on economic growth and has recently been justifiably re-emphasized by Berg and Bruland and their collaborators. At the most elementary level, literacy and the quality of general education (as well as purely technical education) are assigned a crucial role in much of the 'new growth theory' and in the World Bank (1992) *World Development Report*. Over the longer term, the classic works of Max Weber (1930) and of R.H. Tawney (1926) on *Religion and the Rise of Capitalism*, although still controversial (see Kitch 1967 and Castells 1998), demonstrated that a change in attitudes towards usury, the rate of interest, work, consumption and accumulation was important for the rise of acquisitive entrepreneurial behaviour in medieval Europe. The fact that these changes were made by Catholic as well as Protestant theologians does not diminish their importance. Some historians might be inclined to treat religious activities as part of the ideological 'superstructure' of society, but the relative autonomy of many religious orders and traditions, as well as the conflicts between Church and State and the role of religion in establishing cultural norms, mean that it cannot be regarded simply as a part of the political system.

Nor, even more obviously, can politics be denied some independent role, as indeed Engels (1890: 477) himself recognized. Throughout Part II, and certainly in the final chapter [Freeman and Louçã, 2001], we shall emphasize the role of the 'regime of regulation' and of political power in dealing with social conflicts arising with each successive technological regime.

Clearly, there are important points of resemblance as well as difference between a simplistic Marxist scheme and that which is tentatively proposed here. It tries to avoid some of the rigidities and classification problems of that scheme while recognizing its major original contribution to historiography.

This first part of the book [Freeman and Louçã, 2001] has attempted to outline a theoretical framework for the study of economic growth and to provide tentative definitions of five historical processes, which are believed to be of the greatest importance for the explanation and understanding of growth. It suggests that each one of these should be studied, both in its own autonomous development within each society and in its reciprocal interactions with the other elements, with a view to identifying and analysing retardation or acceleration phenomena. However, an historical approach to economic growth is unlikely to be acceptable, unless it not only tells a story using this type of theoretical framework, but is also capable of identifying and explaining recurrent phenomena, as well as special cases. As Werner Sombart (1929) put it, 'all history and particularly economic history has to deal not only or mainly with the special case, but with events and situations which recur, and, recurring, exhibit some similarity of feature – instances which can be grouped together, given a collective label and treated as a whole' (Sombart 1929: 18).

3   Recurrent Phenomena

In Part II [Freeman and Louçã, 2001] we shall identify some recurrent phenomena, but we should re-emphasize here our belief that this recurrence is limited in scope and content. Each technological revolution and each phase of economic growth has its own unique features.

This does not mean, however, that we cannot learn a great deal from even this limited recurrence as well as from unique events. Both meteorology and seismology are natural sciences, which have difficulty with long-term prediction but provide probabilistic forecasts useful for policy-making. In fact, since the entire universe is evolving, even those long-term predictions in which we have great confidence, such as the date of the next eclipse are really no more than conditional probabilistic forecasts with a very high degree of probability attached.

It is in this context that Sidney Winter's recollection of the Heraclitean standpoint that 'we cannot bathe in the same river twice' is so thought-provoking. There is no doubt that Heraclites (and Sidney Winter) were right that, whatever river we may choose to bathe in tomorrow, it will not be the same as the one we bathed in yesterday or today, even though it may have the same name and look the same to all outward appearances. This is also true of the entire physical universe. It is indeed evolving all the time and no part of it is exactly the same today as it was yesterday. Nevertheless, there are sufficient relatively stable characteristics of most rivers for a sufficiently long time (centuries if not millennia) that we can use the knowledge of these characteristics, and of recurrent patterns of change, to navigate some and to use them or others for irrigation. Useful generalizations can be made about rivers, even though they will certainly not be valid for all time. For example, one of the earliest great human civilisations was based on such scientific observations and identification of recurrent patterns in the behaviour of the Nile and the use of this knowledge for large-scale irrigation of agriculture. Models can be made of the silting of estuaries or of the influence of rainfall on the rate of flow, which may be useful both for the advance of science and for technology. Of course, it would be foolish to ignore processes of change, such as climatic change, erosion, or pollution, which may affect the behaviour of those who might wish to drink the water or bathe in it, but the regularity of recurrence has been sufficient for many practical human purposes. This is still true despite the recent occurrence of some catastrophic flooding in various parts of the world and despite the fact that problems of access to water supply have assumed an alarming new importance in some areas.

Thus, despite the validity of Heraclites' statement, we can nevertheless agree with Popper that we can make limited conditional generalizations, both about the recurrent behaviour of rivers and about the human institutions that make use of this knowledge. However, the latter statement is subject to greater qualifications. The questions for historical research are: how much similarity persists and over what periods, what brings an end to the identifiable recurrent patterns, and how do new patterns emerge?

These are indeed the questions that have preoccupied economists in the study of *business cycles*, whether these are inventory cycles (Kitchin cycles), the (now 'traditional') business cycles (Juglars), or long (Kondratiev and Kuznets) cycles. Analysis of economic growth must certainly be concerned with repetitive behaviour, whether in modern capitalist economies or older civilizations. Although there have been many irregularities, there has also been sufficient recurrence, at least in recent times, to provide some useful indications for generalization and for policy-making. The work of Carlota Perez (1983, 1985, 1988) on long waves has shown that, even if *identical* behaviour is ruled out, as it must be, there may still be striking similarities or dissimilarities and some hidden ones too, which are helpful in understanding the phenomena and even in making probabilistic forecasts and indications for policy. In the Conclusions to Part II [Freeman and Louçã, 2001] we shall discuss some recurrent phenomena which we believe to be helpful to an understanding of economic history over the last two centuries.

There are also some fundamental characteristics of the evolution of human societies that have endured for millennia, although their manifestations may have varied very much. Such characteristics would be those that primarily distinguish human behaviour from animal behaviour. These have been enduring characteristics of all human societies from a very early period of differentiation of humans from higher apes, and they depend on learning in various ways, so that the analysis of changes in the modes of *learning* should be a central feature in the study of economic growth.

In earliest times, the learning of humans probably closely resembled that of the foraging animals from which we are descended. It was essentially a search and observation process, based on trial and error and the accumulation of knowledge of edible and poisonous, potential and actual, sources of food. With the domestication of other animals, the use of fire, and above all with settled agriculture, the learning and dissemination became far more complex, but it was still based essentially on search, experiment, language communication, and of course serendipity. Contrary to many theories of history, it would therefore be possible to date the origins of science not in the Middle Ages but in Palaeolithic times or even earlier. What has changed is not the search, observation and learning, but the modes of conducting, and organizing search, re-search, learning, accumulating, recording, validating and disseminating knowledge about the natural world (science) and about ways of producing, using and improving tools and artefacts (technology). As the division of labour proceeded within families and tribes and in varying different geographical environments, learning about production and exchange systems (economics) became increasingly important. As some knowledge became routinized in customs and traditions (culture) and in forms of regulating social behaviour (politics, war, slavery), so the separate streams of knowledge became increasingly important as well as their intermingling in general culture.

Every human economy has been a 'knowledge economy' and not only the contemporary one, which we, in our arrogance, proclaim today. Consequently, the distinction we have made at the outset between the various historical processes is not something that emerged only in very recent times, or in the Middle Ages, but has been a feature of human history for millennia. What have been changing are the ways of learning and accumulating knowledge and passing it on, interacting with changing ways of organizing production, and of regulating economic activities and social behaviour. Learning by doing, even if it was once mainly learning by gathering and eating, has always been with us. Learning by producing and using have been with us since the early use of tools of various kinds. Learning by interacting has always been with us. These are persistent human activities across all civilisations. What have changed are the modes of learning, of recording and disseminating what has been learnt, and the ways in which different modes of learning interact with each other.

Another unique but related feature of human evolution is the extent and nature of the division of labour in human societies at least for several millennia. It is true that some animal species, such as ants and bees, also exhibit a fairly complex pattern of social organization. In the study of these animal societies, too, it is essential to pay close attention to the patterns of communication and control, as well as to hierarchical patterns of organization (Fabre 1885; Marais 1975). The division of labour in human societies, however, is unique, both because of its complexity and because of the speed of emergence of new specializations, associated with the rate of knowledge accumulation, the rate and direction of change in techniques, and the associated changes in the patterns of communication and hierarchical organization. The behavioural routines of colonies of ants and bees have, of course, evolved over biological time, but they are so stable that relatively firm predictions can be made, which may be useful to bee-keepers. The behavioural routines, which also affect human behaviour, are less predictable and stable.

Nevertheless, here too there are some deep and very persistent rivers, even though modes of navigation may appear to change beyond recognition. We have argued that the search for new knowledge, inventive behaviour in relation to techniques, innovation and routine behaviour in relation to economic and political organizations and relatively autonomous, but persistent, streams or historical processes. Analogies with the behaviour of bees or ants break down, above all, because of the role of imagination and changing purpose in these activities. As Marx so cogently pointed out, what distinguishes the worst of architects from the best of bees is that the architect first of all constructs a building in the imagination.

As we have already emphasized in Chapter 4 [Freeman and Louçã, 2001], the role of imaginative, conscious, purposeful activity is important in all spheres of social life and is undoubtedly one of the most important distinctive features of the evolution of human societies. There are, of course, some scientists and theologians who believe that there is a purposeful element in the evolution of the universe in general, or of this planet or of a chosen nation in particular (for example, Gaia theories). Still others believe that the mode of evolution is itself sufficient to impart the appearance of purpose without its actual presence ('blind watchmakers', some versions of chaos theory, etc.). Whatever may be the truth in any of these theories, the element of purpose is overtly present in human history in the conscious activities of human beings in a way that is manifestly not the case either in the evolution of other animal species or geological evolution.

Of course, there are some similarities with the animals from which we have evolved, even in the purposeful use of tools on a very small scale, or in language, communication, and forms of social organization. But at least for the last five thousand years, the differences have become so great that it would be absurd simply to follow biology (or any other natural science) as a model for a theory of human history.

It is for this reason that we cannot accept Popper's restrictive approach to the purposeful action of social groups, as well as individuals. Popper tends to dismiss the effectiveness of purposive action by groups of people, maintaining that 'groups, nations, classes, societies, civilizations, etc.' are 'very largely postulates of popular social theories rather than empirical objects' (Popper 1963: 341). He emphasizes that 'the best laid schemes of mice and men gang oft agley' and lead to pain and tears rather than to promised joys. He is very wary of 'conspiracy theories' that attribute social purpose to entities that can have no such collective purpose, and formulates 'the main task of theoretical social sciences' as the disclosure of the unintended social repercussions of intentional human actions' (p. 342). This type of analysis has certainly played an important part in economic theory, especially Keynesian theory, and it is obviously important in considering the unintended environmental consequences of the widespread application of some new technologies. However, sometimes groups do achieve at least some of the objectives they set out to achieve, just as individuals do, even if they are involved in conflicts and failures. Therefore, historical analysis cannot restrict itself to analysis of 'unintended consequences', but should also take account of 'intended consequences'. The possibility for individuals to imagine a desirable future and to associate with other individuals to achieve a variety of collective purposes, such as catching up in standards of living or improving the environment, is surely an important difference between human beings and other animals, and an essential part of the study of economic growth. Certainly, this study should include unintended as well as intended consequences; for example, falling behind rather than catching up may be the actual outcome of some policies designed to accelerate economic growth. But, in spite of Popper's well justified aversion to conspiracy theory, we cannot rule out the study of purposeful actions, both by individuals and by groups, as well as both their intended and their unintended consequences. In this study, comparisons between success and failure in achieving intended objectives may be especially fruitful. Even though human beings often may not attain the ends that they seek or may even court disaster by persisting with conflicting or irreconcilable objectives, or because the outcome of many different purposes may be quite different from each taken separately, nevertheless, the role of purposeful activity cannot be ignored.

REFERENCES

Abramovitz, M.A. (1979), 'Rapid Growth Potential and its Realization: The Experience of Capitalist Economies in the Postwar Period', in E. Malinvaud (ed.) *Economic Growth and Resources, Volume 1, The Major Issues: Proceedings of the Fifth World Congess of the IEA*, London: Macmillan, pp. 1–51.

Abramovitz, M.A. (1986), 'Catching Up, Forging Ahead and Falling Behind', *Journal of Economic History*, **46**: 385–406.

Abramovitz, M.A. and P.A. David (1994), *Convergence and Deferred Catch-up: Productivity Leadership and the Waning of American Exceptionalism*, CEPR Publication No. 401, Stanford: Stanford University Press.

Adelman, I. (1963), *Theories of Economic Growth and Development*, Stanford: Stanford University Press.

Castells, M. (1998), *The Information Age: Economy, Society and Culture, Volume 3, End of Millennium*, Oxford: Blackwell.

Dobb, M. (1947), *Studies in Economic Development*, London: Routledge.

Dosi, G. (1982), 'Technological Paradigms and Technological Trajectories', *Research Policy*, **11** (3): 147–62.

Engels, F. (1890), Letter to J. Bloch, in *Selected Correspondence of Marx and Engels*, London: Lawrence and Wishart.

Fabre, J.H. (1885), *The Social Life of Insects*, Avignon.

Freeman, C. and F. Louçã (2001), *As Time goes By: From the Industrial Revolutions to the Information Revolution*, Oxford: Oxford University Press.

Gille, B. (1978), *Histoire des Techniques*, Paris: Gallinaud.

Hughes, T.P. (1982), *Networks of Power Electrification in Western Society, 1800–1930*, Baltimore: Johns Hopkins University Press.

Kautsky, K. (1906), *Ethics and the Materialist Conception of History*, Chicago: Kerr.

Kitch, M.J. (1967), *Capitalism and the Reformation*, London: Longman.

Kuznets, S. (1971), *Economic Growth of Nations*, Cambridge: Harvard University Press.

Leibenstein, H. (1957), *Economic Backwardness and Economic Growth*, New York: John Wiley.

Marais, E. (1975), *The Soul of the White Ant*, Harmondsworth: Penguin.

McNeil, I. (ed.) (1990), *An Encyclopaedia of the History of Technology*, London: Routledge.

Needham, J. (1954), *Science and Civilisation in China*, Cambridge: Cambridge University Press.

Nelson, R.R. and S.G. Winter (1977), 'In Search of a Useful Theory of Innovation', *Research Policy*, **6** (1): 36–76.

Pavitt, K. (1995), 'Academic Research and Technical Change', in J. Krige and D. Pestre (eds), *Science in the 20th Century*, Amsterdam: Harwood Academic, pp. 143–58.

Perez, C. (1983), 'Structural Change and the Assimilation of New Technologies in the Economic and Social System', *Futures*, **15**: 357–75.

Perez, C. (1985), 'Micro-electronics, Long Waves and World Structural Change', *World Development*, **13**: 441–63.

Perez, C. (1988), 'New Technologies and Development', in C. Freeman and B.-Å. Lundvall (eds), *Small Countries facing the Technological Revolution*, London: Pinter, pp. 85–97.

Popper, K. (1963), *Conjectures and Refutations: In Growth of Scientific Knowledge*, London: Routledge.
Price, D. de Solla (1984), 'The Science-Technology Relationship', *Research Policy*, **13** (1): 3–20.
Rosenberg, N. (1969), 'Directions of Technological Change: Inducement Mechanisms and Focusing Devices', *Economic Developments and Cultural Change*, **18**: 1–24.
Rosenberg, N. (1974), 'Science, Inventions and Economic Growth', *Economic Journal*, **100**: 725–9.
Rosenberg, N. (1976), *Perspectives on Technology*, New York: Cambridge University Press.
Rosenberg, N. (1982), *Inside the Black Box: Technology and Economics*, Cambridge: Cambridge University Press.
Sombart, W. (1929), 'Economic Theory and Economic History', *Economic History Review*, 2 (January): 18.
Tawney, R.H. (1926), *Religion and the Rise of Capitalism*, Harmondsworth: Penguin, 1936.
Weber, M. (1930), *The Protestant Ethic and the Spirit of Capitalism*, London.
World Bank (1992), *World Development Report*, New York: Oxford University Press.
Ziman, J. (ed.) (2000), *Technological Innovation as an Evolutionary Process*, Cambridge: Cambridge University Press.

Name index